FOOD · SAKE · TOKYO

FOOD

SAKE

TOKYO

{ BY }

YUKARI SAKAMOTO

PHOTOGRAPHS BY TAKUYA SUZUKI

A Terroir Guide

THE LITTLE BOOKROOM

© 2010 Yukari Sakamoto
Photographs © 2010 Takuya Suzuki

Book Design: *ll*DESKTOP.
based on a series design by Louise Fili Ltd
Maps: Adrian Kitzinger

Library of Congress Cataloging-in-Publication Data
Food sake Tokyo / by Yukari Sakamoto ; photographs by Takuya
Suzuki.
p. cm.
Includes bibliographical references and index.
ISBN 978-1-892145-74-1 (alk. paper)
1. Restaurants—Japan—Tokyo—Guidebooks. 2. Bakeries—Japan
—Tokyo—Guidebooks. 3. Markets—Japan—Tokyo—Guidebooks.
4. Tokyo (Japan)—Guidebooks. 5. Food—Japan. 6. Rice wines—
Japan. 7. Cookery, Japanese. 8. Cookery—Japan—Tokyo.
I. Title.
TX907.5.J32T657 2010
647.9552'135--dc22
2009046873

Published by The Little Bookroom
435 Hudson Street, suite 300
New York, NY 10014
editorial@littlebookroom.com
www.littlebookroom.com

Printed in The United States of America.

DEDICATION AND THANKS

Takuya Suzuki who captured the food and the city in these gorgeous photos; Junko Nakahama who coordinated the project in Tokyo; Lisa Ekus who saw that this book found a publisher who shared the vision; Angela Hederman, Linda Hollick, and The Little Bookroom team who embraced me from the beginning—there could be no better publisher for my first book; Adrian Kitzinger who created the maps and put the whole book together; my mother and my family in Japan for keeping me well fed; Elizabeth Andoh who has generously mentored and guided me through Japanese cuisine, writing, and so much more; Takashimaya department store for going out on a limb and hiring a Westerner to work in the *sake* department—this book is the result of my two years in the Nihonbashi flagship store.

And, to my husband, Shinji, whose smile captured my heart and nourishes me daily. Food tastes better when I am with you.

This book is dedicated to the fishermen, farmers, purveyors, and chefs of Japan.

TABLE OF CONTENTS

....

INTRODUCTION

·····················

*T*HIS BOOK IS THE RESULT OF MY EXPERIENCE WORKING IN THE EPICUREAN FOOD hall (*depachika*) at the Takashimaya department store in Nihonbashi, Tokyo, where being a Westerner on staff was exceptionally rare, if not unheard of. Watching many non-Japanese peruse the *depachika* in a daze is what inspired me to write this book.

The wide variety, complexity, and subtleties of Japanese

food are almost completely unknown to most Westerners. As a Japanese American trained as a chef at the French Culinary Institute, and, almost more important, speaking both English and Japanese, I've been able to navigate this dazzling culinary cosmos. I've come to want nothing more than to share my ever-growing knowledge.

My Japanese culinary journey began in Tokyo. Tokyo is a city unlike any other. The contrast of old and new in the city ranges from old temples to robots that help

customers at department stores. One minute you are enchanted with an elegant woman walking gracefully in a kimono, and the next minute you find yourself on the subway squeezed between two young girls dressed up like Lolita-esque *manga* characters. In areas around Ryogoku where the *sumo* stadium is located, you may see young wrestlers wearing thin summer kimonos shopping at local supermarkets. Although the widely held image of Tokyo is that of a fast-paced modern city, neighborhoods like Tsukuda and Tsukishima are historic, charming, and without crowds.

The masses of people on crowded trains in the morning are mind-boggling; white-gloved station staff will push commuters into the cars. Neon signs in English and Japanese characters advertising restaurants, *pachinko* parlors, and *karaoke* bars fill the skies, particularly in Shibuya, Ginza, and Shinjuku. Tokyo Tower stands above Roppongi like a giant candle.

Terroir

Japan is made up of four major islands: Hokkaido, Honshu, Shikoku, and Kyushu. The tiny island nation, about the size of California, extends from the tropical islands of Okinawa to the northern lush, green island of Hokkaido. Tokyo is on the island of Honshu; Kanto refers to Tokyo and the area around it.

As with any country, food changes regionally, but in Japan regionality is particularly revered and observed. Many Japanese chefs are surprised to see that *sushi* menus around the United States are all the same. In Japan, part of the thrill of eating in different parts of the country is being introduced to local fish, often not seen outside of that region, and appreciating it as being as fresh as is only possible when eaten locally.

Even in Tokyo, regionality plays a major role in the cuisine. The core of Tokyo consists of twenty-three wards, but the city extends west towards Mount Takao. Tokyo also encompasses about three dozen cities and villages, parts of which have lush, green mountains with rivers, whose delicious water is used for making *sake*.

The popularity of the Slow Food movement has created a renewed appreciation for *kyōdo ryōri*, or local foods, and Tokyo is filled with many regional restaurants that serve specialties of certain prefectures. These restaurants are often part of Antenna Shops (page 188–189) and are particularly worth seeking out for rare *sake* and *shōchū*.

Food Philosophy

Japanese cuisine is so complex and based on so many observed traditions that a guide such as this can only address a few fundamentals, but a few important concepts are briefly noted.

A Japanese cook generally tries to include each of the following in each meal:

Go shiki (five colors) Red, yellow, green, black, and white
Go mi (five tastes) Salty, sour, sweet, bitter, and spicy
Go hō (five cooking methods) Simmering, boiling, steaming, frying, sautéeing, pickling, etc.
Go kan (five senses) Taste, sight, sound, smell, and texture of the food

Another common phrase that is heard when referring to a Japanese meal is *ichiju sansai* ("one broth three dishes"). This practice dates back more than four hundred years. In modern days, *ichiju sansai* has come to mean a balanced meal of rice, soup, and three dishes, one of the three usually containing protein. The three dishes all prepared in different manners (grilled, simmered, sautéed, etc.).

The seasonality of food is of great significance in Japan. As the temperature cools down, mushrooms seem to start sprouting from the vegetable vendors' baskets. In spring, when snowcapped mountains melt, green buds of the cherished wild mountain vegetables burst from under the carpet of leaves. Seasonality is observed in two ways: by micro-season, of which there are twenty-four; and by *shun*, a unit of ten days (each month has three different *shuns*). In essence, Japan has twenty-four to thirty-six seasons recognized by *kaiseki* chefs.

Etiquette

Japan is a polite country. People are bowing constantly. When a person can't physically be present, the ATM will have one bowing on the screen. When leaving on the Limousine Bus, a staff member will come on the bus, thank travelers for using their company, wish them a safe trip, and return curbside to join her colleagues. The porters and ticket girl then bow deeply as the bus departs.

Throughout this guide, in appropriate chapters, I have included basic etiquette. These small gestures will be greatly appreciated by the Japanese.

Attire

In Japan you may have to take your shoes on and off several times in a day. A pair that is easy to slip in and out of will make this easier. Make sure you don't have holes in your socks. At some restaurants you will be expected to leave your shoes at the front door. When you go to the restroom, there may be a separate pair of slippers in the toilet area. Use these while in the restroom, and leave them there when you depart.

Tipping

Service is included in a bill; tipping is not part of Japanese culture.

Cancellations

Cancel reservations as soon as you know you can't keep them. You may be charged a fee by a small restaurant that purchases food for each meal.

Allergy/Dietary Restrictions

If a restaurant has a set menu, advise the restaurant of any allergies or dietary restrictions when making your reservation. If you order an *omakase* (chef's selection) at a *sushi* counter, be sure to advise the chef of any allergies or dietary restrictions.

Cost

If you are unsure how expensive a restaurant is, it is best to call ahead and consult over the phone rather than do it in person after you have arrived.

Credit Cards

Don't assume you can pay by credit card. Many shops and restaurants accept cash only.

HOW TO USE THIS BOOK

....

EVEN RIDING ON THE BULLET TRAIN, YOU CAN OBSERVE THE JOY THAT IS DERIVED FROM A BENTO box. At *tachigui* (stand-up bars) where customers quickly slurp up bowls of *soba* for a few hundred yen, food is made with attention and care. Everywhere you look, food is being eaten with gusto in Tokyo. There are more than 100,000 restaurants in the city. This guide is my attempt to take you to the best and most representative of Japanese cuisine, at all price levels, and demystify what you will find there.

The first part of the book is devoted to the major foods and beverages of Japan. Each description includes, where appropriate, vocabulary to use in a restaurant or shop, seasonal lists, and other essential information, followed by my recommendations for the best restaurants and shops for that particular food or drink.

There is no denying that Tokyo is an expensive city, but you don't have to spend a lot of money to eat well if you know where to go. Good food is ubiquitous; even neighborhood convenience stores (*konbini*) will carry mixed salads, *bentō* lunch boxes, and gourmet snacks like dried or smoked seafood to accompany a cup of *sake*, also sold on the premises. There are casual restaurants that specialize in modestly priced meals such as hot pots, *soba*, *tonkatsu*, *tempura*, or *sushi*. Concentrating on one dish allows the cook to focus on minutiae such as how thick to cut a piece of fish, or the type of charcoal to use for grilling chicken. Passionate shop owners perfect an item such as *ramen* broth, a special blend of oils for *tempura*, or a curry roux. These are all wonderful places to experience the best of Japanese cuisine at reasonable prices.

The second part of the book focuses on shops and restaurants by neighborhood.

Getting Around

Navigating the city can be difficult. Most streets do not have names. Japanese themselves have a hard time finding shops. Police officers stationed in boxes (*kōban*) throughout the city are helpful and will help you to find what you are looking for. For the most part the Japanese are sympathetic to people who are lost, so put on a big smile and don't be afraid to ask for help. Japanese is included in the book so that you can point to it for assistance.

Listings

Each listing includes, where possible, the name of a shop or restaurant in Japanese. The website, even if in Japanese, may help you to recognize the shop or its signature items. Closing times listed for restaurants are when the last order is taken. For the most part the Japanese dine on the early side. If a restaurant asks you to leave, it may be because they need to close the shop in order for the staff to catch the last train home.

Here is a sample listing:

Ginza Kyūbey • 銀座久兵衛
(Restaurant or shop name in English and Japanese)
Chuo-ku, Ginza 8-7-6 • 中央区銀座8-7-6
(Address in English and Japanese)

Tel. 03-3571-6523   (Phone number)
11:30—13:30, 17:00—21:45;   (Hours)
closed Sunday and holidays   (Holidays)
www.kyubey.jp/index_e.html   (Website)
RESTAURANT   (Type of establishment)
LUNCH MODERATE, DINNER EXPENSIVE   (Budget)
MAP PAGE 245, #24   (Where to find location on map)

Note: Shops and restaurants that appear in **boldface** type in the text are mentioned at greater length elsewhere in the book.

How to Read the Addresses

Chuo-ku, Ginza 8-7-6 The full address in Japanese would be: Chuo-ku (ward), Ginza (neighborhood), 8-*chōme* (area), 7-*ban* (block), 6-*go* (building). In Tokyo the words "*chōme*," "*ban*," and "*go*" are often omitted and the three numbers are written with hyphens between them.

Hours

Every attempt has been made to verify the accuracy of the information included in this guide but businesses close and hours of operation change. To avoid disappointment, call ahead and confirm that an establishment is open. While some shops are listed as open daily, many will close for the New Year holidays and sometimes in the other holidays in August (*obon*) or May (Golden Week).

Maps

The overall map of central Tokyo on pages 156–157 shows the page number, area, and orientation of each of the eleven neighborhood maps. Here is a guide to reading the maps (please note that the overall Tokyo map and the Tsukiji Market map on pages 160–161 have a slightly different format for the book reference numbers):

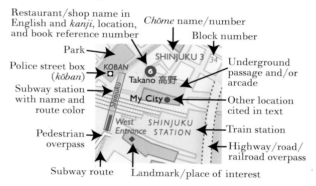

Restaurant/shop name in English and *kanji*, location, and book reference number
Chōme name/number
Block number
Park
Underground passage and/or arcade
Police street box (*kōban*)
Subway station with name and route color
Other location cited in text
Pedestrian overpass
Train station
Highway/road/railroad overpass
Subway route
Landmark/place of interest

Prices

The following terms are assigned to the estimated cost of a meal for one person, excluding alcoholic beverages:

Inexpensive—under $25; Moderate—$25–75;
Expensive—$75–125; Very expensive—over $125

Updating Information

Every effort will be made to update information on my blog: http://foodsaketokyo.wordpress.com/

Phone Numbers

Most numbers in central Tokyo start with 03 and are followed by eight digits. Some numbers may start with three digits (042, for example, would denote a shop in the suburbs). When calling from outside of Japan, the country code for Japan is 81 and the zero is taken out of 03. For example, a Tokyo number of 03-5324-6987 when called from the U.S. would be 011-81-3-5324-6987.

Through this book I hope that you can discover the rich food culture that is unique to this island nation.

"*Ichigo ichie.*" Treasure every encounter, for it may occur only once in a lifetime.

—Yukari Sakamoto
New York, January 2010

CHAPTER 1

EATING OUT

DINING ETIQUETTE

食べ方

TABEKATA

JAPANESE CULTURE IS FILLED WITH MANY RULES AND RITUALS. IF YOU ARE NOT JAPANESE, YOU WILL BE forgiven for not knowing these practices. However, by showing that you are familiar with at least some of these customs, you will be rewarded with great appreciation for your efforts.

Kata is a way of doing something. *Tabekata* is the way of eating—and there are many rules for eating Japanese cuisine properly. That being said, enjoyment of your meal is the most important, so don't let these rules dominate your experience.

If you have allergies, and are dining at a *kaiseki* (a restaurant which serves multi-course meals, probably in a private room) or *kappō ryōri* (a restaurant which serves multi-course meals where diners are seated at a counter across from the chef), call ahead and let the kitchen know.

Starting the Meal

It is common to start a meal with a beer and then move on to *sake* or *shōchū* (or stick with the beer). "*Toriaezu beer*" is the way to tell the waitress that you will start off with beer while you are perusing the menu.

Pouring Beverages

Never pour for yourself. If you are thirsty, offer to pour for your dining partners; they should then return the favor and pour for you. As a good dining companion, you should take notice that your companions' cups never go empty, and they will do the same.

Drinking

When you order an alcoholic drink, you are expected to order some snacks with it, to help digestion.

Wet Towels

Oshibori are used to wipe your hands (never your face) at the start of the meal. In the summer, the *oshibori* will be cold, in the winter, warm. When you are done using the towel, fold it, and set it off to the side. While you are eating, if you need to wipe your fingers, use the *oshibori*. Upscale restaurants will bring you a fresh *oshibori* at the end of the meal.

If you spill some soy sauce or other liquid, do not use your wet towel to wipe it up, but ask for a paper napkin.

Chopsticks

Never stick chopsticks into a bowl of rice—this is a custom practiced at funerals. When you are not using them, set them on the chopstick rest.

If the chopsticks are surrounded by a small piece of paper, like a belt, slide the chopsticks out of the paper ribbon. Do not tear it or rip it apart. Slide one chopstick out first, then the other.

If the chopsticks are disposable chopsticks connected at one end, try separating them one-third of the way from the unconnected end. Do not brush the chopsticks together as it is a gesture that implies that the chopsticks are cheap.

Hashioki are chopstick rests. Set the tips of your chopsticks on the *hashioki* between courses.

Sharing Food

It is not uncommon to share food with your dining companions. Ask for some small dishes and place the food to share on the dish.

Handling Food

When sitting at the counter, the chef will place the food on the diner's tray. This allows him to place it so that it is presented the way it should be viewed by the diner.

When eating from small bowls and plates, it is fine to pick up the bowl and bring it up to your mouth.

To drink *miso* soup, pick up the bowl, bring it up to your mouth, and sup. If there are pieces of food in the broth, hold the bowl with one hand and use your chopsticks with the other hand to dish out the items.

When served a dish with a lid, take the lid off and place the lid off the tray with the inside part facing up. Do not place the lid on the tray or with the inside part facing down. When you are done with the dish, return the lid to its original place on the bowl.

If you find it difficult to take the lid off the bowl, try squeezing the bowl with one hand while lifting the lid with the other hand. The lid helps to preserve the aroma of the food, so when you remove it, be sure to take a long, deep whiff.

When eating *wasabi* with *sashimi*, it is recommended that you do not put the *wasabi* directly into the soy sauce as this causes the essence of the *wasabi* to be lost. Instead, put a little bit of the *wasabi* on the fish, and then lightly dip it into the soy sauce.

When you pick up *sushi* with your fingers, if there is not a sauce on it, you can dip the fish side into soy sauce. The *sushi* chef will often advise you if there is already a sauce on the fish (as in *anago*, eel which is customarily served with a sauce): "*Sono mama de tabete kudasai.*"

Tsuma are the edible garnishes that are served with *sashimi*— perilla leaf (*shiso*), julienned *daikon*, etc. You can wrap the *shiso* leaves around a piece of fish and then dip it into the soy sauce.

Do not pour soy sauce or any other sauce over a bowl of rice, unless it already comes with a sauce.

If any of the bowls or dishes interest you, it is fine to pick them up after you are done eating to look at the bottom to see where they are made. If you think a dish is beautiful, compliment the chef.

BASIC JAPANESE TO USE IN RESTAURANTS

THE CHANCES OF HAVING ENGLISH-SPEAKING STAFF AT RESTAURANTS ARE SLIM UNLESS YOU ARE DINING at an upscale hotel. Knowing a few Japanese words will make the experience easier for you and for the restaurant staff.

At the beginning of a meal it is polite to say "*itadakimasu*," which is an offering of thanks to the chef and to those who provided the meal (the farmers, fishermen, etc.) as well as an expression of gratitude for the produce, animals, and products. At the end of the meal, "*gochisō sama deshita*" ("it was a feast") is the customary way to say thank you.

The word for allergy is *arerugi*; the word *taberarenai* encompasses other food restrictions.

Arerugi ga arimasu. I have allergies.
Ebi no arerugi ga arimasu. I am allergic to shrimp.

Other useful words and phrases:

Konnichiwa Hello, good afternoon
Konbanwa Good evening
Aite imasu ka? Are you open?
Hai Yes
Iie No
Hitori One person
Futari Two people
Sannin Three people
Yonin Four people
Te-buru seki Seat at a table
Kaunta- seki Seat at the counter
Kudasai Please
Mizu o kudasai Water please
Sumimasen Excuse me (all-purpose phrase for calling the server)
Kitsuen seki Smoking area
Kinen seki Non-smoking area
Manseki All seats are taken
Machimasu We will wait.
Rasuto o-da The last order for the evening
Mizu Water
Kanpai "Cheers" (before drinking)
Bi-ru Beer
Nihonshu Japanese sake
Aka wain Red wine
Shiro wain White wine
Shōchū Traditional Japanese distilled spirit
Kore o kudasai I would like this (if you are pointing at a menu or plastic food sample in front of the store)
Bejitarian desu I am a vegetarian
Osusume wa nan desu ka? Do you have any recommendations?

Tabetai desu I would like to eat . . .
Sushi o tabetai desu I would like to eat sushi
Niku o tabetai desu I would like to eat meat
Arimasu ka? Do you have . . . ?
Sashimi arimasu ka? Do you have *sashimi?*
Hashi Chopsticks
Fo-ku Fork
Supun Spoon
Naifu Knife
Amai Sweet
Karai Hot or spicy
Suppai Sour
Shoppai Salty
Nigai Bitter
Karakuchi Dry (for beverages)
Amakuchi Sweet (for beverages)
Agemono Fried
Mushimono Steamed
Itamemono Sautéed
Nimono Simmered
Nama desu ka? Is this raw?
Okawari Refill
Okanjō The check
Kurejitto ka-do Credit card
Genkin Cash
Oishii Delicious
Menyū Menu
Domo arigatō Thank you
Dō itashimashite You're welcome
Gochisō sama It was a feast (at the end of a meal)

JAPANESE FOOD WORDS

JAPANESE CUISINE HAS LONG BEEN ASSOCIATED
with pleasing all five senses. Sound is an integral part of
this aesthetic, and the Japanese language is rich with ono-
matopoetic words that are used to describe food and whose
pronunciations mirror the attributes they describe. Some
describe the texture, temperature, or consistency of food;
others describe sounds coming from the kitchen and heard at
the table. The slurping of *soba* noodles, the gurgling of a hot
pot, or the sound of *tempura* frying in oil are just some of the
sounds that fill the air and that are echoed in many Japanese
words.

Here are some of the most evocative words, and their
meanings:

Atsu atsu Steaming hot, almost too hot to eat, like *ramen*
Beta beta Cloyingly sticky, like a dessert wine
Fuwa fuwa Fluffy, like a marshmallow
Gabu gabu Drinking wholeheartedly
Hoka hoka Hot, at just the right temperature, like a bowl of rice
Hoku hoku Steamy, like baked sweet potatoes
Jyū jyū Juicy meat being grilled
Kori kori Crunchy, like pickled cucumbers
Koto koto Sound of a bubbling pot
Mochi mochi Chewy, like *mochi* (rice taffy)
Neba neba Slimy and sticky, like *nattō* (fermented soybeans)
Nuru nuru Slimy and slippery, like okra
Paku paku Eating wholeheartedly
Pari pari Thin and crispy, like potato chips or *nori*
Piri piri Something that is spicy, like too much *wasabi*
Puri puri Resistant, like fresh shrimp
Puru puru Wiggly, like sesame *tōfu*
Saku saku Delicate and crispy, like *tempura*
Shari shari Sound of ice being shaved
Shiko shiko Chewy, like *udon*
Shuwa shuwa Fizzy and frizzante, like sparkling wine
Ton ton The sound of a knife rhythmically hitting the cutting board
Toro toro Melts in your mouth, like fatty tuna
Tsubu tsubu Chunky bits, like the pulp in freshly squeezed orange
   juice
Tsuru tsuru The sound of slurping noodles

KAISEKI

会席 OR 懐石

KAPPO RYORI

割烹料理

THE ULTIMATE DINING EXPERIENCE IN JAPAN MAY BE A KAISEKI MEAL, A REFINED AND COMPLEX EXPERIENCE in which carefully sourced seasonal ingredients are served in eight to fourteen courses. A *kaiseki* meal honors the taste and texture of the ingredients through sublime preparation and presentation designed to appeal to the spirit as well as to all five senses. An exquisitely choreographed *kaiseki* meal is often served by kimono-clad waitresses in traditional settings in private rooms with low tables on straw mats (*tatami*).

Kappō ryōri also includes several courses of seasonal food, but without the accoutrements of a private room or garden. Diners sit at a counter facing the *itamae* (literally "chef in front of the cutting board"). *Kappō* can be very intimate because the location allows the diner to converse with the chef about the seasonal ingredients and the cooking methods he chooses. *Kappō ryōri* meals are usually less expensive than *kaiseki*; *kappō* chefs will often say that a diner gets better value from a *kappō* meal than a *kaiseki* meal because the ingredients and preparation are often on par with a *kaiseki* meal, but the diner is not paying for a private room and servers. A *kappō* meal will be a more comfortable experience for a solo diner because of the interaction with the chef, even if there is a language barrier.

Both *kaiseki* and *kappō ryōri* dining include a type of service often referred to as *omotenashi*, in which every effort is made for the customer to have a fully satisfying experience. Hospitality reigns, and meticulous attention is paid to insure that the experience will be memorable. At some restaurants, when seeing you off, the staff will bow until you are out of sight.

No detail is overlooked. Care is taken in the choice of foods, and many factors are considered. On a cold day a first course might be a hot savory custard, to warm up the diner and help open the appetite for the rest of the meal. A celebratory meal would differ in subtle ways from that prepared after a funeral. For example, a sea bream is often served at happy occasions because the word *tai* (sea bream) is associated with the word *omedetai* ("congratulations"), but it would never be served after a funeral.

The size of each piece of food is cut so that it is easy for the diner to eat in one bite. If a certain item is hard to chew (raw squid, for example), the chef will score the meat so that it is easier to consume.

The selection of vessels is an essential part of the meal. Some dishes are used to retain heat, some to keep a dish cold. In the summer, glass dishes are used because of their lightness and transparency, but in the winter, thick heavy ceramics and pottery are more appropriate.

Kaiseki cuisine is a celebration of *shun*, the peak of the ingredients' seasonality. *Shun* refers to a ten-day period. Each month is divided into three parts: *jōjun* (the first third), *chūjun* (the middle third), and *gejun* (the last third). A simple flower arrangement will reflect the time of year. Garnishes on the plate often include fresh leaves or flowers picked from the garden just prior to the customer's arrival. If there is calligraphic writing on the wall, it too most likely will refer to the season. Even the chopstick rests may be symbolic of the season, and will change throughout the year.

Kaiseki cuisine is based on the belief that truly seasonal ingredients are best appreciated with minimal manipulation. For example, it is believed that fresh seafood is best served raw as *sashimi* or simply grilled with a bit of salt, without heavy sauces. Vegetables will be warmed in a broth or served with a light dressing.

There are five sets of five rules the chef considers when planning the meal: the five colors (*goshiki*); the five methods (*gohō*); the five flavors (*gomi*); the five senses (*gokan*); and finally the five viewpoints/considerations (*gokan no mon*), a Buddhist treatise on the proper way of eating and being grateful for food that has been prepared.

There are several courses to the *kaiseki* menu and each restaurant will present their own version and number. Each meal contains food prepared in a variety of ways—raw, grilled, in a broth, fried, simmered, and steamed—ending with rice, pickles, and *miso* soup.

Some *kaiseki* and *kappō ryōri* meals can be extremely expensive. Inquire about the cost of a typical meal beforehand. Some of these restaurants are open for lunch, a more affordable meal.

Some of the most common courses in a *kaiseki* meal:

Sakizuke Appetizer or amuse-bouche

Oshinogi or *hitokuchi* One bite or amuse-bouche

Owan or *wan* Soup or steamed dish

Mukozuke Seasonal *sashimi*

Hassun Something from the sea and the mountains (fish or meat and vegetables)

Yakimono Something grilled

Takiawase Assortment of mixed vegetables

Kuchitori Main dish

Takiawase Assortment of cooked vegetables

Sunomono A dish prepared with vinegar

Suimono Soup

Gohan Rice dish (sometimes made with seasonal ingredients) with *ko no mono* (seasonal pickled vegetables) and *miso* soup

Mizumono (or *mizugashi*) Seasonal dessert, may be *kajitsu* (fresh fruit)

Okashi Sweets (or sometimes fruit)

At a *kaiseki* meal, appetizers are often garnished with delicacies (*chinmi*). The three famous *chinmi* are salted, dried mullet roe (*karasumi*), fermented sea slug (*konowata*), and sea urchin (*uni*). Other popular garnishes include:

Karashi Japanese mustard, often served with fish cake stew (*oden*) or some fried foods

Kinome Young leaves of the Japanese prickly ash (*sanshō*) tree

Myōga Fragrant member of the ginger family

Sanshō Dried prickly ash, often served with eel (*unagi*)

Shōga Ginger

Tōgarashi Dried red chili pepper

Wasabi Japanese horseradish, often served with *sashimi* or *sushi*

Yakumi A general term that refers to condiments (some have medicinal properties to aid digestion)

Yuzu An aromatic citrus

Two of the best *kaiseki/kappō ryōri* restaurants in Tokyo are:

Waketokuyama • 分とく山
(*kaiseki* and *kappō ryōri*)
Minato-ku, Minami-Azabu 5-1-5 • 港区南麻布5-1-5
Tel. 03-5789-3838 • 17:00—21:00; closed Sunday and holidays
RESTAURANT • VERY EXPENSIVE • MAP PAGE 156, #25

Revered chef Hiromitsu Nozaki is behind the counter most nights at his flagship restaurant. The flow of the menu will start with lightly flavored foods and continue on to richer, heartier, more flavorful dishes. If you are going to splurge, do it here.

Nihonryōri Ryūgin • 日本料理龍吟
Minato-ku, Roppongi 7-17-24 • 港区六本木7-17-24
Tel. 03-3423-8006 • 18:00—22:30; closed Sunday and holidays
www.nihonryori-ryugin.com/index_en.html (English)
RESTAURANT • VERY EXPENSIVE • MAP PAGE 276, #1

The talented chef Seiji Yamamoto has created a temple to modern Japanese cuisine—a pilgrimage destination for serious foodies from around the world. While many have described his cuisine as

following the tenets of molecular gastronomy, he has recently revisited his classical training, and the food is more traditional than nouveau. The friendly and knowledgeable staff will describe each course eloquently. Chef Yamamoto also trained as a sommelier and this is reflected in a beverage list that includes a finely selected list of wine, *sake*, and *shōchū*. An evening here will be unforgettable. Reservations are hard to get so plan in advance (reservations may be made online).

Three other well-known restaurants are: **Nihonbashi Yukari** for *kaiseki* and *kappō ryōri*, **Ginza Toyoda** for *kappō ryōri*, and **Tsukiji Tamura** for *kaiseki*.

CASUAL DINING

ALTHOUGH TOKYO HAS A REPUTATION FOR BEING EXPENSIVE, IT'S LIKE ANY MAJOR METROPOLIS WHEN it comes to dining out—there are bargains to be found in informal settings where the food is good, or better than good. Dining on a budget in Tokyo is a pleasure, because there are so many options and it is rare to find "bad food" in this city. This section is an overview of the types of places that offer affordable meals; in addition, dozens of individual restaurants are listed throughout the guide in the chapters devoted to specific foods and to neighborhoods.

Noodle restaurants serving *ramen*, *soba*, or *udon* are for the most part, reasonably priced. You can also dine well at a modest price by ordering a set meal (*teishoku*)—usually the house specials with a bowl of rice, soup, and some pickles.

Kaitenzushi (conveyor belt *sushi*) is a fun way to get *sushi* at a bargain without compromising quality. These restaurants are a favorite among families with children but you will also see discriminating fishmongers eating there. And for the price, it can't be beat. Choose the seasonal fish—it will be fresh. If you don't see what you want passing by on the conveyor belt, ask the chef behind the counter and it will be prepared for you. Prices are determined by the color of the plate. When you are ready to pay, a server will come and count your plates, and you will be charged accordingly. **Magurobito**, whose main restaurant is in Asakusa near the Sensoji temple is one of the most popular *kaitenzushi* chains. *Kaitenzushi* are often located near major train stations.

The Tsukishima area is famous for *monjayaki* restaurants that specialize in "grill your own" savory pancakes made with cabbage and other ingredients selected by the diner. Popular additions include cheese, spicy cod roe (*mentaiko*), canned tuna, *kimchi*, and bacon. Similar to the more famous *okonomiyaki* of Osaka, *monjayaki* is the local version—something you will not find much of outside of this neighborhood (see page 251 for *monjayaki* restaurants).

Value-priced restaurants are also found in the shopping complexes near major train stations. Here are a few complexes to check out: TOKIA in the Tokyo Building at Tokyo Station–Marunouchi exit; OAZO at Tokyo Station–Marunouchi exit; Maru Building at Tokyo Station–Marunouchi exit Shin-Maru Building at Tokyo Station–Marunouchi exit.

Many chain restaurants offer good value for money (often $10 or less). The following fast food restaurants have shops throughout the metropolis and are noted for quality food, good service, and cleanliness. There are typically plastic food samples or menus with color photos at these restaurants. Ask the hotel concierge for the nearest location.

Tenya · てんや
www.tenya.co.jp (Japanese)
RESTAURANT · INEXPENSIVE

This restaurant specializes in *tempura* shrimp and seasonal vegetables. *Tendon* is a bowl of rice topped with crispy *tempura*-fried shrimp, a light white fish (*kisu*), squid, squash, and green beans drizzled with a sweet soy dressing. Tenya also offers special menus that are seasonal or based on the seafood of a certain region.

Hanamaru Udon · はなまるうどん
www.hanamaruudon.com (Japanese)
RESTAURANT · INEXPENSIVE

Recognizable by the bright orange sign with the smiling face, Hanamaru Udon serves chewy *udon* and a variety of *tempura*-fried items to place on top of the steaming bowl of noodles. Other toppings that can be added on include okra, fermented soybeans (*nattō*), a soft-cooked egg, or sea vegetables (*wakame*). A classic combination is *kitsune udon*, a hot broth topped with a thin piece of *tōfu* that has been deep-fried and simmered in a sweet sauce. The menu changes throughout the year and includes *udon* salads in the summer. Service is cafeteria-style: pick up a tray, select from the items on display, and place the order for your noodles (small, medium, or large) at the end of the line.

Komoro Soba · 小諸そば
www.k-mitsuwa.co.jp/komoro/mensyoukai.html (Japanese)
RESTAURANT · INEXPENSIVE

Komoro Soba serves buckwheat noodles in a variety of styles. *Soba* with cold sesame dipping sauce (*gomadare*) is popular, as is the hot bowl of *kakiage soba*. *Kakiage* is a mélange of onions, carrots,

鍋料理

NABE RYORI

THE TERM NABE RYORI ENCOMPASSES A VARIETY of hot pots. At home, family and friends gather around the pot while meat or fish and vegetables stew together. *Nabe* are most popular in the fall and winter when it is cold outside. Popular types of *nabe* include *sukiyaki* (*wagyū* beef and vegetables in a sweet soy sauce) and *shabu shabu* (*wagyū* beef and vegetables cooked in a broth and served with a dipping sauce).

The basic broth for the *nabe* can be made from kelp, bonito flakes, soy sauce, *miso*, or chicken stock. Many times the stock is simply water, and its flavor comes from the ingredients of the *nabe*, usually a protein (fish, meat, or *tōfu*), and a colorful variety of vegetables, such as Napa cabbage, leeks, mushrooms, and carrots. The *nabe* can also be served with dipping sauces and garnishes.

Finally, at the end of the meal comes the *shime*. When most of the pot is consumed, the remaining rich broth becomes a vehicle for starchy items that are then added, such as *udon*, *ramen*, or rice.

Many regions are famous for *nabe* based on local products. Here is a list of popular *nabe* that can be found in Tokyo:

Ankō nabe Monkfish (*ankō*) and vegetables

Chankonabe The *nabe* that is an essential part of the *sumo* wrestler's diet, filled with meat, vegetables, and *udon*. If you want to try *chankonabe*, your best bet is to go to Ryogoku station, the neighborhood where the Kokugikan (*sumo* stadium) is and where there are several restaurants that specialize in this dish.

Dote nabe Miso with oysters or other shellfish and vegetables

Fuguchiri Puffer fish (*fugu*) and vegetables served with citrusy soy sauce

Hōtō *Hōtō* are flat *udon* and vegetables in a *miso* broth

Ishikari nabe Salmon, vegetables, and *sake kasu* or *miso* broth

Kamonabe Duck and vegetables

Kiritampo A chicken and vegetable *nabe* with rice that is pounded, molded onto skewers, and grilled

Mizutaki Chicken and vegetables with a citrusy soy sauce

Motsunabe Beef or pork offal, simmered until tender

Oden Fish cakes, *tōfu*, and vegetables

Sakura nabe Horse meat and vegetables

Sukiyaki Thin sliced beef, vegetables, and *tōfu* in a sweet soy broth
   served with a raw egg

Shabu shabu *Wagyū* beef sliced paper-thin that is quickly cooked in
   hot broth with vegetables and served with two dipping sauces,
   ponzu (citrus soy sauce) and sesame. *Shabu shabu* refers to the
   sound of the meat being swished in the hot broth.

Yudōfu *Tōfu* simmered in a kelp broth with vegetables

Yosenabe A popular *nabe* that can include seafood, meat, *tōfu*, and
   vegetables, usually in a *miso-* or soy-based broth

Popular condiments (*yakumi*) for *nabe*:

Goma Toasted sesame seeds
Ichimi Dried red chili peppers
Karashi Japanese mustard
Momiji oroshi *Daikon* and dried red chili pepper, grated
Shichimi Seven spice
Yuzu koshō Salty *yuzu* paste

chrysanthemum leaves, and tiny shrimp shaped into a small disk and deep-fried *tempura*-style. Komoro Soba also has a selection of rice bowls (*donburi*) with toppings like breaded and fried cutlets (*tonkatsu*), deep-fried chicken nuggets (*tori kara-age*), and *tempura*. Some of these shops are *tachigui* (stand and eat—or, in this case, slurp).

Other affordable options include:

For breaded, fried cutlets (*tonkatsu*), **Maisen**; for a *tempura* lunch, **Tenmatsu**; for an all-you-can-eat pickle meal, **Kintame**. **Tsukiji Market** is filled with many good affordable restaurants (see page 159).

FISH CAKE HOT POT

おでん

ODEN

ODEN, THE HOT POT OF STEWED FISH CAKES AND VEGE-
TABLES, KEEPS MANY JAPANESE WARM AND NOURISHED
throughout the winter. For seven or eight months of the year, you'll see big pots of steaming *oden* near the cash registers of convenience stores, and it's not unusual to see a customer walk in, pick up a pack of cigarettes and a beer, and a container of *oden*, too. But it is best at restaurants that specialize in *oden* where chefs stand guard over large hot pots with long chopsticks, carefully coddling the ingredients, adding a ladleful of broth here, adding a few fish cakes there, stirring and keeping watch as the night goes on.

There are three major regional styles of *oden*: Kansai-fu, Kanto-fu, and Nagoya-fu. Kansai-fu *oden* is light and delicate,

based on a simple broth of kelp and bonito flake broth with salt. Kanto-fu *oden* starts with the Kansai-fu base, which is then enriched with the addition of soy sauce and sugar. The intense, *miso*-based Nagoya-fu style is rarely found outside that region.

At an *oden* restaurant, there is one pot that serves all the diners, filled with as many as two or three dozen items in broth. The pot always includes fried fish cakes, and often includes *tōfu*, hard-boiled eggs, and *daikon*, but, according to the season, you will find a changing assortment of seasonal vegetables.

When ordering *oden*, ask for two or three items at a time; you'll ask for additional items as the meal progresses. *Oden* is often garnished with some Japanese mustard (*karashi*) or a salty, citrusy paste (*yuzu koshō*). Toward the end of the meal ask for rice. You'll often be served *chameshi*, the signature rice dish of *oden* restaurants. *Chameshi* can be rice cooked with tea, or, in many places, cooked with tea, soy sauce, and *sake*. Or, you may be served rice cooked with, or topped with, the broth of the *oden* pot. Popular *oden* menu items include:

Age bō-ru 揚げボール Deep-fried fish cakes (called *Satsuma-age*) shaped into the form of balls

Atsu-age 厚揚げ Thick-cut *tōfu* that has been deep-fried; the outer part has a light golden color while the inside remains white and tender

Chikuwabu 竹輪麩 Gluten pounded into a cylindrical shape; it has a chewy texture

Daikon 大根 One of the most popular items in *oden*; it is cooked until tender

Fukuro 袋 A deep-fried *tōfu* packet that is stuffed with vegetables, ground meat, *shirataki* (*konnyaku* noodles), etc.; there is no set recipe, so it is always a surprise bag

Ganmodoki がんもどき *Tōfu* into which different items (which may include carrots, burdock root, *shiitake*, kelp, and gingko nuts) are mixed and then deep-fried

Gobō maki ごぼう巻き Julienned burdock root surrounded by fish cake and deep-fried

Hanpen はんぺん A steamed fish cake (with a light, marshmallow-like texture) often made from shark's meat and grated *yamaimo* potato

Ika maki いか巻き Deep-fried fish cake enveloping sliced squid

Konnyaku こんにゃく A jelly-like cake made from a root vegetable; also referred to as devil's tongue

Musubi kombu 結び昆布 Kelp, tied in a knot, whose flavor contributes *umami* to the rich stock

Negima ねぎま Leeks and tuna skewered onto sticks

Rōru kyabettsu ロールキャベツ Pork-filled cabbage rolls

Satsuma-age 薩摩揚げ Whitefish that is ground and formed into a paste and deep-fried in oil; vegetables may be added to it

Shirako 白子 The sperm sac of a fish

Shirataki しらたき Strings of the root vegetable *konnyaku*

Suji すじ In the Kanto region, whitefish to which cartilage is added that is then rolled into a cylinder shape and boiled; it has a crunchy texture

Tako 蛸 Octopus; *madako* are the bigger ones, which, for *oden*, are cut into small pieces. *Iidako* are tiny bite-size octopus.

Tamago 玉子 Hard-boiled egg

Tōfu 豆腐 In *oden*, often grilled (*yakidōfu*)

Tsumire つみれ Fish paste, made from silver-skinned fish such as sardines

Yaki chikuwa 焼き竹輪 Fish paste shaped into a cylinder and grilled

Three recommended *oden* restaurants are **Otafuku**, **Ogura**, and **Otako**.

Shops that specialize in fish cakes include **Kanmo** and **Tsukugon**.

JAPANESE-STYLE WESTERN FOOD

洋食
YOSHOKU

YOSHOKU IS WESTERN FOOD ADAPTED TO THE Japanese palate. This style of cuisine started in the Meiji restoration period, 1868–1912, when, after centuries of isolation, Japanese citizens began traveling to other countries and learning about the cuisine outside of Japan. Some of these influences are reflected in the popularity, in Japan, of sauces such as ketchup or Worcestershire, as well as bread. Most *yōshoku* dishes will be eaten with silverware instead of chopsticks; rice at a *yōshoku* restaurant is served on a plate instead of in a rice bowl. **Shiseido Parlour** in Ginza (Chuo-ku, Ginza 8-8-3, Tel. 03-5537-6241, map page 180, #30) is considered the gold standard for *yōshoku* in the city. You can also find *yōshoku* at **Taimeiken** and **Yoshikami.**

Some popular *yōshoku* menu items:

Bi-fu shichū Beef stew

Bi-fu sute-ki Beef steak

Furai Breaded and deep-fried items such as shrimp, scallops, fish, oysters

Guratan Gratin dishes, often macaroni or seafood in cream sauce with cheese

Hamba-gū A meatloaf-like burger served with demi-glace sauce, but without a bun

Hayashi raisu Beef, onions, and mushrooms in a demi-glace sauce

Kare-raisu Curry with rice

Korokke Creamy croquettes, sometimes filled with seafood such as crab

Menchi katsu Breaded and deep-fried hamburger to which chopped onions have been added

Omuraisu An omelet filled with ketchup-flavored rice

Omuretsu Omelet

Rōru kyabettsu Cabbage rolls with tomato sauce

DEPARTMENT STORE FOOD HALLS

デパ地下
DEPACHIKA

EACH OF THE MAJOR DEPARTMENT STORES IN TOKYO HAS AN ELABORATE AND EXTENSIVE FOOD HALL IN ITS basement called *depachika*. The word *depachika* comes from the Japanese words for department store (*depa-to*) and basement (*chika*). *Depachika* showcase the best food that Japan has to offer in opulent and exquisitely designed surroundings. There are scores of shops in each *depachika* carrying every imaginable culinary item both Western and Asian. Iron Chefs, Michelin chefs, and Japanese shops that have been in existence for hundreds of years all have shops in *depachika*.

Usually, *depachika* are conveniently located close to train stations. Within walking distance of the Shinjuku Station, through which 3.5 million commuters pass each day, are several major *depachika*, at Isetan, Takashimaya, Odakyū, and Keio; the proximity is convenient for commuters who want to pick something up for dinner on their way home.

If you can, arrive at *depachika* by 10:00 a.m. when the stores open and you will be greeted by the staff respectfully bowing as you enter and cheerfully calling out "*irasshaimase*" (welcome). Takashimaya in Nihonbashi is one of the few remaining department stores whose antique elevators continue to be operated by elevator girls wearing white gloves and chic designer uniforms—a glimpse of a vanishing tradition.

Presentation and packaging, key components of Japanese culture, are probably most elaborate at *depachika*. There are rows of perfectly stacked fruits and vegetables, cases of delicate pastries, carefully assembled *bentō* boxes, and *sake* bottles with striking calligraphy. The seasons are reflected in most of the prepared foods, like traditional Japanese confections (*wagashi*) decorated with motifs of maple leaves in the fall and cherry blossoms in the spring. *Sushi* may be enclosed in bamboo leaves; *bentō* lacquer boxes are tied in a colorful fabric (*furoshiki*); and the wrapping of gifts is an art in itself. Gift-wrapping is often included in an item's price. If you would like your purchase wrapped, say *purezento* or *gifuto*—and smile.

A service is available to deliver your goods to your home or hotel. This typically costs just a few hundred yen for next-day service in Tokyo. If you would like to send a gift to a friend or business associate, bring along their business card or address and phone number.

Visiting *depachika* at holidays provides an insight into the country's food culture. The New Year is welcomed with luxurious New Year's food (*osechi ryōri*), specific symbolic dishes presented in *bentō* boxes; *Setsubun* in February heralds the start of spring with a certain type of rolled *sushi* (*ehōmaki*) that are eaten while facing the auspicious direction for that year; *Hina Matsuri* (Girls' Day) in March is celebrated with colorful, scattered *sushi* (*chirashizushi*); *Doyō no Ushinohi* marks the end of summer and eel (*unagi*) is eaten on that day. Even Western holidays are celebrated: you'll find plenty for Valentine's Day and White Day (the Japanese version of Valentine's Day) in *depachika* chocolate departments; a stock of Beaujolais Nouveau on the day it is released; and cakes for Christmas.

Depachika will often have a dedicated event space for weekly specials promoting the food items of a particular region, season, or holiday. For larger events some stores will open up a space on an additional floor. Do not miss these, as they often feature items that are usually not available in Tokyo. The vendors at these events are enthusiastic about sharing their products and their knowledge with customers. To find out if a department store is sponsoring a special food event, ask at the concierge or information desk on the first floor, usually near the main entrance.

Some of the most widely attended events in a department store's event space are the chocolate fairs held during the first two weeks in February. The practice of giving chocolates to colleagues, friends, and family during this time of year is a ritual that attracts *chocolatiers* from around the world. The events will get crowded, so it's best to go early in the day.

Most food at *depachika* is for takeout only; individual food boutiques do not provide seating, but there are a few eat-in counters with a handful of seats at some *sushi*, curry, *ramen*, or juice stands. These are good options for the solo diner.

On the upper floors of department stores you'll find a variety of well-known restaurants that provide a variety of quality meal options, whether you're in the mood for *sushi*, *tempura*, or noodles. There are usually plastic food samples in front of each restaurant so even if you don't speak the language, you will understand what is on the menu and what it costs. If you are hungry and are near a department store, you should have no hesitation about eating in one of these restaurants—the quality is nothing like the fast-food options at American shopping malls.

Some stores have picnic areas on the roof. Ask at the information counter on the first floor.

The following departments are common to most *depachika*:

Prepared food The most colorful of all the departments is the prepared foods area, where you'll find classic Japanese dishes including a variety of *sushi*, *tempura*, grilled chicken skewers (*yakitori*), breaded deep-fried cutlets (*tonkatsu*), side dishes (*osōzai*), and *bentō* boxes, as well as Chinese and Western items.

The most striking items in the prepared foods department are the *bentō* boxes. The Japanese attention to the presentation of food is perhaps most evident in *bentō* boxes—both the food and the beautiful boxes themselves. In an exquisite container you will find five colors of seasonal ingredients, prepared five different ways, representing five different tastes.

Foreign purveyors Many top foreign purveyors have a presence in depachika including Italian, German, French, and British brands such as Fauchon, Hediard, Harrods, and **Peck**.

Bakeries This nation of rice eaters also loves bread from around the world; crusty baguettes, airy *focaccia*, and hearty Eastern European breads are all represented at *depachika*. The Japanese also have their own version of flour-based breads, called snack breads (*oyatsu pan*), often served with mayonnaise, corn, or tuna. *Anpan* is a soft bread stuffed with sweet *azuki* red bean paste; another popular Japanese bread is *meron pan*, which tastes like muskmelon. Visit **Kimuraya** for Japanese breads, including their signature *anpan*.

Western-Style confections (*yōgashi*) Some of the world's most famous pastry chefs have boutiques in depachika that cater to the Japanese fascination with *macarons*, *madeleines*, and other Western-style pastries. Two Japanese *pâtisseries*, **Yoku Moku** and **Confectionary West**, also offer items rich with butter, sugar, and flour.

Japanese confections (*wagashi*) Four well-known purveyors with shops in most *depachika* include **Toraya**, famous for its *yōkan* (*azuki* bean cakes); **Kano Shojuan**, for interesting modern takes on *wagashi* flavors, including a cheesecake filled with *azuki* beans and a green-tea cake; **Mamegen**, for snack balls of different flavors; and **Bankaku**, for delicate shrimp-flavored crackers (*sembei*).

Chocolates Many top European *chocolatiers* have shops in *depachika*, such as Neuhaus and Wittamer.

Pickles **Kintame** and Nishiri are popular pickle shops based in Kyoto, which is famous for its pickles.

Tōfu

Meat (*niku*)

Seafood (*sengyō*) The noisiest area of any *depachika* is the seafood department. Japanese fishmongers are notorious for their calls advertising seasonal fish, promotions, or ideas about how to cook a certain fish: "The first *sanma* (Pacific saury) of the season! Rich with fat and perfect for *shioyaki* (grilling with salt). Dear customer, today we are selling it for 200 yen per fish. Come quickly as there are only ten left!"

Here you will see an amazing variety of glistening fresh fish; you can also purchase salt-cured, smoked, *himono* (butterflied, salted, and dried), marinated, and grilled seafood. You might find golden nuggets of creamy sea urchin (*uni*) artfully arranged on a small wooden platter, or tiny white fish (*shirauo*) bagged up in water and still swimming. Yes, these can be eaten while still alive, and they dance in your throat on the way down.

All of the seafood will be designated with where it was caught, whether or not it has been frozen, and if it is wild or farmed. There will also be an indication of whether it must be cooked or may be eaten *sashimi*-style.

This area may have small refrigerated lockers for rent at a nominal fee so that shoppers can store their fish while completing their shopping.

Fruits and vegetables Here you will find the legendary gift melons that can cost as much as $500 a piece, protected in a wooden box and surrounded by a silken cloth. Notable fruit shops include **Sembikiya** and **Takano**. The juice stands in this section blend fresh fruits and vegetables to order.

Groceries The source for Japanese pantry items—including artisanal soy sauce, vinegar, *mirin*, salts, and much more.

Sake/wines/spirits As a generic term, "*sake*" refers to any alcoholic beverage, so the *sake* departments at *depachika* will sell beer, wine, *sake*, *shōchū*, and hard spirits.

Tea **Ippodo** and **Yamamotoyama** are famous tea shops with branches in most *depachika*.

Miso

Kitchenware Not located in *depachika*, but on a separate floor upstairs, the kitchen and housewares section is a must-see.

Depachika to Visit

The tenants in *depachika* are constantly changing: as trends come and go, new shops come and go along with them. I have listed some shops worth checking out at the *depachika* below, but these may change. There is usually a concierge in each *depachika*. Stop by and ask for a map, and ask the concierge to point out the shops you are looking for. Even if the map is in Japanese, it will help you navigate the cavernous halls. Also, be sure to ask if there are any special food events on a separate floor.

Listed under each *depachika* are several shops that should not be missed.

Takashimaya • 髙島屋
Chuo-ku, Nihonbashi 2-4-1 • 中央区日本橋2-4-1
Tel. 03-3211-4111 • Daily 10:00–20:00
www.takashimaya.co.jp/tokyo/index.html (Japanese)
MAP PAGE 223, #28

This is the flagship Takashimaya store. You'll find eat-in counters at Shunpanro (puffer fish) and **Imahan** (*sukiyaki*). **Kanō Shōjuan** has a small café and counter displaying traditional and modern Japanese confections. Also visit Lemon Fruits Parlour for juices and sliced fresh fruit.

Unlike most *depachika*, the *sake* department at Takashimaya holds tastings of local *sake* (*jizake*).

Minokichi, a Kyoto institution more than three centuries old, has *bentō* boxes in the Kyoto style, in which the dishes are lightly seasoned, allowing the ingredients' flavors to speak for themselves.

Stop by Akatombo Sandwiches if only to see how expensive the Western-style tea sandwiches are.

Meikahyakusen showcases the best sweets from all over Japan. In particular, the sweet *karintō* crackers from Kozakura are popular.

Nihonbashi's Takashimaya has a *fugu* eat-in counter for those brave enough to try the famous poisonous puffer fish. A hidden gem on the third floor of Takashimaya is Pascal Caffet's chocolate shop where you can feast on truffles and a glass of champagne.

There is a small garden with picnic tables on the roof of the building. Purchase a *bentō* box and some *sake* or a beer and head up.

Mitsukoshi • 三越

Chuo-ku, Nihonbashi Muromachi 1-4-1

中央区日本橋室町1-4-1

Tel. 03-3241-3311 • Daily 10:00–19:00

www.mitsukoshi.co.jp (Japanese)

MAP PAGE 223, #8

Mitsukoshi is the oldest department store in the country: it opened in 1904. Don't miss the *baumkuchen* (layered cake) being made behind a glass window at Club Harie, which you can sample at the café. Regional sweets are sold at Kayuan and other regional specialties at Mishyoan where you will find a selection of pickles, *miso*, and other food products from small vendors. Other shops of interest are Sun Fruits for fresh fruit, Wabisa for modern Japanese-style sweets, and Yoshikawa Suisan for its beautiful displays of fresh fish. Eat-in counters include Tempura Yamanoue and Izumoya for grilled eel (*unagi*).

Daimaru • 大丸

Chiyoda-ku, Marunouchi 1-9-1 • 千代田区丸の内1-9-1

Tel. 03-3212-8011 • Daily 10:00–20:00

www.daimaru.co.jp/english/tokyo.html (English)

MAP PAGE 222, #26

Do what the Japanese do: visit Daimaru, located on the Yaesu exit side of the mammoth Tokyo Station, and select a *bentō* box and a beer or *sake* before boarding the bullet train. The selection of food and drink at the *depachika* is far superior to what is sold in the station or on board.

The *baumkuchen* (European layer cake) shop Nenrinya on the first floor is extremely popular.

On the twelfth floor is a unique restaurant, a branch of the Kyoto pickle shop, **Kintame**, where you can have an entire meal based on pickles.

Isetan • 伊勢丹
Shinjuku-ku, Shinjuku 3-14-1 • 新宿区新宿3-14-1
Tel. 03-3352-1111 • Daily 10:00–20:00
www.isetan.co.jp
MAP PAGE 263, #3

If your time in Tokyo is limited, this is the *depachika* to see. The food at Isetan is displayed as in a museum. If the weather is nice, Isetan offers one of the best rooftop gardens in the city. The manicured gardens juxtaposed against huge exhaust fans and giant neon lights looks like a scene out of a *manga* comic book.

The *sake* shop includes a rare collection of aged *sake* (*kōshū*) housed in a special cellar.

At Jean-Paul Hevin, chocolates are kept in a guarded, temperature-controlled cellar. The adjacent café serves hot chocolate and chocolate desserts. (The shop should be avoided at all costs before Valentine's Day, as there is usually a long line of customers. Guards stand at attention outside the temperature- and humidity-controlled boutique allowing a limited number of customers in at a time so as not to warm up the room.)

Ameya Eitarō is a confectioner that serves up cute and trendy candies that make good souvenirs.

Suzukake is a Japanese confection (*wagashi*) shop whose dainty sweets are packaged in bamboo boxes that cradle and protect them.

Buy an order of bite-sized dumplings (*hitokuchi gyōza*) at Tenten and take them along with a cold beer to the roof for an impromptu picnic.

Next door, **Pierre Hermé**'s *macarons* are available in a variety of pastel colors. Isetan is the only place in the city where you can purchase the world-renowned Henri LeRoux caramels.

Eat-in counters include a bar for imported ham, another for

wagashi, and another at the Kitchen Stage with a rotating cast of chefs from popular restaurants in the city and beyond.

Takashimaya • 髙島屋
Shibuya-ku, Sendagaya 5-24-2 • 渋谷区千駄ヶ谷5-24-2
Tel. 03-5361-1111 • Daily 10:00–20:00
www.takashimaya.co.jp/shinjuku/ (Japanese)
MAP PAGE 263, #7

Takashimaya is located at the south exit (*minamiguchi*) of the Shinjuku JR Station, in the Times Square building. Takashimaya has three entire floors filled with restaurants at the top of the building, including Katsukura, a popular breaded and fried cutlet (*tonkatsu*) shop and Din Tai Fung, a Chinese restaurant known for its soup dumplings. If you want to dine *al fresco*, Takashimaya also has some outdoor space on the roof where you can eat a *bentō* purchased in the *depachika*.

Shops in the *depachika* to seek out include one offering the food of Kyoto's well-known *kaiseki* restaurant, Kikunoi; **Peck** for Italian bread; and the Aji Hyakusen regional foods section, which features pickles from Murakami Ju in Kyoto and kelp (*kombu*) from **Okui Kaiseidō**.

Other don't-miss shops in the Times Square complex are **Tōkyū Hands**, for kitchen and housewares, and **Kinokuniya** bookstore with a selection of English books.

Mitsukoshi • 三越
Chuo-ku, Ginza 4-6-16 • 中央区銀座4-6-16
Tel. 03-3562-1111 • Daily 10:00–20:00
www.mitsukoshi.co.jp (Japanese)
MAP PAGE 181, #16

At the main crossing in Ginza, you'll find another department store on a par with Takashimaya and Isetan. With lion statues guarding the door, it's hard to miss Mitsukoshi. Its *depachika* is divided between two floors, and like Takashimaya and Isetan it is a treasure trove of high-quality, beautifully packaged gourmet delicacies.

Tobu • 東武
Toshima-ku, Nishi Ikebukuro 1-1-25 • 豊島区西池袋1-1-25
Tel. 03-3981-2211 • Daily 10:00–20:00
www.tobu-dept.jp/ikebukuro/ (Japanese)
MAP PAGE 156, #1

Tobu department store in Ikebukuro is home to Japan's largest *depachika* with about 250 vendors. If you spent two minutes at each stall, it would take you more than eight hours to complete your culinary adventure in this one store. The *depachika* is divided into two buildings, the Honkan Shokuhin and Plaza Shokuhin.

The beer selection at the *depachika* is among the best in the city, including many imported labels.

Shops to look for include **Tsukugon** for *oden*, and Pao Pao for fried and steamed dumplings (*gyōza*). There are three notable *wagashi* boutiques that specialize in Japanese confections: **Shiose**, Ryoguchiya Korekiyo, and Sentaro. This is just a tiny sample of what is available—for the best experience, take the plunge and meander around.

Tobu houses more than fifty restaurants on floors 11 to 15 in an area named "Spice." Chinese Iron Chef Chin Kenichi has a branch of his Szechwan restaurant, Shisen Hanten, here, where you can try his signature dish, *mābō dōfu*, *tōfu* and ground pork in a spicy sauce.

Tōkyū Tōyoko-ten Food Show • 東急東横店
Shibuya-ku, Shibuya 2-24-1 • 渋谷区渋谷2-24-1
Tel. 03-3477-3111 • Daily 10:00–21:00
www.tokyu-dept.co.jp (Japanese)
MAP PAGE 156, #24

Shibuya is a hot, trendy area that provides a snapshot of the youth of Japan. Here you'll see young kids—many of them wearing more makeup than a Broadway showgirl—coming to shop at one of the many stores in the area, such as Marui and 109. Located in the Shibuya JR Station building, the food shops here are divided into two sections, Tōkyū Food Show and Norengai.

Tōkyū Food Show is located in the basement of the station building. The *sake* department usually does weekly promotions of locally-produced *sake* (*jizake*), so be sure to try whatever they are pouring—it's a nice way to learn about *sake*, and to support the small producers by picking up a bottle if you like what you try.

For a quick bite, the eat-in En Dashi Chazuke has a selection of hot bowls of rice in a savory broth served with a variety of toppings (*ochazuke*).

Uoriki, one of the fishmongers in the *depachika*, has an eat-in counter with nine seats and serves good *sushi* at a reasonable price. There are photos of the popular menu items—so you can simply point at what you want. There is often a line, but it moves quickly, so put your name on the waiting list posted in front of the shop.

The rest of the food shops are located in Norengai, which is on the first floor by the entrance to the Tōyoko train line. Some popular shops include **Kibun** for fish cakes, and a branch of the revered Kyoto *kaiseki* restaurant, Kikunoi, for its gorgeous offering of seasonal side dishes and *bentō* boxes to go. It is always hard to resist Kamonka's dumplings and pot stickers (*gyōza*), decoratively displayed in the large steamers.

While in Shibuya, you may also want to visit:

Beard Papa • ビアードパパ

Shibuya-ku, Shibuya 2-24-1, Tōkyū Tōyoko-Ten

渋谷区渋谷2-24-1東急東横店

Tel. 03-5428-3560 • Daily 10:00–22:00

www.muginoho.com/english/products/ (English)

MAP PAGE 156, #23

Just outside of the Norengai is a branch of the Beard Papa cream puff shop. The sweet aroma of freshly baked *pâte à choux* permeates the area.

CHAPTER 2

....

FOOD

THE JAPANESE PANTRY

....

BASIC INGREDIENTS

FAMILIARIZING YOURSELF WITH THE BASIC ITEMS FOUND IN MOST JAPANESE PANTRIES WILL ENABLE you to stock your own home kitchen and to better understand the cuisine of Japan. The sections on *dashi* and *umami*, soy products, sea vegetables, and dried goods (*kanbutsu*) have additional information on essential Japanese ingredients.

Sake 酒

In the kitchen, *sake* brings depth to many dishes, adds a light natural sweetness, and when added to seafood helps get rid of any fishy aromas. Avoid *ryōri shu* (料理酒), or cooking *sake*, often sold in the same area of the grocery store as *mirin*; it is an inferior product. Instead, purchase *nihonshu* 日本酒 or *seishu* 清酒 from the *sake* section. As with wine, if you cook with *sake*, the food will naturally pair well with *sake* (see pages 140–146).

Mirin みりん

Used to add sweetness, to soften flavors, and hide unwanted aromas such as strong fish smells. The key is to purchase high-quality *hon mirin* (本みりん). It is sweet, but mellower than sugar. It is good in simmered foods such as *yakitori* and *teriyaki*. *Mirin* will put a nice glaze on these foods.

Vinegar 酢 *Su*

Vinegar is a very delicate product and should be added towards the end of cooking or it loses its aroma. Vinegar, too, can help disguise aromas of fish. Rice wine vinegar, *komesu* (米酢), is most often used. It has an inherent sweetness and makes for flavorful salad dressings and other vinegared dishes.

Soy Sauce 醤油 *Shōyu*

Made from soybeans, wheat, salt, and *kōji* mold (also used to make *sake* and *shōchū*), soy sauce requires a lengthy fermentation.

Types of soy sauce:

Koikuchi 濃口 Regular, or dark soy sauce; the most popular type
Usukuchi 薄口 Soy sauce that is lighter in color than *koikuchi*, and also saltier; used when the cook does not want to darken a food
Tamari たまり Supposed to be wheat free, but this is not always the case, so be sure to check; often served with *sashimi*

Miso みそ

See *Miso*, page 76

Stock 出汁 *Dashi*

See *Dashi*, page 54

Other common pantry items include:

Katakuriko 片栗粉 A starch originally made from dogtooth violet, it is more commonly found made from potatoes. Used to thicken sauces, it is similar to cornstarch but with a finer texture.
Goma abura ごま油 An aromatic sesame oil used for its aroma and nutty flavors
Wasabi わさび Japanese horseradish, available grated and in tubes; look for products that are one hundred percent *wasabi*, often labeled "*hon wasabi*"
Yuzu koshō 柚子こしょう A salty and spicy paste made from salt, *yuzu* rind, and chili peppers
Yuzu 柚子 The skin of aromatic citron; a popular condiment, it is available freeze-dried
Shichimi 七味 A blend of seven spices, often including dried red chili pepper, dried *yuzu* peel, *ao nori*, hemp seeds, sesame seeds, white poppy seeds, and *sanshō* peppers. Blends vary; often served with noodles such as *udon*
Ichimi 一味 Dried red chili pepper (*tōgarashi*), also called *ichimi tōgarashi*

DRIED PRODUCTS

乾物
KANBUTSU

KANBUTSU, DRIED PRODUCTS OF BOTH THE LAND and sea, are key staples of the Japanese pantry. All have a long shelf life, most are natural and without preservatives; and they can be simply reconstituted in water before use. See **Yagichō Honten**, a shop that specializes in *kanbutsu*.

Aonori 青海苔 Dried laver, often sprinkled on savory pancakes called *okonomiyaki*

Aosa あおさ Dried laver, good in *miso* soup

Hijiki ひじき A black sea vegetable rich in minerals and protein

Kaisō 海藻 Generic term for sea vegetables, often added to salads

Kanten 寒天 Agar-agar made from *tengusa*, a sea vegetable, and used as a gelatin

Kombu 昆布 Kelp, essential ingredient in broth

Nori 海苔 Fried laver, often used for rolled *sushi*

Wakame わかめ A sea vegetable often used in *miso* soup and salads

Goma 胡麻 Sesame seeds

Irigoma 炒りごま Roasted sesame seeds

Kurogoma 黒ごま Black sesame seeds

Shirogoma 白ごま White sesame seeds

Surigoma すりごま Crushed sesame seeds

Hoshi shiitake 干し椎茸 Dried *shiitake* mushrooms

Hoshi warabi 干しわらび Dried bracken, a type of mountain vegetable (*sansai*)

Hoshi zenmai 干しぜんまい Dried royal fern, a type of mountain vegetable (*sansai*)

Kanpyō かんぴょう Dried gourd strips

Kikurage きくらげ Dried wood-ear mushroom

Kinako きなこ Flour made from dried soybeans; a popular ingredient in confections

Kiriboshi daikon 切り干し大根 Dried strips of *daikon*

Koya dōfu 高野豆腐 Freeze-dried *tōfu*

Kuzuko 葛粉 Starch made from the kudzu plant, used as a thickening agent, also referred to simply as *kuzu*

Mame 豆 Generic term for beans

Azuki 小豆 Small red beans, often used in confections (*wagashi*)

Daizu 大豆 Soybeans

Kintoki 金時 Kidney beans

Kuromame 黒豆 Black beans

Menrui 麺類 Generic term for noodles

Soba 蕎麦 Buckwheat flour noodles

Sōmen そうめん Thin wheat noodles

Udon うどん Thicker wheat noodles

STOCK
出汁
DASHI

UMAMI-RICH INGREDIENTS LIKE KELP (KOMBU), BONITO FLAKES, AND DRIED SARDINES ARE ALL KEY ingredients of *dashi*, the basic broth on which much of Japanese food is based. The most basic *dashi*, *ichiban* (number-one) *dashi*, is made from kelp and bonito flakes. In parts of Japan, *niboshi* (dried sardines) are used instead of bonito flakes. Dried *shiitake* and scallop ligaments can also be used in *dashi*, as can the head and bones of sea bream (*tai no ara dashi*). Vegetarian *dashi* can be made from kelp (*kombu*), along with dried *shiitake* mushrooms or other dried vegetables such as gourd (*kanpyō*), daikon (*kiriboshi daikon*), or soybeans (*daizu*).

The main ingredients in *dashi* are:

Kombu 昆布 The cold, mineral-rich waters surrounding Hokkaido provide 95% of the country's *kombu*. Most *kombu* is sold in long strips, but it is also available in shavings (*tororo* or *oboro*) to add to soup or sprinkle over rice. *Kombu* can also be wrapped around raw fish in a process called *kobujime*, which changes the fish's texture and adds *umami*.

There are more than forty types of wild and farmed *kombu*. The name of a specific variety of *kombu* often reflects where it was harvested. These are the five most popular:

Rishiri kombu 利尻昆布 Harvested near Rishiri Island, this is an aromatic *kombu* that makes a clear broth, popular with chefs in Kyoto. It is considered a high-quality *kombu* and is often used in top restaurants.

Rausu kombu 羅臼昆布 This thick *kombu* has a stickiness to it, and a deep, rich flavor that is slightly sweet. Also a high-quality *kombu*, it is the *kombu* that is used to make other shaved *kombu* products, such as *tororo* and *oboro*.

Ma kombu 真昆布 Thick and rich in *umami*, slightly sweet, with an elegant flavor, this is also considered a top *kombu*.

Hidaka kombu 日高昆布 From the Hidaka region, this *kombu* is a popular variety used by busy home cooks because it quickly imparts its flavor when simmered in water. It is also reasonably priced and can be used as an ingredient for fish cake stew (*oden*), sea vegetables and seafood simmered in soy (*Tsukudani*), and other kombu dishes.

Naga kombu 長昆布 A very long kombu (more than ten meters long), *naga kombu* is also used in dishes such as *oden* and *Tsukudani*. It is found only in the wild—not farmed—and is reasonably priced.

Okui Kaiseidō 奥井海生堂 is one of the most highly regarded producers of *kombu*. Not available in local supermarkets, this top-quality product may be found in shops in most *depachika*, including **Isetan** and **Takashimaya.** www.konbu.co.jp/ (Japanese)

Katsuobushi かつお節 Dried and shaved bonito flakes, a key ingredient in *dashi*, brings a smoky richness to the broth. It can be made from a variety of fish including yellowfin tuna, mackerel, and anchovies—each, of course, with its own flavor profile. To make *katsuobushi*, the bonito is simmered and its bones are removed, after which it is dried and smoked. Sometimes a mold that promotes fermentation is added to the bonito. Other fish are processed in a similar fashion. There are two major types of *katsuobushi*:

Arabushi 荒節 Light in flavor, this dried and smoked *katsuobushi* is the most popular type, especially in the Kyoto/Osaka region.

Karebushi 枯節 A mold that promotes fermentation and imparts a stronger *umami* flavor is added to *arabushi*, resulting in this type of *katsuobushi*, popular in the Tokyo region.

There are different ways to shave fish flakes, depending on how they will be used in cooking:

Atsu kezuri 厚削り Thick-cut shavings that make an intense *dashi*; used in dishes that are simmered for a long time

Hanakatsuo 花かつお Thinly shaved flakes used for making *dashi* quickly

Hana kezuri 花削り Very thin shavings also used to make instant *dashi*

Ito kezuri 糸削り Thin strands often used as a garnish for *tōfu* or vegetables

Niboshi 煮干し are small fish that are simmered in salty water and sun-dried before being used to make *dashi*. *Niboshi* can be made from a variety of fish. Some popular types include:

Katakuchi iwashi 片口鰯 The most popular type of *niboshi*, made with anchovies; commonly used for making *dashi*

Ma iwashi 真鰯 Made with pilchard; popular for *soba* or *udon*

Urume iwashi 潤目鰯 Low in fat, and odorless; this *niboshi* made with round herring makes a clear-colored *dashi* popular in the Kyoto/Osaka region

Tobiuo 飛魚 *Dashi* made with the flying fish is slightly sweet and popular in the Nagasaki region

Ma aji 真鯵 *Niboshi* made with jack mackerel; results in a delicate and sweet *dashi*

Tai 鯛 Sea bream *niboshi* makes a delicate, elegant *dashi*; found in dishes served at a *kaiseki* restaurant rather than at a neighborhood noodle shop

PRODUCE

....

VEGETABLES

野菜

YASAI

THE BOUNTY OF NUTRITIOUS VEGETABLES IN JAPAN
IS CELEBRATED THROUGHOUT EVERY SEASON.

As snow melts in the hills, bitter and delicate mountain vegetables (*sansai*) spring forth from under ground. The summer garden brims with colorful, sweet tomatoes, eggplant, and the popular *edamame* (soybeans). Autumn brings bamboo shoots and earthy mushrooms from the forest floors, and winter sustenance comes from Japan's many root vegetables, perhaps best represented by the large, icy-white *daikon*.

Vegetable preparations are often minimal—the clean, crisp, pure flavors of raw vegetables are underscored with a satisfying crunch. Light, lively, and refreshing greens are sautéed briefly, blanched, or steamed and topped with simple dressings. *Tempura* showcases vegetables in a crisp, lacy batter. Simmering (*nimono*) is favored in winter because it tenderizes root vegetables and brings out their rich flavors. Another popular dish, *hitashimono*, consists of greens such as chrysanthemum leaves, spinach, and mustard greens that are blanched and then served with soy sauce and garnished with bonito flakes or toasted sesame seeds. These are vegetables most commonly found in Japanese cuisine:

Aka kabu A red-skinned turnip

Aka pīman A red bell pepper

Akajiso A member of the mint family alternately called red *shiso* leaf, red perilla, or beefsteak plant; often used for pickling, especially with *umeboshi* (salted apricots)

Aojiso A green beefsteak plant, or green perilla; this is often called Japanese basil, but tastes mintier than basil

Azuki Small red beans, popular ingredient for *wagashi*

Chingensai Bok choy

Daikon A large, white radish, sometimes called icicle radish

Daizu Dried soybeans

Edamame Soybeans boiled in their skins and salted; a popular summer snack

Enoki A slender, white mushroom; there is also a brown variety

Eringi A king trumpet or king oyster mushroom

Fuki A giant butterbur

Gobō Burdock root

Gōya A bitter gourd

Ingenmame Kidney beans

Hōrensō Spinach

Jagaimo Potato

Junsai A water-shield, often served in a vinegared (*sunomono*) preparation

Kabocha Pumpkin squash

Kabu A turnip, popular for pickling; the leaves of *kabu* can also be eaten

Kaiware Daikon sprouts

Kikurage A wood ear mushroom with an unusually tough and sometimes gelatinous texture

Kinome The young leaves of *sanshō* (see below); when you are served *kinome*, it is suggested that you take the leaves into your hands and clap them together to wake up the flavor

Kinusaya Snow peas

Komatsuna Mustard spinach

Kuromame Dried black beans

Kuwai Arrowhead bulb that is often served in a traditional New Year's meal (*osechi ryōri*)

Kyūri Japanese cucumbers

Maitake Hen-of-the-woods mushrooms

Matsutake A mushroom famed for its aroma

Mitsuba Trefoil, a popular garnish

Mizuna Potherb mustard

Moyashi Bean sprouts

Myōga A ginger bud prized for its aroma and bite, plus the gorgeous blush color it turns when pickled

Nagaimo A Chinese yam, see yamaimo

Nameko A mushroom famous for its slippery texture

Nanohana Rapeseed shoots

Nasu An eggplant

Negi A Japanese leek

Nigauri A bitter gourd, also called *goya* in Okinawa

Ninjin Carrots

Ninniku Garlic

Nira Garlic chives

Nozawana Turnip greens

Okura Okra

Pī-man A Japanese green bell pepper

Rakkyo Baker's garlic

Renkon Lotus root

Sansai Mountain vegetables

Sanshō Japanese prickly ash seeds

Sato imo Taro root

Satsuma imo A sweet potato; Satsuma is a city in Kagoshima

Saya endō Snow peas

Saya ingen Young kidney beans, snap beans

Seri Water dropwort

Shiitake A popular mushroom; dried *shiitake* mushrooms are *hoshi shiitake*

Shimeji A type of mushroom

Shirouri An Asian pickling melon, popular in Narazuke pickles

Shishitō A sweet green pepper, often grilled

Shiso A perilla or beefsteak plant, and member of the mint family; see also *akajiso* and *aojiso*

Shiso no hana The delicate lavender-colored flowers of the *shiso* plant

Shiso no mi The young buds of shiso, a popular garnish for *sashimi*

Shōga Ginger; *benishōga* is red pickled ginger; *gari* are the thin slices of pickled ginger served with *sushi*

Shungiku Chrysanthemum leaves, also called *kikuna*

Soramame Fava beans

Takenoko Bamboo shoots

Tamanegi Onions

Tōgarashi Red chili peppers

Udo Japanese spikenard

Wakegi Spring onions

Wasabi A spicy root vegetable that is a popular condiment for *sushi* and *sashimi*

Yamaimo A yam that is very sticky; when grated, it is called *tororo*

Yurine A lily root

"THE FIFTH TASTE"
旨味
UMAMI

UMAMI IS THE FIFTH CATEGORY OF TASTE AND IS not as commonly known as the other four (sweet, salty, sour, and bitter). *Umami* can be described as savory; it is full, rich, and round on the palate. It exists naturally in many foods, including Parmesan cheese, meat, mushrooms, seaweed, and tomatoes. In 1908 Professor Kikunae Ikeda identified *umami* while sampling his wife's *tōfu* simmered in a kelp broth and later isolated glutamate, inosinate, and guanylate, the naturally occurring amino acids and nucleotides that are the common components in *umami*-rich foods. Professor Ikeda also developed the flavor enhancer monosodium glutamate.

Umami is a concept with which all Japanese people are familiar—the Japanese palate easily recognizes its rich mouth-feel. The *kanji* characters for *umami* translate as "delicious flavor." (When something tastes good, it is often said to be *oishii*, but it can also be called *umai*, and shares the Japanese character for *umami*.) Many Japanese ingredients are rich in natural *umami*, including some of the main players in the Japanese pantry: soy sauce, *miso*, *mirin*, and *sake*. Food is richer in *umami* when dried than when fresh: *shiitake*, scallops, and *daikon*, for example.

Nakaiseki Sen • 菜懐石仙
Setagaya-ku, Shimouma 5-35-5 2nd Floor
世田谷区下馬 5-35-5 2F
Tel. 03-5779-6571
12:00–15:00 Thursday to Saturday;
closed the third week of the month • Reservations required
RESTAURANT • EXPENSIVE • MAP PAGE 156, #31

Chef Yumiko Kano has published more than fifteen cookbooks on vegetarian cooking. Her restaurant, Nakaiseki Sen, offers unique vegetarian *kaiseki* (multi-course fine dining) cooking. But Sen isn't just for vegetarians—anyone who appreciates food will find plenty to enjoy here. Chef Kano's colorful cuisine is inspiring, delicious, and, as it should be in a traditional *kaiseki*, presented beautifully. Some of the vegetables come from the chef's parents' farm in Tottori.

Daigo • 醍醐
Minato-ku, Atago 2-3-1, Forest Tower 2F
港区愛宕 2-3-1 フォーレストタワー 2F
Tel. 03-3431-0811
Daily 11:30–14:00, 17:00–20:00
RESTAURANT • EXPENSIVE • MAP PAGE 157, #22

This *shōjin ryōri* (Buddhist temple cuisine) is presented in private rooms with views of a Japanese garden. It is a *kaiseki*-inspired menu, based purely on vegetables, that offers a rich taste of the garden. The menu may include a soymilk-based soup, wheat gluten (*nama fu*), *soba* noodles, and *miso*—and, often, unusual vegetables you'll be glad to have tried.

Sankōin • 三光院
Koganei-shi, Honchō 3-1-36
小金井市本町 3-1-36
Tel. 042-381-1116
Lunch only • Reservations required
www1.odn.ne.jp/sankouin/index.htm (Japanese)
RESTAURANT • MODERATE

For a truly unique *shōjin ryōri* dining experience, come to Sankōin temple in the Western part of Tokyo. Here you can dine on the traditional Buddhist temple cuisine: very simple and down-to-earth. The temple's cookery techniques are documented in a detailed book, *Zen Vegetarian Cuisine*, authored by abbess Soei Yoneda and published by Kodansha International.

Kushiage Dokoro Hantei • 串揚げどころ はん亭根津

Bunkyo-ku, Nezu 2-12-15 • 文京区根津2-12-15

Tel. 03-3828-1440

11:30–14:00, 17:00–21:30 Tuesday to Sunday; if Monday is a holiday, the restaurant will be open, and closed on Tuesday

www.hantei.co.jp/nedu.html (Japanese)

RESTAURANT • MODERATE • MAP PAGE 157, #3

Nezu is an old downtown neighborhood; a walk through the area offers a glimpse of life in old Tokyo. This handsome, historic three-story building is home to one of the most popular *kushiage* restaurants in the city. While not strictly vegetarian (side dishes may include fish-based *dashi*, and meat is readily available to those who want it), *kushiage* is a unique way to try vegetables: bite-size meats, seafood, and vegetables are threaded on to bamboo skewers, and then breaded and deep-fried. Each day at Kushiage Dokoro Hantei, there are thirty-six options to choose among; these change throughout the year. The easiest way to enjoy a meal here is to order a basic course of skewers accompanied by several side dishes. The meal ends with rice or *ochazuke* (rice with hot tea poured over it), *miso* soup, and pickles, followed by ice cream.

SEA VEGETABLES

海藻

KAISO

SEA VEGETABLES, A NAME FOR AQUATIC VEGETATION MORE ACCURATE THAN THE OFT-USED "SEAWEED," have a prominent place on the Japanese table and are valued for being rich in minerals and low in calories. *Kaisō* is the generic term for sea vegetables; well-known sea vegetables found frequently on the Japanese table include kelp (*kombu*), laver (*nori*), sea tangle (*wakame*), and *hijiki* (no English name). *Wakame* is often used in *miso* soups or on salads; *hijiki* is often simmered in soy sauce and broth (*dashi*). Red algae (*tengusa*) is another major sea vegetable. It won't be found on the dinner plate, but it is widely consumed—it's the major component of agar agar (*kanten*), a low-calorie gelatin.

Kelp 昆布 *Kombu*

Kombu is the king of sea vegetables. It is an essential component in *dashi* (see page 54), the broth used in many Japanese dishes. A natural source for glutamic acid, it is rich in *umami*. *Kombu*

MOUNTAIN VEGETABLES

山菜
SANSAI

EACH YEAR THE APPEARANCE OF WILD MOUNTAIN
vegetables at the market is an eagerly anticipated event
marking the end of a long winter and the arrival of spring.
Sansai are considered precious because they are available
for such a short time—usually a span of a few weeks—and
foraged in the wild. *Sansai* include shoots, greens, and
small and tender young plants; there are more than two
hundred types. *Sansai* are often served in a bowl of *soba*,
the bitterness of the greens offering a nice contrast to the
earthy buckwheat noodles. *Tempura* is one of the best-loved
preparations for *sansai*. Some popular *sansai* include:

Asatsuki Chives
Fuki Japanese butterbur
Fuki no to Unopened bud of
    Japanese butterbur
Katakuri Dog's-tooth violet
Kogomi Fiddlehead fern
Nobiru Red garlic
Seri Water dropwort

Tara no me Shoot of the
    angelica tree
Tsukushi Field horsetail shoot
Udo Japanese spikenard
Warabi Bracken
Yomogi Mugwort
Zenmai Royal fern

thrives in the cool, mineral-rich waters surrounding Hokkaido, Japan's northernmost island.

Some *kombu* products (not the *kombu* used in *dashi*) include:

Komochi kombu *Kombu* layered with herring eggs
Kombu cha *Kombu* that has been dried and crushed into a powder; most often used for tea, soup stocks, or for thickening non-oil salad dressings
Musubi kombu Knots of *kombu*, often found in fish cake stew (*oden*)
Oboro Shaved *kombu*, used for soups
Tororo Shaved *kombu*, used in soups and wrapped around rice and other items

Laver 海苔 *Nori*

Nori is toasted and most often found surrounding rolled *sushi* (*makizushi*). Eighty percent of Japan's *nori* is harvested in the Ariake Bay and Seto Naikai in southern Japan. Before eating, *nori* may be warmed slightly over low heat to bring out its aroma.

Some *nori* products include:

Aonori Green laver that has been dried and flaked; used as a topping on food such as *okonomiyaki*, a savory pancake
Aosa Green laver similar to *aonori*
Ajitsuke nori Laver seasoned with soy sauce and *mirin*; popular at breakfast
Mominori Shredded bits of *ajitsuke nori*; often used as a garnish over noodles
Yaki nori Toasted *nori*, used for rolled *sushi*

PICKLES
漬け物
TSUKEMONO

JAPANESE PICKLES—VARIOUSLY CALLED TSUKEMONO, KONOMONO, OR OSHINKO—CAN BE SALTY, SOUR, tart, piquant, or sweet. Pickling agents include salt, vinegar, soy sauce, *miso*, *sake* lees, and rice bran, to name a few. Pickling time ranges from a few minutes to a few hours to a few years, and some pickles are fermented in the process. They also vary widely in texture: cucumber pickles are crispy, eggplant pickles are soft and may squeak in your teeth. *Takuan*, the popular yellow pickle made from dried *daikon*, is sweet and crunchy.

From the thin-sliced pickled ginger at the *sushi* counter to *kaiseki* meals that traditionally end with them, pickles are present in some form at most Japanese meals. *Benishōga*, or bright red pickled ginger, is a popular accompaniment to fried noodles with vegetables (*yakisoba*). Curry is often served with sweet, red pickles made from seven different vegetables called *fukujinzuke*.

The Japanese are so enthralled with pickles that there are entire shops devoted to one type, such as *umeboshi*. Often called pickled plums, *umeboshi* are actually apricots. The distinctive red color of the *umeboshi* comes from pickling it with red *shiso* (*akajiso*). They can range from soft to hard, and from extremely salty to quite sweet (honey is sometimes used in the pickling process). Consumers have distinct preferences, and at some shops the salt percentages for *umeboshi* are listed: 5% is considered sweet, 7–8% standard, and 14% very salty. *Neriume*, *umeboshi* paste, is used in rolled *sushi* and for salad dressings. A shop that specializes in *umeboshi* is **Godaian**.

Some of the most distinctive pickled items are called *Narazuke*, which originated in Nara, in the Kansai region. These melons, gourds, and other vegetables are pickled in *sake kasu* (*sake* lees) for as long as three years. Many of the melons and gourds are long, thin varieties, and after pickling, are presented in a spiral that resembles a sausage and covered in a brown slurry.

Another distinctive type of pickle, *nukazuke*, uses rice bran (*nuka*) as the fermenting agent. In the market the *nuka* looks like wet sand and covers whole pickled vegetables such as cucumbers, carrots, or radishes. Before eating, the bran is rinsed off and the vegetables are cut up into bite-size pieces. The resulting aroma and flavor are quite different from pickles made with salt or vinegar.

While in Tokyo, be sure to try a local pickle *bettarazuke*: *daikon* pickled in rice *kōji* slurry. These are some other popular pickling styles:

KYOTO'S HEIRLOOM VEGETABLES

京野菜
KYO YASAI

OF ALL THE VEGETABLES RAISED IN JAPAN, THE heirloom varieties of Kyoto are the most famous and are regularly found in the markets and restaurants of Tokyo. The richness—in color, nutrition, and history—of Kyoto's vegetables means they often fetch quite a high price; nonetheless, they're worth seeking out. Forty-one have received an official designation.

Here are just some of the popular varieties of *Kyō yasai*:

Ebi imo A yam, the skin of which resembles a shrimp shell, hence the name (*ebi* means shrimp)

Fushimi tōgarashi A chili pepper from the Fushimi area

Horikawa gobō Burdock root

Kamo nasu A fat, round eggplant from the Kamigamo region of northern Kyoto

Kintoki ninjin A dark red carrot

Kyō takenoko Bamboo shoots that are so sweet and tender they can be eaten raw, *sashimi*-style

Mibuna Similar to *mizuna*, this plant is harvested near the Mibu temple

Mizuna A potherb mustard plant with a thin, white stalk and green leaves, popular as a salad green outside of Japan; in Kyoto it is often pickled or boiled

Shishigatani kabocha Pumpkin squash

Shōgōin daikon A fat and round radish; unlike the omnipresent long *daikon*, this variety has an inherent sweetness

Shiozuke 塩漬け With salt
Suzuke 酢漬け With vinegar
Shōyuzuke 醤油漬け With soy
    sauce

Misozuke 味噌漬け With *miso*
Nukazuke ぬか漬け With rice bran

The best place to see a wide variety of pickles is at *depachika*. At a minimum, there will be separate shops specializing in *umeboshi*, *Narazuke* (pickles from Nara), and *Kyōzuke* (pickles from Kyoto).

Kintame • 近為
Koto-ku, Tomioka 1-14-3 • 江東区富岡1-14-3
Tel. 03-3641-4561 • 11:00–17:00 Tuesday to Sunday
www.kintame.co.jp/ (Japanese)

SHOP/RESTAURANT • INEXPENSIVE • MAP PAGE 157, #18

If you are really passionate about pickles, a meal at Kintame is not to be missed. Ask for the *bubuchazuke*, an array of pickles served with a grilled fish that has been marinated in *miso* or *sake kasu*. (This is the suggested set menu that includes about a dozen types of pickles.) The restaurant is on a small side street that leads up to the Fukagawa Fudoson temple; the neighborhood is off the beaten path and has a nostalgic feel to it. The Monzennakacho location is extremely popular on weekends, so be prepared for a long line. There is also a retail shop a few doors down if you want to purchase any pickles.

Although the main restaurant is listed above, the most convenient location is the branch at **Daimaru**'s Restaurant Floor at Tokyo station.

SEMBIKIYA

特撰

静岡産

マスクメロン

2個桐箱入り

税込 **23,100**円

(本体価格22,000円)

FRUIT

果物

KUDAMONO

THE JAPANESE RESPECT FOR FRUIT PROVIDES AN INSIGHT INTO THE CULTURE'S LOVE OF NATURE AND BEAUTY.

Farmers take great pride in producing an ideal specimen. A farmer raising a muskmelon will select the best melon from each plant and designate it as a keeper; the others are discarded so that the nutrients and water that this plant takes in are given to the chosen one. When it is sent to the market, the melon is delicately wrapped in a silken robe and packaged in a wooden box. It is not uncommon to see these juicy bombs sell for several hundred dollars each.

This same obsessive attention to detail is also lavished on other fruit. Plants are carefully pruned and sheltered from harsh weather conditions with paper umbrellas to shade the fruit from sun and rain. Webs of twine may be used to train vines away from each delicate fruit to prevent mold and to allow direct sunlight.

Brand names for fruit indicate prestige in the same way as do those for *wagyū* beef. The renowned Amaou strawberries of Fukuoka—which may cost as much as $10 each—derive their name from the words *akai* (red), *marui* (round), *okii* (big), and *umai* (delicious). Yubari melons from Hokkaido and Sato Nishiki cherries from Yamagata are just some of the highly regarded brands of fruit that flood the market each year. Try them and you won't be disappointed.

Fruit shops in Japan not only sell fresh fruit but also offer tarts overladen with berries, cakes decorated with cut fruits, citrus fruit jellies presented in the shell of the fruit, fruit confitures, dried fruits, colorful fruit baskets, and more.

Many *depachika* will have at least one fruit shop with an eat-in counter. Go there to indulge in a slice of juicy melon, a freshly squeezed juice, a fruit parfait, or the quirky fruit sandwich of seasonal thinly sliced fruits dressed with whipped cream and sandwiched between crustless slices of white bread.

At the large fruit establishments **Sembikiya** in Nihonbashi and **Takano** in Shinjuku you will find, adjacent to the fruit boutiques, restaurants where you can have a full-course meal based around seasonal fruits, where a spring lunch, for example, may feature mango and strawberries, in both sweet and savory dishes. These fruit emporiums also include casual cafés that offer fruit-based sweets and fresh cut fruit. **Qu'il Fait Bon** is a shop that makes exquisite fruit-laden tarts.

SOY

大豆食品
DAIZU SHOKUHIN

THE SOYBEAN, A RICH SOURCE OF PROTEIN, IS CENTRAL TO THE JAPANESE DIET. SOY PRODUCTS INCLUDE TOFU, soy sauce, and *miso*. *Tōfu* can also be pronounced *dōfu*, as in *Koya-dōfu* (freeze-dried *tōfu*) or *yudōfu* (*tōfu* hot pot).

TOFU

豆腐

TOFU IN JAPAN CAN BE A REVELATION, A FAR CRY FROM THE BLAND BLOCKS COMMONLY FOUND ELSEWHERE. In Japan you will find a wide array of soy products including creamy *tōfu*, golden *tōfu* balls, silken layers of soymilk skin (*yuba*), and much more. If *tōfu* is served chilled (*hiyayakko*), it may be drizzled with soy sauce and garnished with either *myōga* (in the ginger family), grated ginger, bonito flakes, or *wasabi*. A contemporary version of chilled *tōfu* is served with extra virgin olive oil and sea salt.

Tōfu first appeared in Japan in the twelfth century, when the consumption of animal meat in Buddhist temples was forbidden. Soy products are thus an integral part of *shōjin ryōri*, the Zen vegetarian cuisine that originated in Kyoto. Since *tōfu* is composed of 90% water, it is no wonder that Kyoto—famous for its rich water sources—is known for its *tōfu*. The following are popular *tōfu* products:

Abura-age 油揚げ Pieces of *tōfu* from which excess water has been pressed, and then deep-fried

Agedashi dōfu 揚げ出し豆腐 *Tōfu* that is rolled in a starch (*katakuriko*), deep-fried, and covered in a savory soy and *dashi* sauce

Atsu-age 厚揚げ Thick pieces of *tōfu* that are deep-fried

Ganmodoki がんもどき *Tōfu* that is mixed with vegetables from both land and sea, molded into balls, and deep-fried

Hiyayakko 冷奴 Chilled *tōfu*, popular in summer

Kinugoshi dōfu 絹ごし豆腐 Soft or silken *tōfu*

Koya-dōfu 高野豆腐 Freeze-dried *tōfu*, named after Mount Koya where it was originally made

Momen dōfu 木綿豆腐 "cotton *tōfu*" or firm *tōfu*, so called because the *tōfu* was traditionally strained through a piece of cotton cloth

Yakidōfu 焼き豆腐 Grilled *tōfu*, often used in hot pots

Yosedōfu 寄せ豆腐 *Tōfu* with a texture somewhere between silken and firm *tōfu*, creamy but not too firm

Yudōfu 湯豆腐 *Tōfu* hot pot, a popular dish in the winter

Zaru dōfu ざる豆腐 Very soft *tofu* named for the *zaru*, a bowl made from bamboo in which it is formed

OTHER SOY PRODUCTS

Daizu 大豆 Dried soybeans

Edamame 枝豆 fresh soybeans, usually served boiled and seasoned with sea salt

Kinako きなこ Flour made from toasted soybeans; a popular ingredient in *wagashi* (Japanese confections)

Miso 味噌 See page 76

Okara おから The pulp left over after steamed soybeans are pressed to make soymilk; low in fat and rich in fiber, *okara* may be mixed with vegetables, or used as an ingredient in croquettes

Nattō 納豆 Fermented soybeans, famous for a their funky aroma and gooey texture; see page 78

Tōnyū 豆乳 Soy milk

Yuba 湯葉 The skin from soy milk that has been heated; best when served on its own with a bit of soy sauce and *wasabi*, it can also be used to wrap foods or as an ingredient

Tōfuya Ukai • とうふ屋うかい
Minato-ku, Shiba Koen 4-4-13 • 港区芝公園4-4-13
Tel. 03-3436-1028 • Daily 11:00–20:00
www.ukai.co.jp/shiba/tofu/index.html#english (English)
RESTAURANT • LUNCH MODERATE, DINNER MODERATE TO
EXPENSIVE • MAP PAGE 157, #26

In the shadow of the city's landmark Tokyo Tower, Tōfuya Ukai offers one of the most charming dining experiences in the city. The restaurant specializes in *tōfu* and soy products, but also serves seafood and meat. The menu is *kaiseki*-style, with successive courses of exquisitely presented seasonal food, which may include deep-fried *tōfu* in a sweet *miso dengaku* sauce, seasonal *sashimi*, grilled seafood, and hot *tōfu* served in soy milk. Each party occupies its own private room overlooking a Japanese garden and although there are more than fifty-five private rooms and more than five hundred seats in total, you'll feel as if you are the only diners there.

Nebariya • ねばり屋
Shibuya-ku, Hatagaya 2-48-2, Ei Building B1
渋谷区幡ヶ谷2-48-2英ビルB1
Tel. 03-5358-8257 • Daily 11:30—23:00
r.tabelog.com/tokyo/A1318/A131807/13009202/ (Japanese)

RESTAURANT • INEXPENSIVE • MAP PAGE 156, #10

Nebari means "sticky," an appropriate name for this basement
mom-and-pop restaurant that specializes in what may be considered Japan's stickiest food, *nattō*. The menu is composed of simple
rice bowls (*donburi*) of *nattō* served with accompaniments such as
spicy fermented cabbage (*kimchi*), okra, slimy potatoes, and raw
tuna. Counter seats around the open kitchen allow diners to watch
their meals being prepared. On the street in front of the shop is a
menu board with photos of popular set menus.

MISO

味噌 OR みそ

MOST MISO IS MADE FROM ONE OR MORE OF THREE BASE INGREDIENTS: SOYBEANS, RICE, OR BARLEY. Eighty percent of *miso* sold is rice-based (*kome miso*). Barley *miso* (*mugi miso*) is primarily found in Kyushu and soybean *miso* (*mame miso*) in the Nagoya region.

Rich in protein and packed with vitamins and nutrients, many Japanese start the morning with *miso* soup; it is also commonly used as a dip for vegetables, or in salad dressings, or as a flavor enhancer, to add *umami* to hot pots, or as a marinade for fish, meat, and poultry. The sweet rice *miso* can be used as an ingredient for confections.

The palate of *miso* extends from sweet to salty and plays a diverse role in the Japanese kitchen. The color of *miso* ranges from light beige to a deep burgundy or even a dark fudge-like color. The color is determined by the base ingredient and how long it is aged. Its aroma can be light and fruity or rich and earthy. The texture of *miso* also ranges from smooth to chunky. Types of *miso* include:

Awase miso 合わせみそ A blend of two or more *miso*s; the resulting *miso* has properties of both

Dashi iri miso 出汁入りみそ *Miso* with *dashi* in it; often used in *miso* soup

Hatchō miso 八丁みそ Dark red, soybean *miso*, intense in flavor, from Aichi prefecture

Kinzanji miso 金山寺みそ *Miso* with fermented grains and vegetables; slightly sweet, often used as a condiment for vegetables

Saikyō miso 西京みそ Rice-based *miso* from Kyoto, typically on the sweeter side

Sendai miso 仙台みそ Often also called red *miso* (*aka miso*) from the Sendai area

Shinshū miso 信州みそ Rice-based *miso* produced mainly in Nagano prefecture

Shiro miso 白みそ Light-colored *miso*; can be on the sweet side, but can also be salty

There are hundreds of types of *miso* soup. These are a few of the most popular:

Asari jiru Miso soup with clams (*asari*)

Hiyashi jiru An unusual cold *miso* soup, popular in Miyazaki prefecture, with sesame paste, *tōfu*, and leeks

Kenchin jiru Miso soup with vegetables, *tōfu*, sesame oil, and a root vegetable that has been dried, reconstituted and made into a cake (*konnyaku*)

Miso shiru The generic term for *miso* soup, also known as *omiotsuke*

Nattō jiru Miso soup with crushed fermented soybeans

Satsuma jiru Miso soup with chicken and vegetables
Shijimi jiru Miso soup with clams (*shijimi*)
Tonjiru Miso soup with pork and vegetables

Aemono are dressings used on proteins and vegetables in which *miso* is blended with ingredients such as vinegar, sesame seeds, or mustard. The three most common dressings that use *miso* are *goma-misoae* (sesame paste and *miso*), *sumisoae* (sweet rice *miso* and vinegar), and *karashisumisoae* (sweet rice *miso*, vinegar, and mustard).

Some *miso*-based dishes include:

Dengaku A sweet paste of *miso*, sugar, and *sake* made into a thick sauce
   that is used over grilled *tōfu* or vegetables
Furofuki Simmered *daikon* with a sweet *miso* sauce
Misoni Fish (often oily fish such as mackerel or sardines) poached in a
   miso marinade
Misoyaki Fish or meat that is marinated in *miso* and grilled
Misoyaki onigiri Rice ball covered with a thin layer of *miso* and grilled
Misozuke Vegetables that have been pickled in *miso*

Sakamoto Shōten • 坂本商店
Setagaya-ku, Taishido 3-15-5 • 世田谷区太子堂3-15-5
Tel. 03-3413-2361
13:00—18:00 Monday to Saturday; closed Sunday and holidays
SHOP • MAP PAGE 156, #27

Although you can find a selection of *miso* at *depachika*, or even a local supermarket, the selection may be limited. Sakamoto Shōten, a shop that specializes in *miso*, carries about thirty types from small producers throughout Japan.

FERMENTED SOYBEANS

納豆
NATTO

NATTO, FERMENTED SOYBEANS KNOWN FOR their stinky aroma and a slimy texture, is one food that may be hard for a non-Japanese person to appreciate. Popular at breakfast in Japan, *nattō* is stirred with chopsticks until thick and sticky. Soy sauce and Japanese mustard may be added before the *nattō* is spooned over a bowl of rice. Condiments—such as grated *daikon*, leeks, bonito flakes, sea vegetables, pickled apricots (*umeboshi*), Japanese basil, and in some parts of Japan, apples or sugar—may be added. Dried *nattō* with *nori* and other seasonings is often sprinkled over hot rice. Dried *nattō* beans are a popular beer snack.

Not all *nattō* is the same. It varies according to the size of the beans (large, medium, or small), whether the beans are chopped or not, and the type of bean used. Most *nattō* is sold in plastic containers, but *nattō* wrapped in straw will have a richer aroma, texture, and flavor.

Nattō can also be used as a topping for pasta, or as a filling for deep-fried *tōfu* parcels, or as an addition to fried rice or an omelet. In another dish, called *bakudan* (literally, "bomb"), *nattō* is mixed with a raw egg yolk, okra, slimy potato, squid, and raw tuna—the result is a very healthy, very slippery, very slimy mixture that is eaten over rice.

Devotees of *nattō* use special *nattō* chopsticks that are designed to make the *nattō* stickier when stirred.

MEAT

....

肉

NIKU

NIKU IS THE GENERIC TERM ENCOMPASSING BEEF
(GYUNIKU), PORK (BUTANIKU), AND CHICKEN (TORINIKU).

Mention meat and Japan in the same breath, and the first thing that comes to mind for most people is "Kobe beef." Actually, Kobe Beef is a brand name—one of 229 recognized brands of *wagyū*, the Japanese fat-marbled beef that is famous around the world.

Wagyū cattle in Japan lead the most pampered lives imaginable for livestock. Some are fed beer, massaged (not Swedish-style, but by intense brushing), and serenaded with classical music in stress-free environments. *Wagyū* is from four breeds: the most popular is Japanese Black; the others are Japanese Brown, Japanese Polled, and Japanese Shorthorn.

The Japanese are vigilant when it comes to food safety. *Wagyū* is sold with tracking numbers that can be entered into a cell phone as the consumer shops. These numbers trace the meat's origins, document the history of the cow, what it was fed, and where it was processed.

The first time a diner sees *wagyū*, the marbling (*shimofuri*) may be surprising: the beef is uniformly marbled with a large percentage of fat. The most expensive *wagyū* has the most fat, and the fat is white, rather than tinged with yellow, as it may be in lower-quality meat.

Traditional beef dishes include *teppanyaki* (cooked on an iron griddle), *yakiniku* (grilled over a flame), *shabu shabu* (in a sort of hot pot, served hot or cold), and *sukiyaki* (simmered with vegetables in a sauce mixture). Western-style beef dishes that showcase the flavor and texture of the meat include roast beef, beef stew, and carpaccio.

More pork and chicken than beef is consumed in Japan, and the quality of both is excellent. Pork is found in dishes like *tonkatsu* (breaded and deep fried), *shabu shabu*, *shōgayaki* (thinly sliced and stir-fried with ginger), and *kakuni* (soft-simmered). One brand worth seeking out is Hiraboku: the feed mixture used includes the famous rice of Yamagata. Hiraboku's *tonkatsu* can be found at a few shops in Tokyo, including Hirata Bokujo (Minato-ku, Akasaka 9-7-3, Tokyo Midtown) at Tokyo Midtown in Roppongi.

The practice of raising pigs in Japan originated in Okinawa more than four centuries ago. During the late nineteenth century, the prized Berkshire pig (*kurobuta*) was imported from England. *Kurobuta* is famous for its light sweetness, said to come from the Satsuma sweet potatoes fed to the pigs. Try the *kurobuta* at the **Kagoshima Yurakukan** regional shop or at **Maisen**.

Chicken, of course, is served in dishes like *yakitori* (bite-sized chicken on skewers), *teriyaki*, or as boneless fried chicken nuggets called *tatsuta-age* or *kara-age*. The three major chicken brands are Nagoya Kochin, Satsumadori, and Hinaidori. The city of Miyazaki, also famous for its chicken, has a local dish of chicken grilled over *sumi* (charcoal). You can try it at the **Miyazaki Kan KONNE** regional shop.

Some famous brands of *wagyū* 和牛 include:

Kobe Beef 神戸ビーフ This meat has a particular *umami* to it, and aromatic fat; as well as being massaged, Kobe Beef cows munch on a special grass and drink mineral-rich water.

Maesawa Gyū 前沢牛 The cold temperature of the northern prefecture that is home to this breed produces an aromatic meat with fine marbling.

Matsuzaka Gyū 松坂牛 Perhaps the most famous of all, these cattle are fed beer and massaged, resulting in good marbling.

Saga Gyū 佐賀牛 The waters of Saga region are said to contribute to this rich meat with sweet fat.

Yonezawa Gyū 米沢牛 This corn-fed meat with a fine marbling melts in your mouth.

Other names to look for include Iwate Gyū 岩手牛, Hida Gyū 飛騨牛, and Sendai Gyū 仙台牛.

For restaurants specializing in dishes cooked on an iron griddle *(teppanyaki)*, see **Ukai Tei**. Hotels also have top-class *teppanyaki*—Kamon (Chiyoda-ku, Uchisaiwaicho 1-1-1) at the Imperial Hotel, is also recommended.

Depachika offers the best selection for beef, pork, and chicken. For *wagyū*, see **Nihonbashi Hiyama** and **Asakusa Imahan** or **Matsuki**.

Takei • 竹井

Bunkyo-ku, Hakusan 5-17-19 • 文京区白山5-17-19

Tel. 03-3941-2725 • 7:30–19:30; closed Sunday and holidays

SHOP • MAP PAGE 157, #2

In an area peppered with small specialty shops, this meat shop, opened in 1934, has both second- and third-generation family members working behind the counter. Originally the shop specialized in *wagyū*, but due to popular request, it now offers domestic pork and chicken as well. Popular items include the roast beef and potato salad. Takei tries to sell meat at half of the market price by purchasing whole at the Shibaura slaughterhouse and then processing it on premises.

GRILLED CHICKEN SKEWERS

焼き鳥
YAKITORI

YAKITORI RESTAURANTS, ESPECIALLY THOSE UNDER the tracks at Yurakucho station, are popular gathering spots for office workers. Accompanied by a cold beer, the bite-sized bits of chicken, skewered and grilled until the outside is crisp while the inside remains juicy, are often eaten after a long day at the office. They are often very simple places, with only a few seats facing a counter. Often you will be asked if you want the *yakitori* with sauce (*tare*) or simply with salt (*shio*). Popular seasonings include seven spice (*shichimi tōgarashi*)

and a salty citrusy paste (*yuzu koshō*). In Japan, dark meat is generally preferred over white meat because it is juicier and richer in flavor.

Iseihiro Kyobashi Honten • 伊勢廣京橋本店
Chuo-ku, Kyobashi 1-5-4 • 中央区京橋1-5-4
Tel. 03-3281-5864
11:30–14:00, 16:30–21:00 Monday to Saturday;
closed Sunday and holidays
http://r.gnavi.co.jp/g133300/(Japanese)
RESTAURANT • LUNCH INEXPENSIVE, DINNER MODERATE
MAP PAGE 222, #32

Iseihiro dates to 1921 and is a third-generation restaurant. The best seats are at the counter on the ground floor where you can watch the chef, behind a pane of glass, grilling the *yakitori*. Dining on the second floor is *zaseki*-style, at low tables with seating on *tatami* mats on the floor. Iseihiro is one of the standard bearers for *yakitori* in the city. There are two other exceptional *yakitori* restaurants in Tokyo, **Birdland** and **Toritoh**.

Some menu items you may come across at *yakitori* restaurants include:

Aigamo 合鴨 Duck
Bonjiri ぼんじり Fatty part of chicken near the tail
Ginnan 銀杏 Gingko nuts
Hatsu ハツ Heart
Kashiwa かしわ Chicken thigh
Nankotsu なんこつ Cartilage

Negima ねぎま Thigh meat and leeks
Reba- レバー Liver
Sasami ささ身 Lean chicken
Tebasaki 手羽先 Chicken wings
Tsukune つくね Ground chicken and cartilage

OFFAL CUISINE
内臓料理
NAIZO RYORI

NAIZO, OR HORUMON, DENOTES THE EATING OF AN ENTIRE COW OR PIG—EVERYTHING FROM SNOUT TO tail, literally, and the organs and innards in between. If you can overcome any reservations you may have, you'll find fresh and well-prepared *naizō* provides a dining adventure unlike any other. You'll find a range of textures, from chewy (intestines) to creamy (brains). Preparations include stewing, grilling, and barbecuing. The key to good *naizō* is freshness, subtle seasoning (with salt or a soy-based sauce), and skillful preparation.

Yamariki • 山利喜
Koto-ku, Morishita 2-18-8 • 江東区森下2-18-8
Tel. 03-3633-1638 • 16:00—21:00; closed Sunday and holidays
www.yamariki.com/ (Japanese)
RESTAURANT • MODERATE • MAP PAGE 157, #8

Yamariki, an institution in the historic district of Morishita, is famous for its signature cow intestine *nikomi* that is slow-simmered until tender. The restaurant has used the same broth for almost forty years—much like a sourdough starter that has been passed down through generations, the broth is replenished daily. Yamariki is also known for grilled pork parts (*yakiton*), including juicy temples (*kashira*) and chewy rectum (*teppō*). Another distinguishing feature of Yamariki is its knowledgeable sommelier, Mizukami-san, who will suggest French or Japanese wines to accompany your menu. *Izakaya*-style restaurants like this one—*izakaya* denotes a Japanese pub that typically serves only beer, *sake*, and *shōchū*—rarely offer wine.

Wagyū Ryōri Sanda • 和牛料理さんだ
Minato-ku, Akasaka 3-19-3 • 港区赤坂3-19-3
Tel. 03-5570-1129 • 17:30—21:30; closed Sunday and holidays
RESTAURANT • MODERATE • MAP PAGE 157, #14

Wagyū Ryōri Sanda in Akasaka serves organ meats *kaiseki*-style (fine dining in several courses). *Naizō* is customarily served in casual settings, so, even for the Japanese, this dining experience in an upscale setting is unusual. Unlike most of the other *naizō* shops around town, Wagyū Ryōri Sanda is not a crowded joint filled with smoke; here you are served by a kimono-clad waitress.

The organs are served many ways, including raw, grilled, and hot pot-style. It is suggested by the staff that you ask what the different bites are *after* you have eaten them—advice well taken. Adventurous diners will find this restaurant well worth a visit.

See **Saiseisakaba** and **Shinjuku Hormone**, two typical *naizō* pubs.

Each restaurant also may have its own nicknames for an item. For example, the small intestines can be called *maruchō*, *maruchan*, and *kopuchan*, among other names. Here are some basic words you may come across:

Burenzu ブレンズ Brains

Fuwa ふわ Lungs

Gatsu ガツ Guts

Gyūtan 牛タン Beef tongue

Hatsu ハツ Heart

Hatsumoto はつもと Aorta

Hizō ひぞう Spleen

Kashira かしら Temples

Komekami こめかみ Temples

Maruchō まるちょう Small intestines

Nankotsu なんこつ Cartilage

Nodochinko のどちんこ Uvula

Nodomoto のどもと Throat

Pai ぱい Breast

Sao さお Tip of the penis

Shikin しきん Esophagus

Sunagimo すなぎも Gizzard

Tan タン Tongue

Tecchan てっちゃん Large intestines

Teppō てっぽう Rectum

Te-ru テール Tail

Tontoro とんとろ Neck from a pig

Yudetan 湯でタン Boiled tongue

HORSE MEAT

馬肉
BANIKU

OR

桜肉
SAKURA
NIKU

HORSE MEAT (BANIKU OR SAKURA NIKU), POPULAR in the southern prefecture of Kumamoto, but also found in restaurants in Tokyo, is low in fat and cholesterol, high in protein, and rich in vitamins—a healthy protein. Like other meats, each part of the animal produces a different cut that lends itself to different methods of cooking. The lean meat of the neck is eaten braised or ground; tender parts like the fillet are eaten rare; the back leg, rich in fat and collagen, is slow-cooked for a long time so that it becomes tender. The liver, sliced thinly, is sometimes eaten raw. Horse meat is also eaten *sashimi*-style (*basashi*), served with a slightly sweet soy sauce and grated ginger. It can also be served in the manner of steak tartare, or like a beef steak, grilled on the outside and rare on the inside, accompanied by *ponzu* sauce. *Hari hari nabe* is a hot pot of thin slices of horse meat, cooked *shabu shabu*–style with mushrooms and vegetables. *Shōchū*, the distilled spirit, in particular rice *shōchū*, a specialty of the Kumamoto prefecture, is the customary accompaniment for horse meat.

Minoya • みの家
Koto-ku, Morishita 2-19-9 • 江東区森下2-19-9
Tel. 03-3631-8298 • 12:00–14:00, 16:00–21:00;
closed Thursday; closed third Wednesday
of the month from May to October
www.e-minoya.jp (Japanese)

RESTAURANT • MODERATE • MAP PAGE 157, #9

Perhaps the most famous restaurant serving horse meat in the Tokyo area is Minoya, which is known for its horse meat hot pot (*sakura nabe*) or *sukiyaki*-style hot pot of leeks, *konnyaku* threads (no English name), and wheat gluten, served with a raw egg. The broth used in horse meat hot pots has a blend of rich Hatchō *miso* and a sweet Edo *miso*, resulting in a hearty broth able to stand up to a strong meat. Minoya is in the charming historic downtown area near Morishita station. This fifth-generation restaurant has been in existence since 1897. The large establishment has 110 seats on two floors.

SEAFOOD

鮮魚

SENGYO

JAPAN HAS THE MOST DIVERSE SEAFOOD CULTURE ON THE PLANET. THIS ISLAND NATION HAS MORE THAN 18,000 miles of coastline, along with many rivers and lakes. The wide climactic range of the country, from cool Hokkaido in the north down to the tropical islands of Okinawa, makes for a wide variety of seafood available year-round.

Certain regions are famous for seafood (and be aware that names for seafood may change by region). To complicate matters, some seafood is in season twice a year and the name of the same fish may change according to the season. *Katsuo* (bonito), for example, is called *hatsugatsuo* in the spring and *modorigatsuo* in the fall. Fish like this is often meatier during one season and fattier during the other.

The taste, texture, and different ways of eating the hundreds of varieties available throughout the year are exhaustive. This rich and integral part of Japanese cuisine deserves to be explored whenever you have the opportunity.

Some seafood (鮮魚) terms include:

Agemono Deep-fried; some fish, like flounder (*karei*), are deep-fried whole

Ankimo Monkfish liver

Asajime A fish that is killed with a special technique on the morning of the day it is served (see *ikijime*)

Buri daikon Yellowtail simmered with *daikon* in a soy broth

Harawata Literally "guts," *harawata* is the seafood equivalent of offal; an example would be the stomach of a mackerel pike (*sanma*), known for its distinctive bitterness

Himono Fish that are butterflied, salted, and air-dried; this brings out the *umami* in the fish and enriches its texture

Honesembei The bones of small fish that are fried to crispy bits and salted; a popular beer snack

Ichiyaboshi Another term for *himono* that are air-dried overnight

Ikijime (also called *ikejime*) A special process in which a thin metal rod is placed down the spine of the fish to kill it quickly; this procedure results in meat that is softer and richer in texture than that of fish killed by other methods

Ishiyaki Seafood, meat, or vegetables cooked on a hot rock

Kabayaki A sweet soy sauce most often served with eel (*unagi*)

Kara-age Deep-fried boneless nuggets of fish

Kobujime A process in which raw fish is marinated in kelp (*kombu*) to change the flavor and texture

Komochi Seafood with its roe

Kunsei Smoked seafood

Kusaya Fish that is fermented, dried, and grilled; known for its stinky smell (*kusai* means "smelly")

Maruage A deep-fried whole fish

Mirinzuke Grilled *mirin*-marinated fish

Misozuke Grilled *miso*-marinated fish; sometimes called *Saikyō yaki* when marinated in *Saikyō miso*

Namero A technique for preparing oily, silver-skinned fish (*aozakana*) in which the fish is chopped up and marinated with *miso*, ginger, and leeks, and served without cooking

Nimono Fish simmered in *sake*, broth (*dashi*), or a soy-based broth

Nitsuke Fish simmered in soy sauce and *dashi*

Nabe A hot pot, can include seafood and vegetables

Nukazuke Fish marinated in rice bran (*nuka*) and then grilled

Sakamushi Seafood steamed in *sake* and salt

Sakekasuzuke The process of marinating fish in *sake* lees, then grilling it

Sashimi Raw slices of seafood

Sushi Raw slices of seafood served with vinegared rice

Shiokara Describes a variety of fermented seafoods; one of the most common examples is squid, where the guts of the squid are mixed with raw squid

Shioyaki Fish sprinkled with salt and grilled

Shirayaki Eels (*anago, unagi*) grilled and seasoned with salt

Shōyuzuke Soy sauce-marinated fish that can be served raw

Shabu shabu Thin slices of seafood cooked quickly cooked in hot broth

Sujime The process of pickling raw fish in rice wine vinegar

Tataki Seafood chopped up into small pieces and served raw

Teppanyaki Seafood, meat, or vegetables cooked on a iron griddle (*teppan*); unlike what you find in chain restaurants outside of Japan, this is a sophisticated cooking style using top-quality ingredients

Teriyaki A sweet soy sauce used to season fish and meat

Tsuboyaki Shellfish grilled in their shell, often with soy sauce, *sake*, and broth (*dashi*) added before grilling

Tsukudani Seafood or sea vegetables cooked in a sweet soy sauce, originating in the Tsukuda district of Tokyo

Ushiojiru Soup made from a rich seafood stock; can be made from fish bones, from the head and collar of fish, or from shellfish

Yakizakana Grilled fish

Below is a list of fish according to when they come into season; they may also be available other times.

SPRING is famous for *mebaru, sawara, madai, kihada maguro, karei,* and *hatsugatsuo*. Other seafood in season in spring (many unknown and unavailable outside of Japan) include:

Ainame Greenling
Asari Japanese littleneck clams
Baigai Cockle
Funa Prussian carp
Hatsugatsuo Lean spring *katsuo* (bonito)
Hotaru ika Firefly squid
Ikanago Sand lance
Ishidai Striped beakfish
Katsuo Bonito (see *hatsugatsuo*)
Kidai Yellowback sea bream
Kisu Japanese whiting
Mategai Razor clams
Mebachi Big-eye tuna
Mebaru Rockfish

Meitagarei Frog flounder
Minami maguro Southern bluefin tuna
Nishin Pacific herring
Sakura ebi Sakura shrimp
Sakura masu Cherry salmon
Shako Mantis shrimp
Shiba ebi Shiba shrimp
Shimaaji Striped jack
Tairagai Pen shell
Takabe Yellow striped butterfish
Tobiuo Flying fish
Tokobushi Ear shell
Yamame Freshwater cherry salmon

SUMMER fish to look for include *aji, isaki, hamo, hiramasa,* and *takabe*, as well as:

Aji Horse mackerel
Anago Conger eel (from the sea)
Aori ika Bigfin reef squid
Awabi Abalone
Ayu Sweetfish
Binnaga Albacore tuna
Chidai Crimson sea bream
Dojō Loach
Ei Skate
Ebodai Japanese butterfish
Hamo Pike conger
Hiramasa Amberjack
Hoya Sea squirt
Isaki Grunt
Ishigarei Stone flounder
Ishimochi Croaker
Iwana Japanese char
Iwashi Sardine
Kamasu Barracuda
Kanpachi Greater amberjack
Karei Right-eye flounder
Kawahagi Thread-sail filefish
Kibinago Silver-stripe round herring

Kihada Yellowfin tuna
Kintokidai Red bigeye
Kochi Flathead
Kurumaebi Japanese tiger prawn
Mahata Grouper
Megochi Big-eyed flathead
Nijimasu Rainbow trout
Okoze Stonefish
Sake Salmon
Same Shark
Sanma Pacific saury
Sawagani Japanese river crab
Shijimi Corbicula clam
Surumeika Japanese common squid
Suzuki Japanese sea bass
Tachiuo Cutlassfish
Tai Sea bream
Tokijake Baby chum salmon
Tako Octopus
Unagi Freshwater eel
Uni Sea urchin
Urumeiwashi Round herring

AUTUMN fish to look for include *sanma, modorigatsuo, nametaga-rei, akagarei,* and *akijake*, as well as:

Akijake Chum salmon (also called *shirojake*)
Ankō Monkfish

Bora Striped mullet
Hamadai Ruby snapper
Haze Goby

Hirame Bastard halibut	*Modorigatsuo* Rich in fat, more
Ikura Salmon roe	than ten times the fat of
Ise ebi Japanese spiny lobster	spring's *hatsugatsuo*
Kaki Oysters	*Saba* Mackerel
Kegani Hairy crab	*Shiira* Dorado
Kohada Gizzard shad	*Shitabirame* Sole
Konoshiro Greater gizzard	*Soi* Black rockfish
shad	*Sumiika* Cuttlefish
Kurodai Black porgy	*Tara* Cod
Madara Pacific cod	*Torigai* Egg cockle
Magarei Little-mouth flounder	*Tsubugai* Whelk

WINTER fish to seek out include *buri, hirame, hotaru ika,* and *honmaguro,* and:

Akagai Ark shell	*Hamaguri* Cherrystone clam
Akagarei Flathead flounder	*Hatahata* Sandfish
Amadai Tilefish	*Hatsugatsuo* Rich in fat from the
Amaebi Sweet shrimp	winter (*modorigatsuo*)
Bakagai Surf clam	*Hokke* Atka mackerel
Budai Parrot fish	*Hokkigai* Sakhalin surf clam
Buri Yellowtail (also called *kanburi*,	*Hotate* Scallop
or midwinter yellowtail)	*Hon maguro* Bluefin tuna (also
Fugu Puffer fish	called *kuromaguro*)
Gazami Swimming crab	*Hōbō* Gurnard

Itoyoridai Golden thread sea bream

Kajika Japanese sculpin

Kajiki Swordfish

Kani Crab

Kasago Scorpion fish

Katakuchi iwashi Anchovy

Kensaki ika Swordtip squid

Kinki Thornyhead

Kinmedai Splendid alfonsino

Koi Carp

Kue Longtooth grouper

Kuro maguro Bluefin tuna (also called *honmaguro*)

Madai Red sea bream

Managatsuo Pomfret

Matōdai John Dory

Medai Japanese butterfish

Mejina Opal eye

Mirugai Trough shell

Mutsu Japanese bluefish

Namako Sea squirt

Sawara Japanese Spanish mackerel

Sayori Halfbeak

Sazae Turban wreath shell

Shirauo Japanese ice fish

Suppon Chinese softshell turtle

Tarabagani King crab

Tokubire Porcher (also called *hakkaku*)

Wakasagi Freshwater smelt

Yagara Smooth flute-mouth

Yari ika Spear squid

Zuwaigani Snow crab

The best place to shop for a diverse variety of seafood is at *depachika*. Here you will also see shops that specialize in one type of seafood—fish eggs, for example—or a single preparation such as *himono* (butterflied, salted, and air-dried fish).

PUFFER FISH

河豚
FUGU

THE FAMED PUFFER FISH (ALSO REFERRED TO as blowfish) is known more for its lethal toxins than its pleasure on the palate. Restaurants in Japan serving *fugu* must be licensed in properly handling and preparing the fish. The majority of poisoning incidents involve fishermen who are not certified to handle the fish. It is rare to be poisoned in restaurants, but not unheard of.

In fact, much of the *fugu* served in restaurants in Japan is the non-toxic, farmed variety. The tingling sensation on the tongue associated with eating puffer fish does not occur with the non-toxic farmed *fugu*—don't be disappointed if you are eating *fugu* and it does not happen. This is a good thing.

IMPORTANT: Do be careful before eating *fugu*. Be sure to confirm that the chef is licensed to handle the fish. To be safe, go to a restaurant that specializes in *fugu*.

Fugu restaurants often have large tanks in the front window, filled with the funny looking fish, swimming around. In addition to the flesh, many other parts of the *fugu* are consumed, including the skin and the sperm sac, which is considered a delicacy.

Some fugu menu items include:

Tessa てっさ *Fugu sashimi*, often beautifully presented in paper-thin slices in the shape of a chrysanthemum flower, and eaten with a citrusy soy sauce (*ponzu*). *Fugu* is a bit on the tough side so cutting it in very thin slices makes it easier to chew; *fugu sashimi* is sliced so thinly that it is almost transparent. To showcase the skills of the chef, it may be served on a decorative plate so that the pattern on the plate is visible through the slices. Since *fugu* is now being farmed, it is possible to eat it all year long, but if you are having wild *fugu*, the best time to have it is in the winter.

Nabe kawa 鍋皮 The skin of the *fugu*; when it is blanched in a hot pot, it has a *purikori* texture—chewy and a bit tough

Yaki fugu 焼き河豚 Bits and pieces of *fugu* marinated in a sauce and grilled

Fugu kara age 河豚から揚げ Meaty pieces of *fugu* that are fried

Shirako 白子 The sperm sac of a fish. The *shirako* of *fugu* is considered by many to be the most desirable of all *shirako* because of its creamy richness. The season is from January to March. It can be grilled, deep-fried, or lightly simmered and served with *ponzu*.

Tecchiri てっちり A hot pot (*nabe*) that is light, yet deeply flavorful. It is presented in a delicate and stunning paper *nabe* (*kaminabe*) that does not burn, even though it is placed directly over fire. The hot pot is filled with *fugu, tōfu,* Napa cabbage, green onions, *shiitake,* and chrysanthemum leaves. The dipping sauce is made with *ponzu*, small green onions, and *daikon* grated with a dried red chili pepper (*momiji oroshi*).

Fugu zōsui 河豚雑炊 A thick soup made from the flavorful broth that remains in the hot pot after eating *tecchiri;* rice and a scrambled egg are added with some salt to make a rich rice porridge

Hirezake. ひれ酒 A drink made by putting a dried and toasted *fugu* fin into a cup of sake

A popular restaurant chain that specializes in *fugu* is **Genpin Fugu**.

The *fugu* restaurant **Shunpanro** has a four-seat eat-in counter in the Takashimaya *depachika* in Nihonbashi.

SUSHI

寿司 OR 鮨 OR すし

SASHIMI

刺身

THE JAPANESE STRONGLY BELIEVE THAT GOOD-QUALITY SEAFOOD IS BEST ENJOYED RAW. A WIDE VARIETY OF supremely fresh fish in a colorful array and a sensual range of textures: the greatest joy of eating *sushi* and *sashimi* in Japan is the chance to try seafood that is hard to find elsewhere. It goes without saying to look for domestic fish 国産 (*kokusan*). Seek out wild fish 天然 (*tennen*) over farmed 養殖 (*yōshoku*). The other key term to keep in mind is *shun* 旬, which designates seasonality; this should be a priority when ordering. Some seafood is only available for a few days or weeks a year—take advantage of this rare opportunity.

When you are looking for a *sushi* restaurant, you may find "*sushi*" written in different ways. There are two ways to write *sushi* using *kanji*: 寿司 and 鮨. The first is a celebratory style, and the more popular, while the second combines the two characters for "fish" and "delicious." The word may also be written in the simple *hiragana* style as すし.

Sashimi is raw fish without any vinegared rice. *Sashimi* is almost always included in an elegant *kaiseki* menu and in most Japanese meals of several courses.

Arranging *sashimi* is much like the Japanese art of flower arranging, *ikebana*. When choosing how to display *sashimi*, attention is paid to the color, shape, size, and texture of the fish and the plate on which it is served. To finish, the chef will accent the plate with *tsuma*, an edible garnish. *Tsuma* is also the word for spouse or companion, and here refers to an accompaniment. *Tsuma* are also paired with certain fish based on the flavor combination. Tuna is often served with *daikon* and *shiso*. Other *tsuma* helps to cut the aroma of some raw fish, making it more palatable.

Popular *sashimi* presentation styles include:

Funamori The presentation of a variety of *sashimi* on a miniature wooden boat
Sugata tsukuri A whole fish that is cut into *sashimi* slices and then returned to its body; a popular method used with small fish such as horse mackerel
Kiku tsukuri Thinly sliced fish presented in the shape of a chrysanthemum flower

Popular edible garnishes (*tsuma*) include:

Ami daikon *Daikon* cut to look like a fishing net

Asatsuki Japanese chives

Benitade Water pepper; often served next to *wasabi*, its tiny purple leaves pack a spicy punch

Daikon Most commonly seen julienned, *daikon*, at finer *sushi* shops, is cut by hand using a intricate technique called *katsuramuki*

Daikon oroshi Grated *daikon* radish

Hōjiso Lavender-colored *shiso* flowers

Kogiku Baby chrysanthemum flowers in yellow or lavender

Murasaki shiso Purple *shiso* leaves

Momiji oroshi Grated *daikon* with dried red chili pepper

Murame Young buds of red *shiso* leaves

Myōga The fragrant buds of this plant, a member of the ginger family, are a colorful purple and can be served pickled or fresh

Ponzu jōyu A citrusy soy sauce

Shiso A member of the mint family, *shiso* is also known as perilla, beefsteak plant, or Japanese basil

Sumiso Sweet *miso* with vinegar

Wakame A sea vegetable

There are many types of *sushi*. The most common style, vinegared rice shaped into bite-sized pieces and topped with seafood, is called *nigirizushi*. It is also referred to as *Edomaezushi*, because it originated in Tokyo, formerly known as Edo.

Wasabi is used to counteract some of the fishiness of a fish, or—with rich, buttery cuts like *toro*—to balance its fat. *Wasabi* should be fresh *Wasabia japonica* that is not mixed with Western horseradish or food coloring—or made from powder, as is often the case outside of Japan. Real *wasabi* is grated on a sharkskin grater with a gentle, circular motion; and it should be grated frequently, as it loses its aroma quickly. At *sushi* counters, the chef will put the *wasabi* between the rice and the fish. If it is too much or not enough, you can ask the chef to adjust it.

Gari, ginger that is thinly sliced and pickled, is used as a palate cleanser between different types of *sushi*. At top shops, the *gari* is made in-house; it will be naturally colored, rather than the pink color you sometimes find at inferior shops.

The tea used at *sushi* shops is often a powdered *konacha* or *mecha*. It has the same aroma, taste and color of other teas, but is made from dried and powdered leaves; as a result, when hot water is added, an aromatic, dark, rich tea emerges. It isn't necessary to wait for the leaves to steep once the hot water is added.

The major types of *sushi* include:

Batterazushi A pressed *sushi*; vinegared rice is placed in a long rectangular box, topped with a salted, oily fish like mackerel, pressed, turned out of the box, and sliced.

Chirashizushi Vinegared rice that has been spread out in a flat box and topped with a variety of toppings, including seafood, pickles, and vegetables. Often referred to as "scattered *sushi*," it is easy to eat, popular at *bentō* shops, and varies from region to region. A *chirashizushi* from Hokkaido would be filled with salmon, salmon roe, and crab.

Edomaezushi The popular *nigiri* style of *sushi* (see *nigirizushi*)

Futomaki Thick rolled *sushi* (*makizushi*), often stuffed with several colorful items such as *tamagoyaki* (omelet), *shiitake* mushrooms, and cucumber

Hosomaki Small rolled *sushi* (*makizushi*), often made with only one or two ingredients. The following are some types of *hosomaki*:

Anakyūmaki *Anago* eel and cucumber

Kanpyōmaki *Kanpyō* gourd that has been cut into strips, dried, and then simmered in a sweet soy sauce

Kappamaki Cucumber

Nattōmaki Fermented soybean (*nattō*)

Oshinkomaki Made from *takuan* pickles, made from *daikon* radish

Tekkamaki Tuna

Umekyū A combination of tart pickled apricots (*umeboshi*) and cucumber (*kyūri*)

Inarizushi Sushi surrounded with a sweet pocket of deep-fried *tōfu*; the rice in the middle can be plain, or mixed with pickles or vegetables

Kaitenzushi *Sushi* conveyor belts

Makizushi *Sushi* wrapped with *nori* and rolled in a mat, also called *norimaki*; types of *makizushi* include *hosomaki*, *futomaki*, *temaki*, and *uramaki*.

Nigirizushi Also called *Edomaezushi*, describes vinegared rice that is formed into bite-sized pieces and topped with raw seafood

Sasazushi Bite-sized *sushi* wrapped in bamboo leaves

Temakizushi Sushi rolled by hand in *nori*, often in a cone shape

Temarizushi A ball-shaped *sushi*

Uramaki "Inside-out" rolled *sushi*, sometimes covered with fish eggs or sesame seeds; a style more popular outside of Japan

Other *sushi* terms:

Asajime Fish killed the day it is eaten, using the *ikejime* process

Chiai Blood vessel of the fish; the rich flavor is an acquired taste

Chūtoro Medium-fatty tuna

Denbu Shrimp or white-fleshed fish that has been cooked, seasoned, shredded, and often colored

Engawa The fatty part on the very edges (the fins) of flatfish

Geso Squid tentacles

Gunkanmaki *Nori* wrapped around *sushi* and then topped with salmon roe or sea urchin

Gyoku Omelet

Handai A wooden tub in which rice is vinegared

Hikarimono Silver-skinned fish

Ikejime Method of killing live fish that maintains a very fresh quality; also called *ikijime*. *Ikejime* fish are revered for the quality of the meat and will garner a higher price at the *sushi* counter.

Ikemono Fish that are still alive

Ikizukuri or ikezukuri Fish that have been killed just moments earlier and may still be moving on the plate; sometimes included on *sashimi* platters

Kobujime Raw fish that is marinated in *kombu* in order to bring out the *umami* and change the texture of the fish

SUSHI ETIQUETTE

IF YOU ARE ORDERING AN OMAKASE MEAL AT A
sushi shop, it is best to inquire about the price when making
your reservation. ("What should we expect to pay for lunch/
dinner?") If you arrive at the restaurant without reservations, it is better to ask before you sit down. At medium- to
top-range *sushi* restaurants, no prices are posted. Prices vary
wildly.

If you are ordering the chef's tasting menu, let the chef
know before you start if you have any food allergies.

If you are not going to order "*omakase*" (a chef's-choice
menu), and instead choose to order each piece à la carte, be
sure to know which fish are in season.

You can use chopsticks or fingers when eating *sushi*. At
top *sushi* shops each *nigiri* will be pre-seasoned so there is
no need to dip in soy sauce. When putting soy sauce into the
saucer, pour just a little bit. It is a sign of wastefulness if you
leave soy sauce in the saucer.

At some restaurants, the *sushi* chef will season each *sushi*
item for you, and there is no need to dip into soy sauce. If
you need to dip *sushi* into soy sauce, it's best to lightly dip
a part of the fish side into the soy sauce and put the whole
piece in your mouth. Be careful not to dip the rice into the
soy sauce because the rice will soak up too much soy sauce
or fall apart. *Gari*, the pickled ginger, is used as a palate
cleanser. This should never be placed on top of a piece of
sushi and eaten. *Sushi* with *nori* should be eaten as soon as it's
served, before the *nori* becomes soggy.

If the *sushi* is not pre-seasoned, turn the *nigiri* over, and
dip just a bit of the seafood into the soy sauce. You should
not add *wasabi* to the soy sauce as the *sushi* chef has already
added *wasabi* to the *sushi*. If you prefer more *wasabi*, or less,
let the *sushi* chef know.

Sushi should be consumed in one bite; don't bite it in half.
If it is too big, ask the chef to use less rice.

If you are served a platter of *sashimi* with a side of
wasabi, the way to eat it is to put a little bit of *wasabi* on
the fish and lightly dip the fish into the soy sauce. If you
put the *wasabi* directly into the soy sauce it will lose its
aroma—plus, putting too much *wasabi* in your soy sauce is
often considered an insult to the chef.

As with a French meal, there is an order to the courses. Of course, you can eat whatever you want, in whatever order you want. However, if you want to make a good impression on the *sushi* chef, save the rich flavored and fatty seafood for the end of the meal. Start off with light, white fish; then move on to meatier fish. From here try some seasonal seafood, incorporating different textures. Finish off with some sweet items, like eel (*anago*) with a sweet sauce and or omelet (*tamagoyaki*). This is a suggested order:

Shiromi White fish, including *hirame, kanpachi, karei, suzuki*, and *tai*

Hikarimono Silver-skinned fish, including *aji* (often topped with ginger), *kohada, iwashi, saba*, and *sayori*

Kairui Shellfish, including *akagai, tsubugai, torigai, hotate*, and *hokki gai*

Akami Red-fleshed fish, including *katsuo* (bonito) or *maguro* (tuna); *chūtoro, ōtoro, akami, zuke maguro, aburi maguro* (grilled), *bintoro*, and *kamatoro*

Nimono Simmered seafood, including *anago, hamaguri*, and *shako*

Makimono: Including rolls stuffed with tuna (*tekka maki*), *umejiso* (*umeboshi* paste and *shiso*), *oshinko* (pickles), *kappa maki* (cucumbers), *kanpyō maki* (made from *kanpyō*), *negitoro maki*, and *nattō maki*

Tamago Omelet

Kan How *sushi* is counted in restaurants: *ikkan* denotes one piece, *nikan* denotes two pieces. High-end shops will serve one piece of *sushi* per serving (*ikkan*); lower-end places, such as *kaitenzushi* (revolving *sushi* counters), serve two pieces per serving (*nikan*)

Kanpyō Dried gourd strips simmered in a sweet soy broth

Kappa Cucumber rolls

Makisu A bamboo *sushi*-rolling mat

Mejimaguro Baby tuna (so named because of its size, not its age)

Murasaki Soy sauce; *murasaki* means purple, which refers to the color of the soy sauce

Neta The seafood that is placed on top of the rice for *sushi*

Nikiri Soy sauce, *mirin*, and sake that have been cooked together

Nori Laver (sea vegetable) that is used to wrap *sushi*

Oboro A paste often made from white fish or shrimp, to which *mirin* and/or sugar is added

Odori Eating seafood that is still alive (*odori* means dancing—you feel the seafood dancing on your tongue)

Oshinko Pickles, often pickled *daikon* served with rolled *sushi*

Otoro The fattiest tuna meat

Otsukuri Small servings of seasonal *sashimi*; these courses may precede the *sushi* course at a high-end *sushi* restaurant

Shiromi A generic term for whitefish

Shōyu Soy sauce used as a dip or marinade

Soboro Minced protein, such as chicken, eggs, or seafood, seasoned and cooked

Su Vinegar used for flavoring rice

Sujime The process of marinating fish in vinegar

Tamagoyaki A thick omelet that can be sweet or savory

Tataki Finely chopped raw fish

Tekka Rolled tuna *sushi*

Tobiko Flying-fish roe

Toro The fatty part of tuna

Tsume A sweet sauce used as a dressing; often made from soy sauce and *mirin*, also called *tare*

Wasabi Japanese horseradish

Yakishimo Searing the outside of the fish

Zuke Fish that has been marinated in soy sauce and other flavorings

Seasonal Sushi

There may be more than one English name for some of the seafood listed below, and names of fish often change from region to region—the following is just a basic guide. Your best bet is to ask the chef to recommend *shun* or seasonal items. Some fish are available year-round due to farming and international imports. (Also see page 92 for seasonal seafood.)

THE FIVE RI'S

THE LANGUAGE SPOKEN IN A SUSHI SHOP
is particular to that world. The terminology of the
sushi shops includes the following five "*ri*" words
that you will hear over and over:

Agari Tea that is served at the end of the meal; green
tea cleanses the palate and prevents the growth of
bacteria

Gari Pickled ginger, which also cleanses the palate and
has antibacterial properties

Nikiri A thick sauce made from simmering soy sauce,
mirin, *sake*, and *dashi* that is brushed on seafood

Nori Black green laver often used for rolled *sushi*

Shari Vinegared rice

SPRING fish to look for include *kasugo* and *madai* from the sea bream family. Other seafood in season in spring include:

Akagai Ark shell
Anago Conger eel
Bafun uni Horse dung sea urchin
Botan ebi Botan shrimp
Hatsu gatsuo First spring bonito, lean with a firm texture and without fat
Iwashi Sardine
Kasugo Young sea bream
Madai Red sea bream
Mirugai Trough shell

Sayori half-beak
Sazae Turban wreath shell
Shako (komochi) Squilla or mantis crab shrimp with eggs
Shirauo Japanese icefish
Shirogisu Japanese whiting
Sumi ika Cuttlefish
Tako Octopus
Torigai Egg cockle
Uni Sea urchin

SUMMER is a good time for the *hikarimono*, or silver-skinned fish.

Aji Horse mackerel
Anago Conger eel
Aori ika Big fin reef squid
Awabi Abalone
Ebi Shrimp
Hiramasa Amberjack
Hoshigarei Spotted halibut
Iwashi Sardine
Karei Righteye flounder
Katsuo Bonito
Kihada maguro Yellowfin tuna
Kisu Sillago

Konoshiro Gizzard shad
Kuruma ebi Tiger prawn
Ma aji Japanese jack mackerel
Magochi Flathead
Makogarei Marbled flounder
Murasaki uni Japanese purple sea urchin
Shako Mantis shrimp
Shima aji Striped jack
Suzuki Japanese sea bass
Tachiuo Cutlassfish
Torigai Japanese cockle

AUTUMN is good for *modorigatsuo*, *sanma*, and other fatty fish.

Akagai Bloody clam
Ikura Salmon roe
Iwashi Sardine, round herring, anchovy
Kanpachi Amberjack
Karei Righteye flounder
Kita murasaki uni Northern Japanese purple sea urchin
Kohada Gizzard shad
Maguro Tuna

Mebachi Bigeye tuna
Mirugai Trough shell
Modorigatsuo Autumn bonito
Saba Mackerel
Sanma Pacific saury
Shako (konashi) Squilla or mantis crab shrimp without eggs
Sumi ika Cuttlefish
Tai Sea bream
Tako Octopus

WINTER is the time for *kanburi* and other fatty fish.

Aka uni Red sea urchin
Ama ebi Sweet shrimp
Akagai Bloody clam
Buri Yellowtail
Hamaguri Orient clam

Hirame Bastard halibut
Hon maguro Bluefin tuna
Hotategai Japanese scallop
Ikura Salmon roe
Iwashi Sardine

Kanbirame Winter bastard halibut	*Saba* Mackerel
Kanburi Winter yellowtail	*Sayori* Half-beak
Kawahagi Thread-sail filefish	*Shirako* Sperm sac of fish
Kohada Gizzard shad	*Shirogisu* Sillago
Kuromaguro Bluefin tuna	*Sumi ika* Cuttlefish
Kuruma ebi Tiger prawn	*Tai* Sea bream
Madai Red sea bream	*Tako* Octopus
Mirugai Trough shell	*Yari ika* Spear squid

The best place to see a wide variety of *sushi* is at *depachika*. *Inarizushi, oshizushi* (pressed *sushi*), *chirashizushi, Edomaezushi*, and more are available, so you can see the different styles. Very few *sushi* places are open on Sundays. A safe bet is to go to *sushi* restaurants in department stores or hotels.

Kaitenzushi are the counters that have a conveyor belt loaded with pre-made *sushi*. These are a nice, affordable option, and popular with families in Japan. The Magurobito chain does a nice job. See **Magurobito** in Asakusa.

For the ultimate experience, there are many high-end *sushi* counters where you can sit at the counter and have a revelatory experience (see **Ginza Harutaka**). If you have the budget for this, it is highly recommended. However, you can also have a rewarding experience on a more modest budget by visiting the more expensive places at lunchtime (see **Kizushi** or **Kyūbey**).

A *sushi* breakfast at Tsukiji Market can be a delicious experience, but… many of the dozens of *sushi* shops are crowded, and the market can become a circus when busy. You may have to stand in line for more than an hour, and, once inside, you may be pushed out the door the minute you finish. Be forewarned.

RICE AND NOODLES

RICE

KOME

THERE ARE CURRENTLY MORE THAN FIVE HUNDRED VARIETIES OF RICE GROWN IN JAPAN, EACH WITH its own aroma, texture, and flavor profile. *Koshihikari* is the most widely cultivated variety. Other popular varieties include

Akitakomachi, known for its strong flavor, the mild *Milky Queen*, known for its sticky texture, and *Kirara* 397, said to have a hint of sweetness. These varieties are different from the rice cultivated for *sake*. *Kodaimai* refers to heirloom strains of rice that have been cultivated for many generations.

The cultivation and harvest of rice is celebrated in May, when the rice seedlings are transplanted into water-filled fields, and in the autumn, at harvest. Rice is grown throughout Japan.

As throughout the culture, there are some rules of etiquette that apply to rice. Rice is so treasured in Japan that it is considered disrespectful to waste it. If you don't think you will finish a full bowl of rice, ask for a smaller portion before you begin eating (*"Gohan sukuname o kudasai"*). Never pour soy sauce over rice. It should be enjoyed as it is.

If the rice you are served has some charred bits in it, this is considered a good thing; the charred bits are referred to as *okoge* and are often a sign that the rice was cooked in a ceramic pot instead of a rice cooker.

Some types of rice include:

Akamai Red rice (a form of *kodaimai*)

Genmai Unpolished brown rice

Hakumai Polished white rice

Kodaimai A hearty heirloom strain of rice

Kuromai Black rice (a form of *kodaimai*)

Midorimai Green rice (a form of *kodaimai*)

Mochigome Sticky rice

Shinmai Newly harvested rice that appears on the market each fall

Zakkokumai are beans and grains are added to rice before it is cooked. The colorful flecks are not only attractive, but add essential vitamins and minerals to the rice. These grains can be purchased separately or pre-mixed. Following are some of the popular *zakkokumai* ingredients:

Amaransu Amaranth

Awa Foxtail millet

Azuki Dried *azuki* beans

Daizu Dried soybeans

Hadaka mugi Rye

Hato mugi Job's tears barley

Hie Japanese barnyard millet

Kibi Common millet

Kinia Quinoa

Kuromame Black beans

Maru mugi Uncracked grains of barley

Mochi Sticky rice

Oshi mugi Rolled barley

Donburi are large bowls of hot rice with toppings. These one-bowl meals are popular at lunchtime. Here are some common toppings:

Anagodon Tempura-fried eel
(*anago*)
Ikuradon Salmon roe
Kaisendon Seasonal fresh, raw
seafood
Magurodon Raw tuna
Magurozukedon Raw tuna
marinated in soy sauce and
mirin
Oyakodon Literally "mother
and child," *oyakodon* is
made of chicken and loosely
cooked eggs with a soy and
dashi broth. The restaurant
Tamahide in Ningyocho is
famous for its *oyako donburi*.
Shirasudon Salted, boiled sardines
Sukiyakidon Thinly sliced beef in
a sweet soy sauce
Tendon Tempura drizzled with a
sweet soy sauce
Unidon Sea urchin

Mazegohan, literally "mixed with rice," is cooked rice into which ingredients are folded. Some popular *mazegohan*:

Shiso gohan Fresh green Japanese
basil leaves
Takana meshi A pickled green leaf
Yukari gohan Dried, purple *shiso*
leaves

Literally "boiled with rice," *takikomigohan* has the additional ingredients added to the pot before the rice is cooked. This is a wonderful way to express the time of year by using seasonal ingredients such as fish or vegetables. The fish is often grilled before it is added to the pot. The liquid in which the rice is cooked may be seasoned with ingredients such as soy sauce, *sake*, or *mirin*. *Okowa* is a variation of *takikomigohan* using sticky rice. Yonehachi Okowa is a popular shop with stalls in many *depachika* selling seasonal *okowa* bentō boxes.

Some types of *takikomigohan*:

Gomoku gohan Five different
ingredients, such as chicken,
carrots, mushrooms, bamboo
shoots, and burdock root
Kuri gohan Chestnuts
Mame gohan Beans, usually green
peas
Matsutake gohan Matsutake
mushrooms
Sekihan A dish made from sticky
rice and *azuki* beans served at
celebrations
Shijimi gohan Clams
Shōga gohan Julienned ginger
Taimeshi Grilled sea bream

Onigiri, or *omusubi*, are rice balls stuffed with different ingredients and are commonly seen at convenience stores. These are carefully packaged along with a *nori* wrapper that is protected in a plastic sleeve so that it stays crispy until eaten. These are simple meals that travel well. Often when taking a short trip, a family member may be sent off with a few rice balls and some pickles. Hikers often carry *onigiri* in their backpacks.

Zōsui, or *okayu*, is creamy rice porridge.

Suzunobu • スズノブ
Meguro-ku, Nakane 2-1-15 • 目黒区中根2-1-15
Tel. 03-3717-5059 • 7:30–20:00; closed Sunday and holidays
www.suzunobu.com (Japanese)

SHOP

Perhaps Tokyo's most famous rice shop, Suzunobu has an impressive display of rice harvested from all over Japan, with over fifty varieties on display at a time. The rice is milled at the shop. The bespectacled and friendly Nishijima-san, is a five-star *komemaisuta*, a rice specialist. He can advise you on flavor profiles and textures, or suggest rice depending on what kind of dish you are cooking.

BUCKWHEAT NOODLES
蕎麦　そば
SOBA

OF ALL OF THE TYPES OF NOODLE IN JAPAN, SOBA IS THE MOST BELOVED. CONNOISSEURS BELIEVE THAT THESE buckwheat noodles are best appreciated served cold with a dipping sauce as *mori soba*. Eating *soba* this way, one can most fully enjoy the aroma and texture of the noodles. Some serious *soba* aficionados refer to themselves as *sobaliers*—essentially, *soba* "sommeliers."

The dipping sauce (*tsuyu*) is made from a blend of *kaeshi* and *dashi*. *Kaeshi* is made from a blend of soy sauce, sugar, and *mirin*, and ranges in sweetness. *Dashi* can be made from kelp and bonito or other smoked fish flakes and varies in intensity and smokiness.

Soba noodles are made with buckwheat flour, wheat flour, water, and salt. How much of the buckwheat is milled away determines the color and flavor of the noodles. The percentage of buckwheat flour to wheat flour also affects the flavor and texture. If a shop states their noodles are "7/3," that indicates a blend of 70% buckwheat flour and 30% wheat flour.

If you want to eat *soba*, look for signs that say *teuchi soba* 手打ちそば (handmade *soba*). Some shops have a large window where you can see the dough being rolled out into a thin sheet and being cut into thin strands with a special *soba* knife.

To eat *soba* properly, dip the bottom third of the noodles in the dipping broth, carefully slurping up the noodles and enjoying the flavor, texture, and aroma. Condiments from which you can choose include scallions, *wasabi*, grated *daikon*, and seven-spice blend. After finishing your noodles, the waiter will bring out *soba yu*, some of the hot water in which the noodles were cooked. This slightly starchy, flavorful water is poured into the remaining broth to make a savory, creamy hot soup to finish your meal. These are some common *soba* terms:

Inaka Rustic noodles, dark in color
Kake *Soba* topped with a hot broth
Kamo Namban Slices of duck served with scallions in hot broth
Kawari *Soba* dough flavored with different ingredients such as citrus, sea vegetable, Japanese perilla, green tea, sesame, etc.
Kitsune Hot *soba* served with sweetened deep-fried *tōfu*
Mori Cold *soba* served with a dipping broth
Sansai *Soba* served with young mountain vegetables, popular in spring when *sansai* are harvested
Sarashina White, delicate *soba* noodles that result when most of the shell of the buckwheat is milled away
Sobagaki A dense cake made from *soba* flour that may be served with a sweet or savory dressing
Sobagaki zenzai *Soba* flour cake served with sweet *azuki* bean paste
Tanuki Hot *soba* served with *tempura* bits
Tempura soba *Soba* served with a side of *tempura* seafood and vegetables
Teuchi Handmade noodles
Tororo *Soba* served with grated *yamaimo* mountain potatoes that have symbolic meanings including long life and health in the New Year
Zaru *Soba* noodles served on a *zaru* (bamboo tray) and garnished with laver (*nori*)

Kanda Yabu Soba • かんだやぶそば
Chiyoda-ku, Awajicho 2-10 • 千代田区淡路町2-10
Tel. 03-3251-0287 • Daily 11:30–19:30;
closed some holidays in January and August
www.yabusoba.net (Japanese)
www.norenkai.net/english/shop/yabusoba/index.html (English)
RESTAURANT • INEXPENSIVE TO MODERATE
MAP PAGE 157, #6

If you are to visit only one *soba* restaurant in Tokyo, it should be Yabu Soba. *Soba* aficionados from around the country trek to this fifth-generation establishment that opened in 1880. Enter the old building through a small garden and step back in time. The room is traditionally Japanese, with dark-colored wood and paper-covered lights. Listen carefully and you can hear the girl behind the cash register sing out each order to the kitchen. This is the only place in Japan that I have seen this done. The elderly, kimono-clad waitresses efficiently manage the busy dining room. If you are hungry the diverse menu allows you to order a few dishes (such as *sashimi yuba*, *tempura*, and grilled *nori*) prior to closing the meal with noodles. There is also a full menu of *soba*, both hot and cold.

Matsugen Ebisu • 松玄恵比寿
Shibuya-ku, Hiroo 1-3-1, Hagiwara Building
渋谷区広尾1-3-1萩原ビル
Tel. 03-3444-8666
11:30–27:00 Monday to Saturday;
11:30–24:00 Sunday and holidays
www.pewters.co.jp/shops/matsugen/index.html#ebisu (Japanese)
RESTAURANT • INEXPENSIVE TO MODERATE
MAP PAGE 156, #30

Contrast Yabu Soba in Kanda with the modern Matsugen in Ebisu. Matsugen's communal tables are set in a softly lit room. If you are lucky enough to be there at the right time, you can watch the noodles being rolled out and cut. Matsugen's full menu includes an unusual *bukkake soba* that is garnished with twelve different toppings. The aromatic, toasty *shirogomadare* sesame dipping sauce is a nice contrast to the *soba* noodles. Matsugen has opened a branch in Manhattan in collaboration with chef Jean-Georges Vongerichten.

Toranomon Sunaba Honten • 虎ノ門砂場本店
Minato-ku, Toranomon 1-10-6 • 港区虎ノ門1-10-6
Tel. 03-3501-9661
11:00–20:00 Monday to Friday; 11:00–15:00 Saturday;
closed Sunday and holidays
www2.ttcn.ne.jp/sobasake/soba/tokyo/052.html (Japanese)
RESTAURANT • INEXPENSIVE TO MODERATE
MAP PAGE 157, #20

This historic two-story wooden structure adds a picturesque element to this modern neighborhood. The brightly-lit interior feels more modern. There are tables and chairs on the first floor and *tatami* seating on the second floor. The menu is that of a classic *soba* restaurant; the dipping sauce is a bit on the sweet side without being cloying.

Also see **Narutomi** and **Nagasaka Sarashina**.

WHEAT NOODLES
うどん
UDON

THE THICK WHEAT-FLOUR UDON ARE POPULAR IN THE SHIKOKU REGION AND HAVE BECOME INCREASINGLY popular in Tokyo with many fast-food chains offering *udon* as a quick meal at a reasonable price (see Casual Dining, page 29, for **Hanamaru Udon,** the chain restaurant easily identified by its bright orange signage and flower logo, found throughout the city).

The three main popular regional styles of *udon* include *Sanuki* (thick), *Inaniwa* (thin noodles from Akita), and *Mizusawa* (thin, hard noodles from Gunma).

If looking for good *udon*, look for a sign that says *teuchi* 手打ち (handmade). Some *udon* terms include:

Bukkake **Udon** often eaten in the summer and served cold; toppings may include okra, fermented soybeans *(nattō)*, and grated *yamaimo* potato

Kake **Udon** served in a hot broth often topped with julienned leeks

Kama age **Udon** served hot in a *kama* pot

Kare- udon **Udon** served in a rich, curry sauce

Kishimen Flat *udon*

Kitsune **Udon** topped with sweetened deep-fried *tōfu*

Nabeyaki A hot pot of seafood and vegetables often topped with a raw egg

Tanuki **Udon** topped with deep-fried bits of *tempura* batter

Tempura **Udon** topped with *tempura* shrimp or *tempura* vegetables

Tsukimi **Udon** topped with a raw egg, which poaches in the hot broth; said to resemble the moon, hence the name, which means "moon-viewing"

Udonsuki **Udon** served *sukiyaki*-style (in a sweet soy broth with meat and vegetables)

Wakame **Udon** topped with sea vegetable

Yakiudon Vegetables and pork stir-fried with *udon* in a savory sauce

Zaru Cold *udon* served on a bamboo strainer plate, served with a dipping sauce

Konaya • 古奈屋
Chiyoda-ku, Marunouchi 1-6-4,
Marunouchi Oazo Building 5th floor
千代田区丸の内1-6-4丸の内オアゾビル5F
Tel. 03-5220-5500 • Daily 11:00–22:30
www.konaya.ne.jp/ (Japanese)
RESTAURANT • INEXPENSIVE • MAP PAGE 222, #14

A popular *udon* trend is curried soup (not stew) to which *udon* are added. Konaya is a chain of stores specializing in these hearty bowls with a slurry of curry, made from twenty-two different vegetables and spices and stewed for three days, blended with bonito flakes, soy sauce, and sugar, and rounded out with some milk. Beware: when you slurp, the curry tends to splatter—and stain. There are several Konaya branches throughout the city.

RAMEN
ラーメン

RAMEN IS COMFORT FOOD TO MANY JAPANESE. IT IS ALSO CALLED CHUKA MEN. EVEN THOUGH MUCH OF the *ramen* consumed in Japan is instant, the best place to eat *ramen* is at a *ramen* shop.

Behind the counter there is usually a pot gurgling with stock and another pot with hot water for cooking the noodles. The steaming hot *ramen* should be consumed quickly before the noodles get too soggy and the fat starts to congeal. The secret is to slurp—slurping cools down the broth as it enters your mouth and helps you appreciate its aroma.

Deconstructed, a bowl of *ramen* consists of stock blended with *motodare* (the concentrated flavor), noodles, toppings, and fat. As documented in Juzo Itami's movie, *Tampopo*, attention must be paid to each of the components.

The soup stock defines the type of *ramen*. The basic stocks are *tonkotsu* (made from pork bones), *marudori* (mostly chicken, with a bit of pork), and "*W*" a blend of fish *dashi* and chicken stock. ("*W*" is a play on the word for "double.") Each shop will tweak the stock; some shops add apples, for example, to make it sweet.

Motodare is added to the stock in each bowl. The three most popular flavors of *motodare* are salt (*shio*), soy sauce (*shōyu*), or *miso*. The *motodare* may also include onions, garlic, and ginger. Dried fish powders like powdered bonito *may* be added to give the *motodare* more *umami* and depth.

Each bowl of *ramen* is topped with oil, compounding the richness of the broth and enhancing the aroma. Types of oil include chicken fat, lard, sesame oil, chili oil (*ra-yu*), garlic oil, or leek oil.

The noodles (*men*) can be straight or curly, thick or thin. The most important function of the noodle is to carry the broth. At top shops, the noodles will be served al dente.

A wide array of toppings may be used for *ramen*. Typical toppings for a soy sauce *ramen* are *cha-shu* (soft slices of pork), *menma* (bamboo shoots), and *negi* (leeks). Pork bone *ramen* might be garnished with toppings that include *cha-shu*, *negi*, and wood-ear mushrooms. Other popular items served on top of *ramen* include eggs (raw, hard-boiled, simmered, or soft-boiled), *nori*, fish pâté, or vegetables.

Greens are often added, including spinach, *wakame*, or *nori*, which adds a unique aroma. Butter may be added to enrich the broth—this is common in the northern prefecture of Hokkaido, famous for its dairy products. Other vegetables that are added to *ramen* might include bean sprouts, corn, cabbage, and carrots. The acidity and bite of red pickled ginger can help to cut through a rich pork bone broth. Shrimp and other seafood might also be added.

Regionality plays into *ramen* styles as well. Hokkaido, the northernmost island in the Japanese archipelago, is home to *miso ramen*. Tokyo is famous for its soy sauce *ramen* and Fukuoka on the southern island Kyushu, is home to the renowned pork bone (*tonkotsu*) *ramen*.

In the basement of Tokyo Station is an area called Tokyo Ramen Street (map page 222, #30) in which you'll find branches of four of Tokyo's popular *ramen* shops. If you are really curious about *ramen*, then consider a day trip to the Shin Yokohama Ramen Museum, in a city next to Tokyo, which covers the history of *ramen* and has several restaurants. www.raumen.co.jp/ramen (English). Some common items found on *ramen* menus include:

Cha-shu ramen **Ramen** topped with slow-cooked pork
Hiyashi chūka Cold *ramen* noodles with toppings and dressing
Mazemen **Ramen** with minimal broth and toppings
Negi ramen **Ramen** topped with minced leeks
Tantan men **Ramen** topped with a spicy meat sauce
Tsukemen **Ramen** in which the noodles are served in a separate bowl
   from the broth
Yasai ramen **Ramen** topped with vegetables

Ivan Ramen • アイバン　ラーメン
Setagaya-ku, Minami Karasuyama 3-24-7
世田谷区南烏山3-24-7
Tel. 03-6750-5540 • 17:30–22:30 Monday to Friday;
11:30–17:30 Saturday to Sunday; closed Wednesday and 4th
Tuesday of the month (best to call ahead to confirm it's open)
www.ivanramen.com (English)
RESTAURANT • INEXPENSIVE

Run by a New Yorker, Ivan Orkin, this shop in suburban Setagaya-ku is always on the lists of top *ramen* shops in the city. The shop has lines on the weekends and holidays so go on a weekday if you can. Speak with Ivan before you order to inquire if there are any seasonal (*gentei*) items on the menu; this is where Ivan really shines. The Culinary Institute of America–trained chef sharpened his skills under the tutelage of André Soltner at Lutèce, so it is no wonder that his broth is elegant as well as rich with flavor. His bowls are delicately balanced with handmade noodles and just the right toppings.

Also see **Ippudō**, **Sapporoya**, and **Kyushu Jangara Ramen**.

SWEETS

....

JAPANESE CONFECTIONS
和菓子
WAGASHI

WAGASHI'S RICH HISTORY DATES BACK TO THE NARA PERIOD (AD 710–794). IT'S NOT UNUSUAL TO FIND *wagashi* purveyors established hundreds of years ago that are still in business, and still following recipes that have been handed down through the generations. Some *azuki* bean cake (*yōkan*), skewered rice ball (*dango*), and stuffed pastry (*manju*) recipes date back more than a thousand years. *Wagashi* is popular at temples, where some originated.

The beauty of *wagashi* is in their presentation. The Japanese have an affinity for seasonal motifs, which are artfully represented in *wagashi*. Spring brings pastel-colored flowers of plum and cherry trees; salted cherry blossoms are also used as ingredients this time of year. Summer symbols include hydrangeas, fireworks, and images of cool waters. Autumn *wagashi* highlight the brilliant red, orange, and yellow of fall foliage.

Ingredients are simple, often sticky rice or rice flour, *azuki* beans, and sugar. In stark contrast to Western pastries, butter and cream are not used, hence *wagashi* are considered a healthy dessert. Some are intensely sweet and best paired with a bitter green tea.

There are hundreds of *wagashi*, many with regional roots. Yamanashi prefecture is famous for *shingenmochi*, small packets of soft jelly-like confections (*warabi mochi*), sprinkled with soybean powder and served with a small bottle of brown sugar syrup. Each portion is wrapped in a clear wrap and comes with its own wooden toothpick. The chestnut delicacy *kurikinton* is a specialty of Gifu prefecture and is in season in the fall. Perhaps one of the most famous regional *wagashi* is *yatsuhashi* from Kyoto, a cinnamon-flavored, flour-based confection. *Wagashi* also include savory rice crackers (*sembei*).

Wagashi are an important part of holidays in Japan. Certain *wagashi* appear in shops around a certain holiday. During the *shichi-go-san,* or the Children's Festival, if you are fortunate enough to see children dressed up in kimonos, chances are they will be carrying around long, narrow bags of *chitoseame* candy. During *setsubun,* marking the end of winter and the beginning of spring, you will find *fukumame,* or good luck beans.

Green tea, toasted soybean powder, *azuki* beans, brown sugar syrup, and sticky rice are the most common *wagashi* flavors, but you will find that these are just the tip of the iceberg. Recently, sales of *wagashi* have declined, and some shops are incorporating Western ingredients and techniques to create "modern *wagashi.*" Examples are a fluffy cheesecake surrounding a green tea cake with black beans, butter cookies made with sweet *miso,* and *tuiles* made with black sesame seeds.

Wagashi are served in traditional cafés called *kanmidokoro,* that are characterized by simple seating, small tables, paper-paneled walls, and *kimono*-clad waitresses. They are a comfortable place to retreat and relax and unlike coffee shops, tend to be quiet. To attract younger customers, some *kanmidokoro* have updated their recipes with Western ingredients such as cream cheese, caramel, or cacao. The venerable *wagashi* producer Toraya has opened up a **Toraya Café** and Ryoguchiya Korekiyo, also an institution, has opened up R Style. Both of them have successfully rebranded themselves with modern-style sweets. Both shops are in the **Omotesando Hills** building.

The world of *wagashi* is vast and complex, and has been carefully codified. The three major groups are moist confections (*nama*), half-wet confections (*hannama*), and dry confections (*higashi*).

The moist *wagashi* include sticky rice, often pounded into cakes (*mochimono*); rice balls made from sticky rice (*ohagi*); sticky rice with *azuki* beans (*sekihan*); as well as steamed items such as steamed buns.

The half-wet confections include *monaka* cakes—two light wafers sandwiching *azuki* paste.

Many of the dry confections, *higashi,* are made from rice flour and sugar, often the prized *wasanbon,* a premium, fine-grained sugar. *Sembei* rice crackers are part of the *higashi* category. Grilled items are also considered "dry," and include a sweet *castella* cake (*kasutera*) and small pancake-like cakes (*dorayaki*) often stuffed with *azuki.*

Variations on *mochi,* pounded sticky rice, are popular. *Dango* are small *mochi* balls skewered and dressed with an *azuki* paste, ground sesame seeds, toasted soybean powder, or a sweet soy sauce. Or, the sticky glutinous rice can be wrapped in bamboo leaves and steamed to make *chimaki*, a popular *wagashi* for the Children's Day holiday on May 5th.

Perhaps the best places to explore a wide variety of *wagashi* are in *depachika*. Isetan in Shinjuku elevates *wagashi* to its highest level and presents the confections like museum pieces. Some *depachika wagashi* shops also have eat-in cafés.

Seasonal items will be designated by the word *kisetsu* 季節. *Genteihin* 限定品 denotes limited production items, often seasonal. *Wagashi* shops in *depachika* to look for include:

Kanō Shōjuan • 叶匠壽庵
www.kanou.com

This Kyoto-based shop has both traditional and modern sweets. In the summer *azuki* cakes are presented in bamboo. You will find them at most *depachika*. The Kano Shojuan counter in Takashimaya in Nihonbashi has a small eat-in counter.

Suzukake • 鈴懸
www.suzukake.co.jp

This Fukuoka-based shop presents exquisite *wagashi* in cool, sleek packaging of bamboo baskets. Signature items include a *monaka* in the shape of a bell (*suzu*) and delicate crisp wafers of lotus root, sweet potato, and other vegetables, coated with sugar and baked. The department store Isetan is the only location of Suzukake in Tokyo.

Toraya Akasaka Honten (main shop) • とらや赤坂本店
Minato-ku, Akasaka 4-9-22 • 港区赤坂4-9-22
Tel. 03-3408-4121 • 8:30–20:00 Monday to Friday;
8:30–18:00 weekends and holidays
www.toraya-group.co.jp (Japanese)
SHOP AND CAFE • MAP PAGE 156, #13

Toraya, founded in the 1600s, is a purveyor to the Imperial Family. The signature item is the *azuki* cake wrapped in bamboo leaves (*yōkan*) which comes in flavors like green tea and brown sugar. Toraya has outlets in most *depachika*.

Shiose • 塩瀬
www.shiose.co.jp (Japanese)

Shiose dates back to 1349 and offers a wide selection of high quality *wagashi*. You can find this shop at major *depachika*.

Kagetsu • 花月
Bunkyo-ku, Yushima 3-39-6 • 文京区湯島3-39-6
Tel. 03-3831-9762
9:30–18:00 Monday to Saturday; closed Sunday and holidays
www.karintou-kagetsu.com (Japanese)
SHOP • MAP PAGE 219, #9

Kagetsu is known for rice crackers that are deep-fried and then covered in a black sugar syrup (*karintō*), packaged in the shop's signature orange cans. The crackers have a nice crunch and the outer coating of sugar is not too sweet. Kagetsu also carries savory rice crackers.

Hōraiya • 宝来屋
Chiyoda-ku, Kudanshita Minami 2-4-15
千代田区九段下南2-4-15
Tel. 03-3261-4612 • 9:00–18:00 Monday to Friday;
10:00–16:00 Saturday; closed Sunday and holidays
wagashi.houraiya.co.jp (Japanese)
SHOP • MAP PAGE 157, #4

Hōraiya is a small shop offering beautiful, handmade *namagashi* in a variety of decorative shapes. The selection changes with the season. Popular items include a *matsufu* baked sweet of egg and flour and the chestnut *yōkan*.

Sasama • さゝま
Chiyoda-ku, Jimbocho 1-23 • 千代田区神保町1-23
Tel. 03-3294-0978 • 9:30–18:00 Monday to Saturday; closed
Sunday and holidays • www.sasama.co.jp (Japanese)
SHOP • MAP PAGE 157, #5

This shop is known for its small selection of carefully produced handmade *namagashi*. It is a small shop with an atmosphere that has not changed with the times.

Also see **Harajuku Mizuho, HIGASHIYA Man, Kinozen, Baikatei, Umezono, Mugitoro, Kuuya, Minamoto Kitchoan, Toraya Akasaka Honten, Ginza Akebono, Matsuzaki.**

These are some words you may come across while choosing *wagashi*:

Amanattō A variety of beans that are cooked in sugar water until sweet and tender, then dried

Amazake A sweet drink, very low in alcohol, made from fermented rice and served hot or cold

An Sweet bean paste often made from *azuki* beans, either smooth (*koshian*) or chunky (*tsubuan*). *Shiroan* is a sweet bean paste made from white beans. *An* can also be made from chestnuts or sweet potatoes.

Anmitsu Many variations exist, but the most popular is made with agar agar jelly and fresh fruit topped with a brown sugar syrup

Azuki beans An essential ingredient in Japanese sweets

Daifuku A generic term for pounded sticky rice that is stuffed with *azuki* paste

Dango Three or four rice-flour balls skewered on a bamboo stick and dressed with a variety of sweet and savory toppings

Dorayaki Two sweet, round pancakes sandwiching *azuki* paste; variations of this include butter or whipped cream mixed with the *azuki* paste.

Goma Sesame seeds. *Shirogoma* are white sesame seeds. *Kurogoma* are black sesame seeds.

Hannamagashi Confections with 10-30% moisture content

Higashi Dry, pastel confections made from flour and sugar, often pressed into decorative molds, 10% or less moisture

Imo yōkan Dense cakes made from sweet potatoes, sugar, and agar agar

Jōnamagashi Soft and delicate *namagashi*, usually with seasonal motifs

Jōshinko Flour made from non-sticky rice that is used as an ingredient in *wagashi*

Kakigōri Shaved ice topped with sweet syrups, popular in summer

Kanten Also known as agar agar, *kanten* is made from *tengusa*, a red sea alga; it has no calories and no taste, and takes on the flavor of whatever it is mixed with; it solidifies at room temperature, making it simple to work with

Karintō Candy made from flour, water, and egg that is deep-fried and coated with sugar

Kashi Generic term for confections; *wagashi* are Japanese confections and *yōgashi* are Western confections

Kashiwa mochi *Azuki* and sticky rice wrapped in an oak leaf

Kasutera *Castella* sponge cake

Kinako Dried soybean powder, tan in color, with a toasty aroma and nutty taste

Kintsuba A thin cake batter surrounding a block of chunky *azuki* paste and grilled until crisp

Kokutō Brown sugar

Koshian Sweet, smooth *azuki* paste

Kuri Chestnuts

Kuriimu Often refers to ice cream but may also refer to whipped cream

Kuromitsu Syrup made from brown sugar that is almost black in color

Kusa mochi While the word *kusa* means grass, the green color of the sticky rice is from mugwort, and surrounds an *azuki* paste

Kuzu ko A starch made from the kudzu plant, famous for its delicate aroma and smooth texture, often used as an ingredient for *wagashi*

Kuzu mochi Arrowroot *mochi* cakes, often topped with toasted soybean powder and brown sugar syrup

Kuzu kiri Arrowroot noodles often served with brown sugar syrup

Mame daifuku Sticky rice studded with beans surrounding *azuki*.
   A popular variation is *ichigo daifuku* that includes a juicy whole
   strawberry in the middle
Mamekan Simply steamed red beans and agar agar
Manjū Steamed dumplings stuffed with *azuki*
Mattcha Powdered green tea
Miruku Often refers to sweetened, condensed milk. It is a popular
   topping on shaved ice paired with green tea and *azuki*.
Mitsumame Popular dish of agar agar jelly, canned fruit, and steamed red
   beans, topped with brown sugar syrup
Mizu yōkan Similar to the *azuki yōkan* cakes, *mizu yōkan* has a higher
   percentage of water and hence is not as dense
Mochi A taffy made from sticky rice that has been steamed and pounded.
   It can be served sweet or savory (with soy sauce and *nori*)

SEASONAL WAGASHI MOTIFS

January Pine leaves

February Plum blossoms

March Cherrystone clams

April Cherry blossoms

May Sticky rice wrapped in oak leaves and used to
   celebrate Boys' Day on May 5th

June Eggplant

July Cool waters with swimming fish

August Sunflowers

September Chestnuts

October Autumnal leaves

November Persimmons

December Chrysanthemum flowers

Mochigome Sticky rice that is the base for many *wagashi*

Monaka Sandwich-like delicate, crispy rice wafers surrounding *azuki an* paste

Nama wagashi Freshly made *wagashi*, with 30% or more moisture content

Ogura aisu Chunky *azuki* mixed with ice cream

Ohagi *Azuki* paste surrounded by steamed sticky rice

Oshiruko A popular sweet dating back to the Edo period, this is a sweet soup made from chunky or smooth *azuki* paste and sugar served with small rice-flour dumplings or chestnuts

Sakura mochi *Azuki* paste wrapped in a thin cherry cake, or steamed sticky rice, packaged in a salted leaf from a cherry tree

Shiratamako Flour made from sticky rice

Shiro koshian Sweet, smooth bean paste made from white beans

Taiyaki A grilled fish-shaped cake filled with *azuki*

Tokoroten Noodles made from agar agar served with a tart, soy sauce with vinegar, often garnished with mustard

Tsubuan Sweet, chunky *azuki* paste

Warabi mochi Produced from the root of bracken, this very soft *mochi* can be topped with toasted soy bean powder and brown sugar syrup

Wasanbon A very high-grade Japanese sugar, delicate in texture and flavor, a key ingredient for *higashi*

Yasai sembei Thin crisps of vegetables (such as lotus root, sweet potatoes, and ginger), laced with sugar and baked

Yōkan A dense cake made from agar agar, sugar, and *azuki*. *Yōkan* can be smooth, chunky, or filled with chestnuts.

Zenzai A thick soup made from *azuki*, often served with steamed millet or rice-flour dumplings; very popular in the cold winter months, especially in the Asakusa area

Zerii Jelly, can be flavored with powdered green tea or other flavorings

CRACKERS

煎餅

SEMBEI

CRACKERS (SEMBEI, ALSO CALLED OSEMBEI) ARE A TYPE OF CONFECTION THAT CAN BE SWEET OR savory. There are three main types of *sembei*—rice-, flour-, or egg-based.

The style of *sembei* changes according to region. In Tokyo you will find thick and hard types made from non-glutinous rice. *Sembei* made in Kyoto is made from glutinous rice, resulting in delicate *sembei*. The texture of the Kyoto cracker is described as *saku saku* (crispy) while the Tokyo crackers are *kari kari* (crunchy). Aichi prefecture is known for *sembei* that include seafood such as shrimp dried and flattened between two hot metal plates.

Sembei made with roasted beans or sesame seeds pack a nutty crunch. While some *sembei* are baked or grilled, others can be deep-fried, adding a layer of richness. *Sembei* are available in a variety of flavors including salad (*sarada*), sea urchin (*uni*), spicy cod roe (*mentaiko*), *wasabi*, or curry. Others can be wrapped in *nori* while some are dusted with dried red chili pepper. *Sembei* are popular as an afternoon snack with tea, or in the evening with beer. They are a practical portable snack for travel, and beautifully packaged assortments are often given as gifts.

Some popular types of *sembei*:

Agesembei Deep-fried rice crackers

Arare Literally, "hailstones," or tiny pellet-like rice crackers, that may also be in the shape of seasonal motifs such as autumn leaves or spring blossoms

Ebi sembei Crackers that include small shrimp that have been flattened and baked

Genkotsu Very crunchy, jaw-breaking rice crackers

Goma sembei Rice crackers studded with sesame seeds

Kakimochi Bite-size rice crackers

Kakinotane Crescent-shaped, soy-sauce-flavored bite-size *sembei*

Karintō Fried crackers with a sweet coating

Nattō maki *Nori* surrounding dried *nattō* (fermented soybeans)

Nekonbu arare Small rice crackers with chopped *kombu* (kelp)

Norimaki arare Small rice crackers wrapped in *nori*

Nure sembei Drenched in a sweet soy sauce, these crackers are very soft and squishy

Renkon sembei Crackers, similar to potato chips, that are made from thinly sliced and deep-fried lotus root

Shio sembei Salted rice crackers

Shōga sembei Ginger-flavored crackers

Tōgarashi sembei Rice crackers flavored with a layer of *ichimi* (dried red chili pepper)

Usuyaki sembei Very thin rice crackers, popular in Kyoto

Wasabi peas Although not a cracker, these dried peas with a *wasabi*-flavored coating are considered *wagashi*

Yasai sembei Crisp, thinly sliced vegetables, such as lotus root and sweet potatoes, that are laced in sugar and baked

Yatsuhashi A popular *wagashi* of Kyoto made from rice flour, sugar, and cinnamon; it can be crisp or soft

Zarame Rice crackers covered with sugar crystals

Kanda Awahei • 神田淡平
Chiyoda-ku, Uchi Kanda 2-13-1 • 千代田区内神田2-13-1
Tel. 03-3256-1038 • 9:00—20:00 Monday to Friday;
9:30—18:00 Saturday; closed Sunday and holidays
www.awahei.com/ (Japanese)
SHOP • MAP PAGE 157, #7

Awahei is a fun place to shop for *sembei* because there are so many unique flavors to try including garlic (*ninniku*), squid ink (*ikasumi*), ginger (*shōga*), and Japanese prickly ash (*sanshō*). Awahei is known for its *ichimi tappuri*, the bright red *sembei* coated with dried red chili pepper—your eyes start watering before you even put one near your mouth. If you go in the spring, check out the beautiful cherry blossom (*sakura*) *sembei*.

Department store food halls (*depachika*) are also good places to find a wide variety of high-end *sembei*. Local supermarkets as well as convenience stores carry a selection of everyday *sembei*.

These are popular *sembei* shops with branches at most *depachika*:

Kyoto Ogura Sansō • 京都小倉山荘
www.ogurasansou.co.jp/ (Japanese)
Famous for Kyoto-style, delicate and light rice crackers.

Ginza Matsuzaki Sembei • 銀座松崎煎餅
http://matsuzaki-senbei.com/ (Japanese)
Known for sweet egg and wheat crackers artfully painted with designs such as fireworks and flowers.

Mamegen • 豆源

www.mamegen.com/ (Japanese)

A shop well known for its wide variety of flavored beans, nuts, and crackers.

Bankaku • 坂角

www.bankaku.co.jp (Japanese)

This shop specializes in shrimp crackers called "Yukari."

Keishindō • 桂新堂

www.keishindo.co.jp (Japanese)

Keishindō also sells shrimp crackers.

Also see **Iriyama Sembei**.

WESTERN-STYLE CONFECTIONS
洋菓子
YOGASHI

IN JAPAN, SWEETS AND CONFECTIONS ARE DIVIDED INTO TWO CATEGORIES, WESTERN-STYLE (YOGASHI) and Japanese-style (*wagashi*). *Yōgashi* has found a place in the food culture of Japan because of the country's growing observance of Western holidays. Chocolates are given on Valentine's Day and cakes are eaten on Christmas. Walk through any *depachika* and you'll find an impressive selection of Western-style cakes, tarts, chocolates, and sweets, and branches of many French *boulangeries*, *pâtisseries*, and *chocolatiers*.

The Japanese adore chocolate. Award-winning European chocolatiers such as Jean-Paul Hevin and Pierre Marcolini have taken Tokyo by storm. These temples to chocolate have consumers lined up in orderly queues for the opportunity to indulge in truffles and bonbons.

Chocolate has become a popular part of the nation's food culture, with the Japanese developing their own variations on international traditions and customs. In Japan, on Valentine's Day, girls give chocolate not only to their boyfriends, but also to their fathers, work colleagues, and friends. Chocolate given to a boyfriend is called *honmei choko* (the "real" chocolate), while chocolate given to colleagues is called *girichoko* ("obligatory" chocolate). Exactly a month later, these gifts are repaid on March 14th, which is known as White Day. The name White Day comes from the tradition of the return gift being white chocolate (no regifting possible), although recently return gifts are not limited to white chocolate.

In addition to faithfully duplicating Western confections, the Japanese have incorporated Western ingredients and techniques to create their own unique products. Hokkaido prefecture, a region known for its dairy products, produces Marusei Bata-Sando, two cookies sandwiching a rum-flavored butter cream studded with raisins. These usually can only be purchased in Hokkaido, at regional shops in Tokyo, or during special promotions in *depachika*. This limited availability makes them more treasured. www.rokkatei.co.jp (Japanese). Many Japanese *chocolatiers* skillfully incorporate Japanese flavors into traditional Western chocolates. Some Japanese *chocolatiers* to visit include Hironobu Tsujiguchi of Le Chocolat de H, Le Patissier Takagi, and Theobroma.

Many of these pastry and chocolate shops are quite pricey. If you are on a budget, window-shop at these boutiques and make your purchases at convenience stores. The boutiques offer an amazing array including chocolates filled with salted caramel, *mattcha*, and seasonal flavors.

Ice cream can be a revelation in Japan. Uniquely Japanese flavors include *mattcha* with brown sugar syrup (*kuromitsu*), toasted soybean powder (*kinako*), and black sesame seed (*kurogoma*). Ice cream shops to look for include Kihachi and **Pierre Marcolini**. Check out convenience stores for their Häagen-Dazs selection that includes Japanese flavors not available outside of the country.

Mochi cream is a trendy sweet made from a thin layer of sticky rice (*mochi*) surrounding flavored pastry creams, sold in some *depachika* at shops called Mochi Cream. *Mochi daifuku* is a thin layer of *mochi* surrounding ice cream that can be in flavors that change with the seasons, sold at convenience stores.

Sadaharu Aoki
Chiyoda-ku, Marunouchi 3-4-1, Shin Kokusai Building
千代田区丸の内3-4-1新国際ビル
Tel. 03-5923-2800 • Daily 11:00–20:00
www.sadaharuaoki.fr
SHOP AND CAFÉ • MAP PAGE 157, #15

Japanese pastry chef Sadaharu Aoki produces classic French pastries, but incorporates Japanese ingredients—one of his most popular is an éclair filled with *mattcha* cream, for example.

Pierre Hermé • ピエール・エルメ

Shibuya-ku, Jingumae 5-51-8, Laporte Aoyama

渋谷区神宮前5-51-8 ラ・ポルト青山

Tel. 03-5485-7766 • 11:00–21:00 Monday to Saturday;
11:00–20:00 Sunday and holidays

www.pierreherme.co.jp/ (Japanese)

SHOP AND CAFÉ • MAP PAGE 255, #12

The darling of the French, *pâtissier* Pierre Hermé, famous for his *macarons*, has opened an upscale café, Bar Chocolat, above his boutique in Aoyama. A taste of Japan is present in his *wasabi macaron* and *mattcha* truffle.

Oriol Balaguer

Minato-ku, Shiroganedai 4-9-18, Barbizon Building 32, 2F

港区白金台4-9-18バルビゾンビル32, 2F

Tel. 03-3449-9509 • call for hours

www.oriolbalaguer.com

SHOP • MAP PAGE 156, #32

A former pastry chef at El Bulli, Spaniard Oriol Balaguer creates chocolates flavored with *wasabi*, soy sauce, *yuzu*, and *mattcha*.

Matsunosuke • 松乃助

Shibuya-ku, Sarugakucho 29-9, Hillside Terrace D-11

渋谷区猿楽町29-9ヒルサイドテラスD-11

Tel. 03-5728-3868 • Daily 10:00–20:00

www.matsunosukepie.com/about/en_about.html (English)

SHOP AND CAFÉ • MAP PAGE 156, #28

Akiko Hirano studied pie making in America and her popular shop Matsunosuke is in Daikanyama. Here you can satiate a craving for authentic pies such as apple and banana cream, and New York cheesecake.

Confectionary West

Chuo-ku, Ginza 7-3-6 • 中央区銀座7-3-6

Tel. 03-3571-1554

9:00–23:00 Monday to Friday;
11:00–20:00 weekend and holidays

www.ginza-west.co.jp/ (Japanese)

SHOP AND CAFÉ • MAP PAGE 180, #20

Confectionary West, known for its Leaf Pie, a delicate version of a *palmier*, has shops in most *depachika*.

Ogawaken • 小川軒
Minato-ku, Shinbashi 2-20-15 • 港区新橋2-20-15
Tel. 03-3571-7500
9:30–18:00 Monday to Friday;
Saturday until 17:00; closed Sunday and holidays
www.ogawaken.co.jp (Japanese)
SHOP • MAP PAGE 180, #33

Ogawaken is known for its Raisinwich, two almond *sable* cookies sandwiching alcohol-infused raisins and cream.

BAKERIES
パン屋
PANYA

ONE MIGHT NOT IMMEDIATELY EQUATE TOKYO WITH WORLD-CLASS BAKERIES—BUT SOME OF THE BEST French, Italian, and German bakeries in the world have set up shop in the land known for rice and noodles.

The Japanese appreciation for *dekitate* 出来立て or *yakitate* 焼き立て (hot out of the oven) bread is perhaps best observed at *depachika* than at individual bakeries. Fauchon, at Takishimaya, for example, will post the baking schedule so that consumers can come and line up to pick up a hot loaf at the scheduled time. And, since this is Japan, the baking schedules are as reliable as the train schedules—run with military precision.

Although if you are reading this book, you probably have come to Japan to eat Japanese food, chances are you will get a craving for bread after eating rice every day. Here is a very short list of the many great bakeries in Tokyo:

Viron • ヴィロン
Chiyoda-ku, Marunouchi 2-7-3, Tokia Building 1st Floor
千代田区丸の内2-7-3トキアビル
Tel. 03-5220-7289 • Daily 10:00–21:00
SHOP AND CAFÉ • MAP PAGE 157, #16

Viron's "Retrador" baguette is made from flour milled in France specifically to create a classic baguette with an exceptional crumb and crust. Viron has a wide selection of breads, pastries, and sandwiches with traditional French fillings, including *rillettes*, *pâté de campagne*, and *jambon* with gruyère.

SNACK BREADS
おやつパン
OYATSUPAN

OYATSUPAN REFERS TO SNACK BREADS, OFTEN
consumed between meals. Fillings may include canned
corn, canned tuna, sausage, or cheese, often with generous
portions of mayonnaise. Sandwiches can also be made from
yakisoba (noodles stir-fried with meat and vegetables) laid
in a hot dog bun; breaded and deep-fried croquettes served
on a hamburger bun are another *oyatsupan*. *Curry-pan* are
deep-fried breads stuffed with a spicy curry. *Mentaikopan*
is spicy cod roe, spread with some butter, on a baguette and
then baked until crispy.

Oyatsupan can be sweet as well as savory. *Anpan* are
sweet breads stuffed with sweet red bean (*azuki*) paste.
Meronpan, meant to resemble a muskmelon, is light-green
bread topped with a sweet layer of melon-flavored frosting
that is scored and then baked. *Kuri-mupan* is sweet bread
stuffed with whipped cream. *Mushipan* are sweet breads
that have been steamed.

In Ginza, across the street from Mitsukoshi, and located
between Wako department store and Yamano music shop,
is **Kimuraya** (founded in 1869), an institution that features
anpan and variations such as *sakurapan*, an *anpan* topped
with a salted cherry blossom. (There is even a popular car-
toon character named Anpanman.) The secret to Kimuraya's
anpan is the use of *sake* lees. Not only does it give the bread
an inherent sweetness, it helps the bread brown quickly as it
bakes, giving it a nice sheen.

Maison Kayser • メゾンカイザー

www.maisonkayser.co.jp (Japanese)

Maison Kayser's buttery and flaky croissants have received awards in France. Maison Kayser has shops in many *depachika* including Takashimaya and Mitsukoshi. Its chewy sourdough bread calls out to be sliced and dressed up with cheese and sliced meats, or toasted and topped with *confiture*, available at other shops in the *depachika*.

L'Atelier de Joël Robuchon • ラトリエ ド ロブション

Minato-ku, Roppongi 6-10-1, Roppongi Hills Hillside 2F
港区六本木 6-10-1 六本木ヒルズヒルサイド 2F
Tel. 03-5772-7500 • Daily 11:00–22:00
www.joel-robuchon.com (English)
SHOP • MAP PAGE 276, #2

At the base of the Roppongi Hills complex is the renowned restaurant l'Atelier de Joël Robuchon. Adjacent to the restaurant is a small but efficient *boulangerie* and *pâtisserie* with exquisite *ficelles* and authentic French sandwiches. Do not miss the *tarte au citron*, perhaps the best in the city.

Peck • ペック

www.takashimaya.co.jp/store/others/gourmet/peck/index.html
(Japanese)

The famous Milanese food shop, Peck, only in Takashimaya, is the place to find *focaccia* drenched in olive oil, airy *ciabatta*, and other breads that would bring tears to the eyes of an Italian *nonna*.

CHAPTER 3

....

BEVERAGES

TEA

CHA

TEA IN JAPAN CAN TASTE PUNGENT, SWEET, SOFT, GRASSY, OR EARTHY, AND IS RARELY SWEETENED. Most tea consumed in Japan is made from the *Camellia sinensis* plant, but some teas may be made from grains such as buckwheat (*soba*), black beans (*kuromame*), or flowers (*sakura*, or cherry blossoms).

The first harvest each spring in late April or early May is celebrated when the new tea (*shincha*) reaches the market. Green tea may be harvested up to three or four times per year, though the first harvest is considered the best. Leaf tea is picked, steamed, processed (dried and rolled), and refined (the stems and debris removed), or it can be ground for *mattcha* or roasted for *hōjicha* (see below).

There are two types of *mattcha*. The *mattcha* used in traditional tea ceremonies is expensive. *Mattcha* is also sold in an instant form—like instant coffee—that can be used for making *mattcha au lait*, or for mixing with vanilla ice cream, or into milkshakes. Be sure to ask before you purchase.

Tea aficionados will want to invest in an iron pot (*tetsubin*) that softens water and brews tea with rounder flavors. If you purchase one, be sure to inquire about whether or not the inside is enamel-coated. Some pots can be put directly over heat; others are used exclusively for steeping. These pots need to be cared for properly, as they can rust easily.

Some well-known tea purveyors include Yamamotoyama, Ippodo, and Itoen.

Tea master Sen no Rikyū (1521–1594) established the traditional tea ceremony, which is also a forerunner of *kaiseki* cuisine. If you'd like to attend a traditional tea ceremony, several hotels offer one, including the Imperial Hotel and the Hotel Okura. The JNTO (Japan National Tourist Organization) has reliable, up-to-date information about tea ceremonies and classes open to the public; you can find them at www.jnto.go.jp/eng/arrange/attractions/practical/sadou.html (English).

Some tea terms you may run across include:

Bancha 番茶 The third harvest of *sencha* (see below). *Bancha* may also refer to tea that is harvested in the late summer or fall. At this point, the soft shoots have grown and the leaves of the plant have become brittle. *Bancha* is a plain-tasting green tea, slightly astringent and yellow in color, made from stems and stalks. It's a good tea to drink with food, as the light flavor of the tea complements food.

Fukamushicha 深蒸し茶 Steamed for two to three minutes when it is processed, on the palate, *fukamushicha* is mellow and has a round flavor.

Genmaicha 玄米茶 A gorgeous tea to look at; *genmaicha* is *bancha* flecked with small roasted, popped brown rice kernels that impart a distinctive aroma. The tea is soft on the palate and a bit savory. It is low in caffeine—a good tea to drink in the evening. This same tea is also sold with *mattcha* powder added (*mattcha iri genmaicha*).

Gyokuro 玉露 This tea bush is shaded from harsh sunlight for about two weeks prior to harvest and the new, mild leaf buds are hand-picked, resulting in a delicate tea. Lightly sweet on the palate and mellow in its aroma, this gentle, top-quality tea is the base for *mattcha*.

Hōjicha ほうじ茶 Heated at a high temperature so as to be slightly roasted, this blend of *bancha* and *kukicha* teas is known for its elegant aroma. It is considered a good after-dinner tea, because it helps the body to digest food and is lower in caffeine than green teas.

Ichibancha 一番茶 The first crop of tea, often picked around May 1st; may also be referred to as *shincha* 新茶.

Mattcha 抹茶 These leaves are also shaded from the sunlight. In the process of making *mattcha*, the leaves are steamed and then dried without crushing. The veins of the leaves and the stalks are removed, and the remaining leaf is ground into a fine powder. This tea is used for the traditional tea ceremony. It has also become a popular ingredient for pastries, ice cream, and other sweets.

Mecha 芽茶 Made from buds and tips and harvested early in the season, this tea is aromatic, slightly bitter, and astringent.

Mugicha 麦茶 Roasted barley tea, popular in the summer served cold, it has a toasty flavor and is brown in color.

Kamairicha 釜入り茶 Pan-fired tea that is light, simple and refreshing, with a roasted taste; common in Kyushu.

Kōcha 紅茶 Black or Western-style teas

Konacha 粉茶 The powdered (but not *mattcha*) tea found at *sushi* shops, where it may be referred to as *agari*. It has a rich flavor, but is light on the palate.

Kobucha 昆布茶 Made from kelp (*kombu*) that is dried and powdered, this tea is round and full on the palate and is naturally rich in *umami*. It can also be used as a cooking ingredient to add richness and *umami* to a dish.

Kukicha 茎茶 Made from the twigs, stalks, and stems of the tea bush. It is slightly nutty and earthy, with a hint of sweetness on the palate.

Kuromamecha 黒豆茶 Made from black beans, this slightly sweet tea retains the beans' subtle fragrance.

Sakuracha 桜茶 A cup of this tea, made from salted cherry blossoms, is a beautiful sight as the cherry blossom opens up in the cup. It is slightly salty on the palate.

Sakuranbocha さくらんぼ茶 Green tea flavored with cherries

Sanpincha さんぴん茶 Jasmine tea, popular in Okinawa

Sencha 煎茶 The most popular type of tea consumed in Japan, *sencha* leaves are steamed for thirty seconds to one minute during processing. *Sencha* is noted for its refreshing flavor and grassy notes, and pairs well with many types of sweets.

Shincha 新茶 The first crop of tea, also called *ichibancha*

Sobacha 蕎麦茶 Roasted buckwheat tea, silky and round on the palate, with a nutty aroma

Tamaryokucha 玉緑茶 Popular in Kyushu, this is *sencha* that has curly, twisted leaves; it has citrusy notes and is slightly astringent on the palate

In much the same way that certain locations in France are known for their wine, the following places in Japan are known to produce highly regarded tea. These are the names to ask for when shopping for tea.

Asamiyacha A village in Shiga prefecture, an area known for its aromatic roasted *hōjicha*.

Chirancha A village in Kagoshima prefecture in the southern part of Kyushu. This area gets very warm, and the first tea harvests often come from here.

Murakamicha A village in Niigata prefecture, a cold region that produces a tea that is round, mellow, and slightly sweet on the palate.

Sayamacha A village in Saitama prefecture, these teas are heated strongly and as a result are known for having a strong toasted flavor with a hint of sweetness.

Shizuokacha One of the most famous regions in Japan for tea

Ujicha The Uji region of Kyoto has an optimal climate for growing tea. Its *gyokuro* and *mattcha* are of the highest quality.

Yamecha A village in Shizuoka prefecture, near Mount Fuji, its *gyokuro* is known for being rich with a strong sweetness.

SAKE

日本酒 OR 清酒
NIHONSHU SEISHU

SAKE IS A GENERIC TERM REFERRING TO ALL ALCOHOLIC PRODUCTS. NIHONSHU IS THE WORD FOR JAPANEse *sake*. *Sake* can be sweet, sparkling, aromatic, creamy, and even thick. Some have an aroma and palate similar to white wine. While many people shun warm *sake* as poor quality, in Japan, there are many great *sake* made specifically to be drunk warm. Casual pubs, *izakaya*, are great places to explore a wide range of *sake*.

Sake is made from rice, water, yeast, and *kōji* (*Aspergillus oryzae*). *Kōji* is used to break down the starch in rice into fermentable sugars. *Terroir* is evident in *sake*, because water and rice are usually locally procured and have distinctive tastes. Many different rice strains are used for making *sake*; Yamada Nishiki is the king, and a good name to remember. A reliable way to choose *sake* is to look for famous producing regions like Niigata or Yamagata, or famous brand names including Sawa no I from Tokyo, Hakkaisan from Niigata, Uragasumi from Miyagi, Dassai from Yamaguchi, and Masumi from Nagano.

One thing to look for on the label is the SMV (Sake Meter Value) or *nihonshudo* 日本酒度. The lower the number, the sweeter the *sake*, the higher the number, the drier. Another number you may see on the label is the *seimaibuai* 精米歩合 that designates the percentage of rice that remains after it is polished. The higher the number, the more impurities have been milled away, and the more delicate and clean the *sake*.

While in Japan you may have the opportunity to try *sake* that is hard to find outside of the country. Interesting *sake* worth searching out include sparkling *sake* that has no official designation; *nigorizake*, an unfiltered *sake* in which some of the lees remain; *kimoto*, a rarely seen *sake* that is full-bodied and complex; and *yamahai*, an aromatic and heady *sake*.

There are thirteen *sake* breweries (*kuramoto*) in Tokyo, mostly in the Western part of the city around the Ome, Hachioji, and the Tama area. Some offer tours but rarely if ever in English. www.tokyosake.or.jp (Japanese)

The retail shop **Hasegawa Saketen** has a well-selected inventory and the staff is friendly and knowledgeable. There are branches at Omotesando Hills, Azabu Juban and in the basement of Tokyo station in the GranSta area. Some of these shops also have small counters where you can enjoy a cup of *sake*.

Some *depachika*, like Nihonbashi's **Takashimaya** and Shibuya's **Tōkyū Tōyoko-ten's Food Show**, often have weekly promotions where local *sake* breweries (*jizake*) will come to promote their *sake*. The promotions include free tastings, often conducted by someone from the brewery.

See *izakaya* chapter for places to drink *sake* in the city.

Some terms pertaining to *sake* terminology (note that some may also include the suffix "*shu*," for example *daiginjō* and *daiginjōshu* are the same thing) include:

Amakuchi 甘口 A slightly sweet *sake*
Daiginjō 大吟醸 A variety of *sake* in which rice is polished to 50% or less and to which a small amount of distilled alcohol is added

Futsuushu 普通酒 A category that encompasses most *sake* in Japan (almost 75%); considered "table *sake*"

Genshu 原酒 *sake* that, unlike most, is not diluted with water; hence, the alcohol percentage is higher

Ginjoshu 吟醸酒 A variety of *sake* in which rice is polished to 60% or less and to which a small amount of distilled alcohol is added; these *sake* tend to be delicate and aromatic

Honjōzō 本醸造 A variety of *sake* in which rice is polished to 70% or less and to which a small amount of distilled alcohol is added

Jizake 地酒 *sake* from small breweries; usually handcrafted

Junmaidaiginjō 純米大吟醸 A variety of *sake* in which rice is polished to 50% or less and which does not contain any distilled alcohol

Junmaiginjō 純米吟醸 A variety of *sake* in which rice is polished to 60% or less and which does not contain any distilled alcohol

Junmaishu 純米酒 A variety of *sake* in which rice is polished to 70% or less and which does not contain any distilled alcohol; these tend to be full-bodied

Karakuchi 辛口 A *sake* dry on the palate

Kimoto 生酛 A rarely seen *sake* that is full-bodied and complex

Kōshū 古酒 Aged *sake*; most *sake* should be consumed young, but some, like *kōshū*, are made to be aged in order to develop richer flavors; some may be sweet on the palate

Muroka 無濾過 Unfiltered *sake*; some may be a bit cloudy

Namazake 生酒 Unpasteurized *sake*

Nigorizake にごり酒 *Sake* in which some of the original lees remain; can be slightly cloudy to thick and chunky

Seishu 清酒 Clear *sake* from which solids have been filtered

Shiboritate 搾立て Freshly pressed *sake*

Taruzake 樽酒 *Sake* that has been aged in cedar barrels, enriching the mouthfeel

Tokubetsu honjōzō 特別本醸造 Similar to honjōzō but made with a special strain of rice that is highly milled

Tokubetsu junmai 特別純米 Similar to *junmaishu* but made with a special strain of rice that is highly milled

Yamahai 山廃 A variety of *sake* that can be aromatic and heady

SHOCHU
焼酎

SHOCHU, THE DISTILLED SPIRIT NATIVE TO JAPAN, IS OFTEN CALLED "JAPANESE VODKA"—SOMETHING OF a misnomer, as *shōchū* is usually about 50 proof whereas vodka is often 90 proof or more. *Shōchū* is only exported to a handful of countries, so it can be difficult to find outside of Japan, but within the country it is the beverage of choice: *shōchū* has outsold *sake* in Japan since 2003.

Shōchū is made from a variety of base ingredients. Sweet potato (*imo*) *shōchū* can have a heady aroma, chestnuts (*kuri*) may impart a toasty aroma; there is a Japanese basil (*shiso*) *shōchū* that is easily recognizable by its minty aroma. Some common base ingredients are listed later in this chapter; *shōchū* can also be made from a variety of vegetables, *sake* lees, kelp, and much more.

The mold to break down the starches in the base ingredients into fermentable sugars, called *kōjikin* (*aspergillus oryzae*), is what makes *shōchū* different from other distilled spirits, and gives it a distinctive aroma. The taste of a *shōchū* is greatly affected by which of three basic types of *kōji* is used in making it. *Shirokōji* 白麹 (white *kōji*) creates a very soft, gentle-tasting, and often light-bodied *shōchū*. *Kikōji* 黄麹 (yellow *kōji*) is the same *koji* that is used for making *sake*. The resulting *shōchū* is often aromatic with floral tones, and is supple on the palate. *Kurokōji* 黒麹 (black *kōji*) is the famous mold used in Okinawa's *awamori*. *Shōchū* made with *kurokōji* are often bold on the palate and full-bodied.

Shōchū is often mixed with water; the alcohol content of a glass of *shōchū* with water is comparable to that of a glass of wine. The drink's profile and impact on the palate can vary based on the temperature of the water it's mixed with—on a cold winter's day, nothing warms the body like a cup of hot *shōchū*. It can also be consumed straight, on the rocks, or as a mixer. *Shōchū* is the base for *chūhai*, a popular fruit cocktail that comes in a variety of flavors and is sold in cans at about half the price of beer.

The process used to age a *shōchū* will be discerned on the palate. If it has been aged in a stainless steel tank, the *shōchū* will retain more of the taste of the base ingredient. Since ceramic is a material that breathes, *shōchū* aged in a ceramic pot will be softer on the palate. Naturally, aging in a wooden barrel will add tannins and color to *shōchū*, similar to whiskey. Finally, aging a *shōchū* for more than two years will allow it to mellow and come together, making it smoother, with a longer finish. Also important is to ask if the *shōchū* was distilled under high or low pressure. *Genatsu*, *shōchū* distilled under low pressure, is often softer on the palate, while *joatsu*, *shōchū* distilled under high pressure, is more full-bodied.

Shōchū is made in every prefecture of Japan—that can't be said about *sake*, which is not brewed in Kagoshima—but in many ways, *shōchū* is most identified with the southern island of Kyushu where much is produced. If you're new to *shōchū*, and you're ordering it from a menu, it is a good idea to familiarize yourself with the names of the prefectures of Kyushu, and their specialties. This will insure that you have a quality *shōchū*. Listed below are some of the prefectures of Kyushu and the types of *shōchū* they are best known for:

Kagoshima 鹿児島 Sweet potato (*imo*)

Miyazaki 宮崎 Buckwheat (*soba*)

Oita 大分 Barley (*mugi*)

Kumamoto 熊本 Rice (*kome*)

Amami Oshima 奄美大島 Brown sugar (*kokutō*)

Okinawa 沖縄 Thai rice (*awamori*)

Okinawa is famous for its local version of *shōchū*, *awamori*, which is made from Thai rice and a specific black *kōji* mold that imparts earthy and heady notes. A special aged *awamori*, called *ku-su*, must be aged a minimum of three years, often in ceramic pots. This and other notable regional *shōchū* are available in Tokyo at regional shops, liquor stores, and bars and restaurants with *shōchū* on the menu. Check out **Kagoshima Yurakukan** and **Miyazaki Kan KONNE**.

Shōchū can also be pronounced *jōchū*, as in *imojōchū* (sweet potato *shōchū*) or *komejōchū* (rice *shōchū*).

The *shōchū* you drink will be one of two types, depending on the distillation process.

Otsurui 乙類 Made in a pot still (*tanshiki*), a single-distillation *shōchū* with an alcohol content of less than 45 percent; it retains the aroma of the base ingredient. *Otsurui shōchū* is good for drinking straight, on the rocks, or with hot water. It can also be used as a mixer for cocktails. *Otsurui* is also called *honkaku shōchū* 本格焼酎. This is the top-quality *shōchū* that is worth exploring. If purchasing any *shōchū*, make sure it is *honkaku shōchū*.

Kōrui 甲類 Made in a continuous still (*renzoku shiki*) in which the spirit circulates through the still several times, it is very smooth on the palate and is less than 36 percent alcohol. On its own, *kōrui shōchū* does not have any notable aromas and is unimpressive on the palate—it's typically used as a cocktail mixer.

The most common base ingredients used to make *shōchū* include:

Imo 芋 (sweet potato) Highly aromatic, *imojōchū* is usually smooth and slightly sweet on the palate. There are many varieties of sweet potato, all contributing their own characteristics. Recommended brand: Sato

Mugi 麦 (barley) Roasty, toasty, and often dry, *mugijōchū* can be aged in barrels, making it fuller on the palate and reminiscent of whiskey (though lower in alcohol). Recommended brand: Naka Naka

Kome 米 (rice) Light, crisp, and food-friendly, *komejōchū* is a good *shōchū* to try first, as it is quite smooth on the palate. Recommended brand: Torikai

Soba そば (buckwheat) Round on the palate, with strong buckwheat aromas. Recommended brand: Mayan no Tsubuyaki

Kokutō 黒糖 (brown sugar) Only made on the islands between Kagoshima and Okinawa, this is also a good starter *shōchū*. It's sweet on the nose and finish, and even slightly sweet on the palate. Recommended brand: Kikaijima

Awamori 泡盛 (Thai rice) Made with the addition of the black *kōji* mold, *awamori* is full-bodied and pairs well with the rich and well-seasoned foods of Okinawa, where it is produced. Recommended brand: Harusame

Kuri 栗 (chestnuts) Slightly sweet and aromatic, like *marron glacé*. Recommended brand: Kotanba

Goma 胡麻 (sesame seeds) With a nutty aroma and a round mouthfeel. Try it mixed with milk on the rocks for a unique cocktail. Recommended brand: Beniotome

Shiso しそ (perilla leaves) With the unmistakable minty aroma associated with *shiso* leaves. Recommended brand: Tantakatan

Shōchū Authority • 焼酎オーソリティ

Chiyoda-ku, Marunouchi 1-9-1, Tokyo Station,
Yaesu Kitchen Street, 1st Floor

千代田区丸の内1-9-1東京駅八重洲キッチンストリート1F

Tel. 03-5208-5157 • Daily 10:00–21:00

www.authority-online.jp/html/newpage.html?code=2 (Japanese)

SHOP • MAP PAGE 222, #21

Shōchū Authority offers one of the best selections of *shōchū* and *awamori* in the city, and the knowledgeable staff can help you find whatever you are looking for. It is conveniently located inside Tokyo station, outside of the ticket gate.

JAPANESE WINE
日本のワイン

JAPAN'S FIRST COMMERCIAL WINERY DATES BACK TO 1875 IN YAMANASHI, JUST WEST OF TOKYO. JAPANESE wineries do a commendable job, considering the challenges of hot and humid weather conditions. Regions known for producing wines include Yamanashi, Nagano, Yamagata, Tochigi, and Hokkaido.

Japan's most famous native grape, *kōshū* (甲州), produces a light-to medium-bodied white wine with fruity notes that pairs well with Japanese food. Chardonnay and merlot are harvested in Japan and some German grapes do well in the cool climate of Hokkaido.

The restaurant **Nihonbashi Yukari** has a nice selection of Japanese wine. Antenna shops will also have a nice selection of domestic vintages, in particular the Yamanashi shop.

Cave de Relax • カーヴドリラックス

Minato-ku, Nishi-Shinbashi 1-6-11 • 港区西新橋1-6-11

Tel. 03-3595-3697 • Daily 11:00–20:00

http://caverelax.com/english/HOME.html (English)

SHOP • MAP PAGE 157, #21

The selection at Cave de Relax covers both old world and new world vintages along with a nice selection of Japanese wine. There are more than 1,300 wines from which to select; about one-fourth of owner Kunio Naito's wines are priced less than 1,000 JPY. This is one of the most popular shops in the city. The staff is friendly and knowledgeable and there is a delivery service.

Coco Farm and Winery • ココ・ファーム・ワイナリー

Tochigi-ken, Ashikaga-shi, Tajima 611

栃木県足利市田島611

Tel. 0284-42-1194 • Daily 9:30–17:30

www.cocowine.com (English)

WINERY AND RESTAURANT

Coco Farm and Winery in Tochigi is about an hour north of Tokyo. The winery produces a diverse portfolio of wine from sweet to dry, still to sparkling, red, white, and rosé. The winery works with developmentally disabled and autistic students of Cocoromi Gakuen who live at the school next door. There is a café overlooking the vineyard in which to enjoy a flight of wine with food. Grapes are harvested at the winery, but also purchased from vineyards around the country. This is a great place to learn about Japan's *terroir*. The winery also hosts a harvest festival each autumn that attracts thousands of visitors over one weekend. There is a tasting room and tours of the winery. Call ahead to confirm details if you want to schedule a tour. The tasting room and café is open all year long.

To see a few wineries in one day, you may want to visit Yamanashi prefecture, about an hour west of Tokyo by express train. The city of Katsunuma has been producing *kōshū* grapes for more than 1,200 years. Originally these grapes were grown as table grapes and eventually found their way to wine bottles. Here are just some of the many wineries in Katsunuma (call ahead for hours of operation):

Château Mercian • シャトー・メルシャン

Yamanashi-ken, Koshu-shi, Katsunuma-cho,
Shimo-Iwasaki 1425-1

山梨県甲州市勝沼町下岩崎1425-1

Tel. 0553-44-1011

www.chateaumercian.com/cm/english/index.html (English)

Grace Winery • グレイスワイン
Yamanashi-ken, Koshu-shi, Katsunuma-cho, Todoroki 173
山梨県 甲州市 勝沼町 等々力173
Tel. 0553-44-1230
www.grace-wine.co.jp/english/englishnew.html (English)

Marufuji Winery • 丸藤ワイナリー
Yamanashi-ken, Koshu-shi, Katsunuma-cho, Fujii 780
山梨県甲州市勝沼町藤井780
Tel. 0553-44-0043 • www.rubaiyat.jp/ (Japanese)

Lumière Winery • ルミエールワイナリー
Yamanashi-ken, Fuefuki-shi,
Ichinomiyacho, Minaminoro 624
山梨県笛吹市一宮町南野呂624
Tel. 0553-47-0207 • www.lumiere.jp/en/ (English)

UMESHU
梅酒

UMESHU IS A POPULAR SWEET ALCOHOLIC DRINK
BASED ON APRICOTS. UMESHU TRADITIONALLY IS
made from the distilled spirit *shōchū* but recently has been made
with *sake*, brandy, and even *mirin*. On a hot day a glass of *umeshu*
on the rocks is a nice aperitif or nightcap. Some popular brands
of *umeshu* include:

Asabiraki From Iwate, a *sake*-based *umeshu* called Umekanon. It has the
sweet aromas of fresh apricots but on the palate it is elegant, crisp,
and dry.

Chōya The largest producer of *umeshu* in Japan. Its signature green
bottle includes whole apricots that are often spooned into the glass
with the *umeshu*. Choya also produces a rich molasses-like Kokuto
Umeshu made with brown sugar with overtones of dark chocolate,
leather, and dried figs.

Kaga Umeshu From Ishikawa, an *umeshu* aged for three years, called
Manzairaku, that is round, smooth, and mellow on the palate.

Kishu Akai Umeshu From Wakayama, made with red perilla leaves and
has aromas of fresh strawberries and a crisp finish like California
white zinfandel

Oshuku Nigori Umeshu From Tokushima, an unfiltered variety in which
the meat of the apricot has been mashed and mixed with honey, with
the consistency of a thick fruit juice

CASUAL PLACES FOR DRINKS

JAPANESE PUBS
居酒屋
IZAKAYA

IZAKAYA ARE CASUAL PUBS OFFERING BOTH ALCOHOL AND FOOD. PERHAPS THE EASIEST WAY TO FIND AN *izakaya* is to look for a red paper lantern outside. A sign of a good *izakaya* is one with a menu offering seasonal seafood and vegetables. Some *izakaya* feature a certain cuisine like grilled chicken skewers (*yakitori*) or fish cake hot pot (*oden*); other *izakaya*, called *robatayaki*, feature grilled foods. These are neighborhood places with "regulars." Some *izakaya* allow customers to keep a bottle of *shōchū* at the pub so each time they come back a bottle is waiting.

There are many *izakaya* throughout the city where you will be able to find a wide variety of *sake*. Good *izakaya* are so common that it's not necessary to travel far to find one; the best way is to ask your concierge for a recommendation nearby.

Here are two contrasting *izakaya*, the upscale **Sasagin** in Yoyogi Uehara and the casual **Yamariki** in Morishita.

Sasagin • 笹吟
Shibuya-ku, Uehara 1-32-15, Kobayashi Building
渋谷区上原1-32-15小林ビル
Tel. 03-5454-3715 • 17:00–23:00; closed Sunday and holidays
RESTAURANT • MODERATE • MAP PAGE 156, #19

Near Yoyogi-Uehara station, this elegant *izakaya* has a great selection of *sake* displayed in the windowed refrigerator behind the long counter. The menu is diverse, including seafood, and small bites that are perfect accompaniments to *sake*. Popular dishes include *nuta*, seasonal seafood served with a vinegary *miso* dressing, or grilled gingko nuts.

Yamariki • 山利喜
Koto-ku, Morishita 2-18-8 • 江東区森下2-18-8
Tel. 03-3633-1638 • 17:00–22:00; closed Sunday and holidays
www.yamariki.com (Japanese)
RESTAURANT • MODERATE • MAP PAGE 157, #8

Located in the historic Morishita district, this institution, well-known for its *naizō ryōri* (see page 84), is also often ranked as one of the top ten *izakaya* in the city. There is usually a line to get in. (If you don't want to wait, you can try the branch down the street; the staff will direct you there.) What makes Yamariki unique as an *izakaya* is that it has a sommelier on staff, Mizukami-san, who will help you select a bottle of wine to pair with the food. The *sake* list as well is solid and while the *shōchū* selection is short, it is a well-selected list. The signature dish, *nikomi*, of innards, Port wine, *Hatchō miso*, sugar, and bouquet garni, has been using the same broth for more than forty years.

STAND-UP BARS

立ち飲み
TACHINOMI

TACHINOMI (LITERALLY "STAND AND DRINK") ARE CASUAL BARS WHERE YOU CAN GET SOMETHING TO drink and small plates of food. *Tachinomi* long were known for being smoky dives, unwelcoming to women, where salarymen would stop after work before heading home. Modern *tachinomi* attract a younger and hipper crowd with reasonable prices and friendly atmospheres; some even may have wine lists. Ebisu and Shinbashi are two neighborhoods filled with *tachinomi* where you can walk around and dip into these casual establishments.

Tachigui Sakaba buri • 立喰酒場 buri
Shibuya-ku, Ebisu-Nishi 1-14-1 • 渋谷区恵比寿西1-14-1
Tel. 03-3496-7744 • Daily 17:00–3:00
www.takewaka.co.jp/buri/index.html (Japanese)
BAR AND RESTAURANT • INEXPENSIVE TO MODERATE
MAP PAGE 156, #29

Buri has the one of the largest selections in Tokyo of "one cup" *nihonshu*, small single-serving jars of *sake*. This bar provides a fun and unique way to try many types in one evening. There are more than thirty different *sakes* on offer, decorating the wall. Point, pop the top, and "*kampai.*" While you are here try the slush-like frozen *sake*. The menu is filled with small plates of *nihonshu*-friendly foods such as seasonal seafood and grilled meats.

Gohiikini • ごひいきに
Minato-ku, Shinbashi 2-8-9 • 港区新橋 2-8-9
Tel. 03-3502-3132 • 12:00–13:30, 16:00–24:00;
Saturday until 23:00; closed Sunday and holidays
BAR AND RESTAURANT • INEXPENSIVE TO MODERATE
MAP PAGE 180, #35

The neighborhood is filled with *tachinomi*. This popular stand-ing bar just outside of Shinbashi station is one of the friendli-est. Service is cafeteria-style, where food is selected from a long counter; drinks are ordered from the bar. Long communal wood tables are filled with a diverse crowd of both men and women of mixed ages, unlike many in the area, which can be filled with older salarymen.

Stand Bar Maru • マル
Chuo-ku, Hatchobori 3-22-10 • 中央区八丁堀 3-22-10
Tel. 03-3552-9210 • 17:00–23:00; closed weekends and holidays
BAR AND RESTAURANT • INEXPENSIVE TO MODERATE
MAP PAGE 157, #17

Maru may be one of the best bargains among the city's standing bars. Located next door to a wine shop offering about two hundred wines, customers can purchase a bottle and have it opened at the bar for a nominal fee. The first floor is standing only (*tachinomi*), but if you get there early enough you may be able to snag a seat in the second floor restaurant. Following the tapas concept, legs of Iberico ham are shaved to order and other small plates can be shared; the grilled meats are highly recommended. In an out-of-the-way area, Maru is always buzzing with a young crowd.

BEER GARDENS
ビアガーデン
BIA GA-DEN

DURING JULY AND AUGUST, TOKYO'S HOT AND HUMID SUMMER, SOME DEPARTMENT STORES OPEN OUTDOOR beer gardens on their rooftops. It is a striking setting, especially in Shinjuku when you are surrounded by skyscrapers, both a fun experience and a unique glimpse into the drinking culture of Japan. If you are lucky, a breeze will cool you down a bit. The cold beer is served with typical pub fare—sausages and fried potatoes—in a casual atmosphere. Department stores with popular beer gardens include Keio in Shinjuku, Matsuya in

Asakusa, **Tobu** in Ikebukuro, and Matsuzakaya in Ginza. Call ahead to make sure that the beer gardens are open.

Meiji Kinen Kan • 明治記念館
Beer Terrace Sekirei
Minato-ku, Moto Akasaka 2-2-23 • 港区元赤坂 2-2-23
Tel. 03-3746-7723 • call for hours of operation
www.meijikinenkan.gr.jp/english/restaurant/sekirei.html
(English)

MAP PAGE 156, #11

This may be one of the most spectacular beer gardens in Japan. Guests sit in wicker chairs around a garden that is so precisely manicured, it looks as if it was tended to with tweezers — a rare, luxurious treat in this concrete city.

KILOMETERS
0   1   2   3

MILES
0   ¼   ½   1   2

Toshima-ku

1. Tobu 東武

IKEBUKURO

Sankōin 三光院
(Koganei City)

Nakano-ku

Shinjuku-

SHINJUKU
p.263

SHINJUKU

10. Nebariya ねばり屋

11. Meiji Kinen Kan
明治記念館

Meiji-Jingu Shrine

13. Toraya Aka
Honten (main
とらや赤坂オ

12. Daisō ダイソー

19. Sasagin 笹吟

HARAJUKU

OMOTESANDO
pp.254-255

Tokyo Midtow

Ivan Ramen
アイバン ラーメン

Shibuya-ku

Minato-k

SHIBUYA

23. Beard Papa ビアードパパ

24. Tōkyū Tōyoko-ten Food Show
東急東横店

Setagaya-ku

25. Waketokuyama 分とく山

30. Matsugen Ebisu
松玄恵比寿

28. Matsunosuke 松乃助

27. Sakamoto Shōten 坂本商店

29. Tachigui Sakaba buri 立喰酒場

31. Nakaiseki Sen
菜懐石仙

Meguro-ku

32. Oriol Balaguer

Suzunobu スズノブ

TOKYO 東京

2. Takei 竹井

Bunkyo-ku

NEZU

3. Kushiage Dokoro Hantei
串揚げどころ はん亭根津

AMEYOKO
p.218

ASAKUSA/
KAPPABASHI
pp.198–199

UENO

Taito-ku

OKACHIMACHI

NGURAZAKA
273

Chiyoda-ku

AKIHABARA

5. Sasama
さゝま

4. Hōraiya 宝来屋

6. Kanda Yabu Soba かんだやぶそば

KANDA

7. Kanda Awahei 神田淡平

RYOGOKU

8. Yamariki
山利喜

NIHONBASHI
pp.222–223

NINGYOCHO
pp.240–241

9. Minoya
みの家

Imperial Palace

TOKYO

Chuo-ku

Koto-ku

General Post Office

Takashimaya

16. Viron ヴィロン

15. Sadaharu Aoki

17. Stand Bar Maru
マル

Wagyū Ryōri Sanda
和牛料理さんだ

GINZA
pp.180–181

YURAKUCHO

18. Kintame
近為

21. Cave de Relax カーヴドリラックス

20. Toranomon Sunaba Honten
虎ノ門砂場本店

Hotel Okura

TSUKISHIMA
& TSUKUDA
p.249

SHINBASHI

TSUKIJI
pp.160–161

Itō Yōkadō
イトーヨーカド

22. Daigo 醍醐

Tsukiji
Market

Tokyo Tower

26. Tōfuya Ukai とうふ屋うかい

Tokyo Bay

NAGAWA

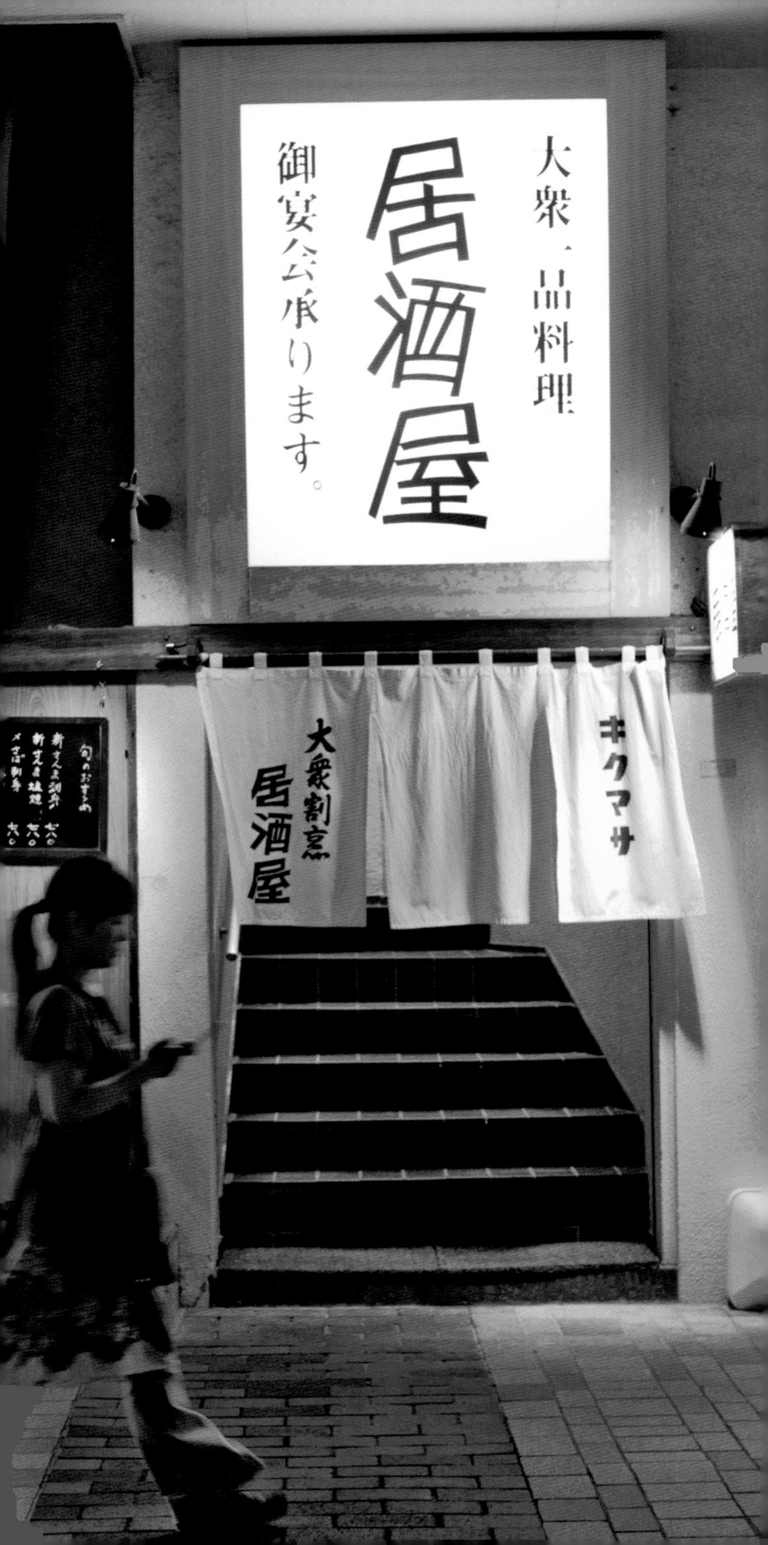
大衆一品料理
居酒屋
御宴会承ります。
大衆割烹
居酒屋
キクマサ
旬のおすすめ
新さんま刺身
新さんま塩焼

CHAPTER 4

....

PLACES TO EAT AND SHOP

BY NEIGHBORHOOD

....

TSUKIJI MARKET

築地市場

TSUKIJI SHIJO

TSUKIJI, IN THE HEART OF THE CITY, IS THE WORLD'S LARGEST FISH MARKET; IT IS PERHAPS ONE OF THE most dynamic culinary destinations in the country. (In total there are twelve wholesale markets in Tokyo. The other popular ones are the Adachi market for seafood and the Ota market, which sells seafood, produce, and flowers; both are open to the public.)

The history of the Tsukiji market dates back to 1603, when it was located in the nearby historic Nihonbashi district. The market moved to its current location in 1923 after the Kanto earthquake, and is tentatively scheduled to move again in 2013, a few kilometers along the bay to Toyosu. The new location will have better access to the highway connecting the market to Narita International Airport, which has become the gateway for much of the seafood that comes in and out of Tsukiji. The move is controversial for a variety of political, environmental, financial, and other reasons. The current facilities are in desperate need of renovation; regardless, you may never have a chance to see this longstanding Tokyo institution unless you visit soon.

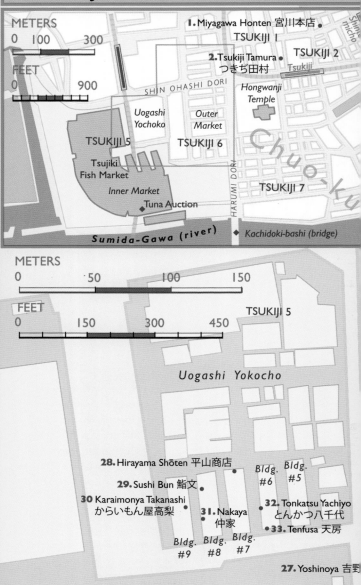

TSUKIJI MARKET 築地市場

METERS
0   100   300

FEET
0   900

1. Miyagawa Honten 宮川本店
TSUKIJI 1

2. Tsukiji Tamura • つきぢ田村
TSUKIJI 2

Tsukiji

SHIN OHASHI DORI

Hongwanji Temple

Uogashi Yochoko

Outer Market

TSUKIJI 5

TSUKIJI 6

Chuo-ku

Tsujiki Fish Market

HARUMI DORI

Inner Market

TSUKIJI 7

◆ Tuna Auction

Sumida-Gawa (river)   ◆ Kachidoki-bashi (bridge)

METERS
0   50   100   150

FEET
0   150   300   450

TSUKIJI 5

Uogashi Yokocho

28. Hirayama Shōten 平山商店

Bldg. #6   Bldg. #5

29. Sushi Bun 鮨文

30. Karaimonya Takanashi からいもん屋高梨

31. Nakaya 仲家

32. Tonkatsu Yachiyo とんかつ八千代

• 33. Tenfusa 天房

Bldg. #9   Bldg. #8   Bldg. #7

27. Yoshinoya 吉野

26. Tomie

Tsujiki Fish Market
Inner Market

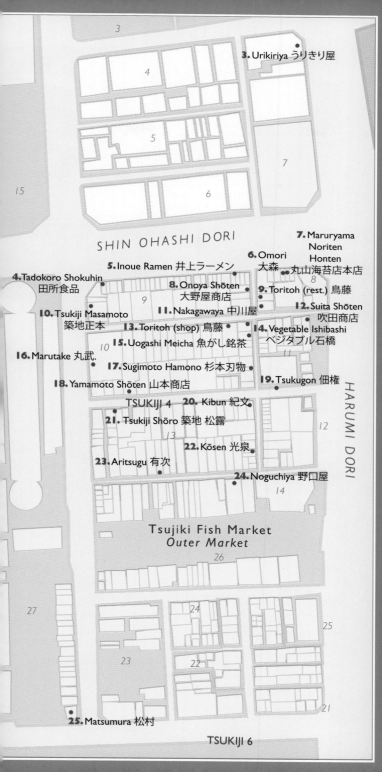

3. Urikiriya うりきり屋

7. Maruryama Noriten Honten 丸山海苔店本店

SHIN OHASHI DORI

5. Inoue Ramen 井上ラーメン

6. Omori 大森

4. Tadokoro Shokuhin 田所食品

8. Onoya Shōten 大野屋商店

9. Toritoh (rest.) 鳥藤

12. Suita Shōten 吹田商店

10. Tsukiji Masamoto 築地正本

11. Nakagawaya 中川屋

13. Toritoh (shop) 鳥藤

14. Vegetable Ishibashi ベジタブル石橋

15. Uogashi Meicha 魚がし銘茶

16. Marutake 丸武.

17. Sugimoto Hamono 杉本刃物

18. Yamamoto Shōten 山本商店

19. Tsukugon 佃権

TSUKIJI 4

20. Kibun 紀文

21. Tsukiji Shōro 築地 松露

22. Kōsen 光泉

23. Aritsugu 有次

24. Noguchiya 野口屋

HARUMI DORI

Tsujiki Fish Market
Outer Market

25. Matsumura 松村

TSUKIJI 6

Tsukiji is very much a working market, with more than 30,000 people coming here daily to trade more than 2,000 varieties of seafood. The market supports the restaurants and retail shops of Tokyo, and sends some of its seafood to famous *sushi* restaurants around the world. Be careful when visiting—an estimated 19,000 delivery trucks and 6,000 carts, often driven by cigarette-smoking workers, weave in and out of the narrow streets. You'll also see rickety bikes with wooden boxes balanced on the back, bearing the names of pricey and elegant *sushi* shops such as "Jiro" (denoting the three Michelin-starred Sukiyabashi Jiro), picking up fish to take back to the restaurant.

The market is divided into two parts: *jōgai*, the outer market,

which is open to the general public, and *jōnai*, the inner market, which is restricted to wholesalers. There are 1600 stalls in the inner market and another four hundred in the outer market. The stores listed below are in the outer market. Beware: the surroundings are overwhelming at first.

The market sets up while the city is just going to sleep, around 2 a.m. The shops start to open by 5 a.m. or 6 a.m. and close in the early afternoon. The frozen tuna auction, a celebrated attraction of the inner market, generally starts at around 5:00 a.m. The king of the marketplace is tuna. The most revered is the bluefin. Tuna is available in both fresh and super-frozen varieties (the latter is cut into pieces at the market with a bandsaw).

In the market you will find a dizzying array of thousands of sea creatures, including spiny sea urchin, salmon roe, shellfish, oysters, squid, octopus, and eels. As seafood comes into the market, the fishmongers see the first sign of the changing seasons. It is often said that fishmongers at Tsukiji Market are more knowledgeable about weather patterns than weather forecasters. In addition to seafood, the market also sells produce, knives, and pantry items. A wide variety of restaurants on site feed, at reasonable prices, the thousands of people working at and visiting the market.

Avoid Sundays and national holidays, when the market is closed. There are also a few weekdays each month when it is closed, so it is best to check on the market's website to see whether it is open http://www.tsukiji-market.or.jp/tukiji_e.htm (English). Many of the shops in the outer market also close on the days when the inner market is closed. If Tsukiji Market is closed, visit Ameyoko near Ueno station: it is open all year long.

The end of the year, right before the New Year's holidays, is one of the busiest times of the year—during this time in 2008, the tuna auction was closed to the public for the first time because the public presence had become disruptive and distracting to the business of the auction. Since then, it has been closed during the holiday season.

Travel lightly and wear comfortable shoes. Leave large backpacks at home.

There is delicious and reasonably priced food available at the market, albeit, for the most part, served in very humble settings. Many of the shops source their food from the market, so ingredients could hardly be fresher. Best of all, there is a wide variety of options to choose from, including *tempura*, *ramen*, curry, and of course, *sushi*; there is even an Italian restaurant that specializes in seafood dishes (Tomiena, Tsukiji 5-24, Building#1, map page 161, # 26).

The most casual places to eat are stand-and-eat shops where you will find one-bowl dishes such as *ramen*, curry, or rice bowls. Many of these are located along Shin Ohashi Dori Street.

Another part of the market filled with restaurants is called Uogashi Yokocho 魚がし横丁. Here you will find long lines of hungry people in the morning queuing for the Japanese breakfast of champions: *sushi*. If you find raw fish unappetizing in the morning, there are other options.

The two most famous *sushi* restaurants in the market are Sushi Dai and Daiwa Sushi. They also have the longest lines. Both restaurants are constantly seen on TV and covered in magazines, and sometimes the wait is more than two hours. While the *sushi* is good, customers are often squeezed into tight spaces and rushed through their meals. Remember, this isn't your only chance to have *sushi*.

Addresses in and around the market are all in Chuo-ku 中央区.

Sushi Bun • 鮨文
Tsukiji 5-2-1, Building #8 • 中央区築地5-2-1ビル8
Tel. 03-3541-3860
www.tsukijinet.com/tsukiji/kanren/susibun/ (Japanese)
RESTAURANT • MODERATE • MAP PAGE 160, #29

Another *sushi* shop with a strong following is the 150-year old Sushi Bun, originally a cart at the former fish market in Nihon-bashi. Sushi Bun only uses wild fish that is domestically caught. The fifth-generation daughter speaks English and can help you with the menu.

Nakaya · 仲家
Tsukiji 5-2-1, Building #8 · 中央区築地5-2-1ビル8
Tel. 03-3541-0211

RESTAURANT · INEXPENSIVE · MAP PAGE 160, #31

Another very satisfying way to satiate a craving for raw fish is to have a *donburi*, or a large bowl of rice topped with seasonal *sashimi*. Nakaya has a selection that includes an *uni don* of creamy, sweet sea urchin. The most luxurious item on the menu is a bowl topped with fatty tuna, salmon roe, and sea urchin. Cooked options include grilled or simmered fish over rice.

Miyagawa Honten · 宮川本店
Tsukiji 1-4-6 · 中央区築地1-4-6
Tel. 03-3541-1292 · Monday to Friday 11:30—14:00, 17:00—20:30; Sunday and holidays 11:30—14:00, 17:00—20:00; closed Saturday

RESTAURANT · MODERATE · MAP PAGE 160, #1

Established in 1893 Miyagawa Honten is synonymous with local eel (*unagi*) that is steamed, then grilled over charcoal and basted with a sweet soy sauce. Despite the popularity of this preparation, connoisseurs suggest having it grilled and seasoned with salt (*shirayaki*) and served with *wasabi* and soy sauce. The *unagi* is cooked to order and may take up to thirty or forty minutes.

Toritoh · 鳥藤
Tsukiji 4-8-6 · 中央区築地4-8-6
Tel. 03-3543-6525
www.toritoh.com (Japanese)

RESTAURANT · INEXPENSIVE · MAP PAGE 161, #9

If the mountains of seafood conjure up a craving for chicken, Toritoh is the place to go. The restaurant is popular for its char-coal-grilled chicken served over a hot bowl of rice (*donburi*). The dish includes nibbles and bits from every nook and cranny of the chicken, from the fatty tail area to the liver, breast, thighs, and gizzard. Also on the menu is *oyakodon*, made of loosely scrambled eggs and chicken simmered in a sweet *dashi* stock. The shop has been in business since 1907; the retail shop is just around the corner (map page 161, #13).

Yoshinoya · 吉野家
Tsukiji 5-2-1 Building #1 · 中央区築地5-2-1ビル1
Tel. 03-5550-8504
www.yoshinoya.com/shop/tsukiji/index.html (Japanese)

RESTAURANT · INEXPENSIVE · MAP PAGE 160, #27

Yoshinoya is a popular fast-food chain specializing in *gyūdon*, thin slices of beef cooked with onions and a sweet soy sauce, and ladled over a bowl of rice. The shop was founded in 1899 and was located near the original fish market in Nihonbashi.

Tenfusa • 天房
Tsukiji 5-2-1, Building #6 • 中央区築地5-2-1ビル6
Tel. 03-3547-6766
RESTAURANT • INEXPENSIVE • MAP PAGE 160, #33

Tenfusa is at the end of the building that also houses Daiwa Sushi and Sushi Dai, so it may be hard to find among the long queues. Tenfusa specializes in eel (*anago*) and shrimp *tempura*. The nutty aroma of sesame oil fills the room—making it hard to wait, especially on an empty stomach. The *tempura* is served over rice and is drizzled with a sweet sauce and served with a side of pickles.

Omori • 大森
Tsukiji 4-8-7 • 中央区築地4-8-7
Tel. 03-5565-3704
RESTAURANT • INEXPENSIVE • MAP PAGE 161, #6

Omori is a curry shop; its signature dish is half curry and half *gyūdon* (thin slices of beef, cooked with onions and a sweet soy sauce). In business since 1923, the restaurant seats only five people at the counter.

Inoue Ramen • 井上ラーメン
Tsukiji 4-9-16 • 中央区築地4-9-16
Tel. 03-3542-0620
RESTAURANT • INEXPENSIVE • MAP PAGE 161, #5

If you are craving *ramen*, head to Inoue, a stand-and-eat restaurant located on Shin Ohashi Dori street. The restaurant serves only one type of *ramen* and is very popular with local businessmen; there is often a long line during the noon hour.

Tonkatsu Yachiyo • とんかつ八千代
Tsukiji 5-2-1, Building #6 • 中央区築地5-2-1ビル6
Tel. 03-3547-6762
RESTAURANT • INEXPENSIVE • MAP PAGE 160, #32

Tonkatsu Yachiyo serves deep-fried *panko*-crusted shrimp and pork. In winter, at the height of oyster season, be sure to try the deep-fried oysters (*kaki furai*). This is a workingmen's restaurant, and portions are generous.

Tsukiji Tamura · つきぢ田村
Tsukiji 2-12-11 · 中央区築地2-12-11
Tel. 03-3541-2591 · 11:30–15:00, 17:00–22:00 Monday to Friday;
11:30–22:00 weekends and holidays
www.tsukiji-tamura.com

RESTAURANT · LUNCH MODERATE, DINNER MODERATE TO
VERY EXPENSIVE · MAP PAGE 160, #2

A few blocks away from the market, Tsukiji Tamura is a top destination for *kaiseki* (elegant, multi-course dining) cooked by third-generation chef Takashi Tamura. The main dining room has several tables and the noon meal is often filled with ladies who lunch. Private rooms are also available for an extra charge. Lunch is a bargain for the several courses you'll receive. The chef's father, Teruaki Tamura, is the author of *The Elegant Art of Japanese Food and Manners* (available in Japanese and English) that demystifies many of the rituals of this stylized cuisine.

Two main streets, Shin Ohashi Dori 新大橋通り and Harumi Dori 晴海通り, are the boundaries of the outer market.

Most of the shops are open from 5:00 a.m. to 1:00 p.m. Some will be open later, but it doesn't make much sense to come to the market after noon. Check the market calendar before your visit; most shops are shuttered whenever the inner market is closed.

The following food shops in the outer market are worth checking out (these are all shops without seating areas, although there are items that you can buy and munch on while walking through the market):

Kōsen · 光泉
Tsukiji 4-13-2 · 中央区築地4-13-2
Tel. 03-3541-8981

SHOP · MAP PAGE 161, #22

Kōsen specializes in *mentaiko*: fish roe, often from pollack or cod that has been marinated and slightly fermented in a spicy mixture of dried red chili pepper. There are many ways to eat it: raw, on a bowl of hot rice; grilled slightly; or in a pasta dish. You know you are eating good-quality *mentaiko* when you're able to feel each individual tiny egg in your mouth.

Tsukiji Shōro • 築地 松露
Tsukiji 4-13-13 • 中央区築地4-13-13
Tel. 03-3543-0582 • www.shouro.co.jp (Japanese)
SHOP • MAP PAGE 160, #21

Savory, fluffy thick omelets (*tamagoyaki*) are sold in several stores around the market. You will find them plain or stuffed with fillings such as grilled eel, herbs, or shrimp. Tsukiji Shōro, formerly a *sushi* shop, became so famous for its omelets that now they are the only items sold. Brilliant yellow, with golden-colored edges, each omelet is seasoned with *dashi*, which makes these omelets so delicious. It is no surprise that top *sushi* and *kappō* restaurants order their *tamagoyaki* from Shōro. Some variations on the menu include *oyakoyaki*, filled with chicken and *mitsuba*, *kamaage* bursting with dried pink shrimp, and the *umaki* with grilled eel.

Another popular *tamagoyaki* shop is Marutake 丸武. The family of a famous TV star, Terry Ito, runs it, which explains in part its popularity. The omelets are good too. Tsukiji 4-10-10 (map page 161, #16). Tel. 03-3542-1919.

Tsukugon • 佃権
Tsukiji 4-9-11 • 中央区築地4-9-11
Tel. 03-3546-6871
www.tsukugon.co.jp (Japanese)
SHOP • MAP PAGE 160, #19

In winter a popular comfort food is *oden*, a stew of fish cakes and vegetables. Tsukugon offers a wide selection of these fish cakes, which are stuffed with vegetables and seafood and deep-fried. While the fish cakes most often end up in the *oden* stew, they are also eaten cold as a snack to accompany *sake*. Another popular shop in the market for fish cakes is Kibun 紀文 Tsukiji 4-13-18. Tel. 03-3541-3321. www.kibun.co.jp (Japanese)

Tadokoro Shokuhin • 田所食品
Tsukiji 4-9-11 • 中央区築地4-9-11
Tel. 03-3541-7754
www.tsukiji-monzeki.com/tadokoro.htm (Japanese)
SHOP • MAP PAGE 161, #4

Known for *umami*-rich fish roe, Tadokoro Shokuhin showcases salmon roe (*ikura*), spicy cod roe (*karashi mentaiko*), and salted cod roe (*tarako*), among others. *Ikura* on a hot bowl of rice is a treat. The *karashi mentaiko* is often eaten on angel hair pasta with a bit of butter and mayonnaise, or spread onto a toasted baguette with a little butter and garlic.

Noguchiya • 野口屋
Tsukiji 4-14-18 • 中央区築地4-14-18
Tel. 03-3544-8812
www.table-mono.co.jp/2008/index.html (Japanese)
SHOP • MAP PAGE 161, #24

Noguchiya, a stall specializing in soy products, serves small baskets of creamy *tōfu* (*zarudōfu*), thin gossamer films of soymilk skin (*yuba*), and rich soy milk beverage (*tōnyu*). The deep-fried, thick (*atsuage*) and thin (*aburaage*) *tōfu* are both rich in flavor. In the summer months enjoy a cone of soft soy milk ice cream.

Matsumura • 松村
Tsukiji 6-27-6 • 中央区築地6-27-6
Tel. 03-3541-1760
www.katsuobushi.jp (Japanese)
SHOP • MAP PAGE 161, #25

Matsumura specializes in the smoky flakes of bonito (*katsuobushi*). In front of the shop are large wooden boxes filled with what look like wood shavings from a lumber mill. These delicate shavings are from dried and smoked fillets of bonito, and are a key ingredient when making the smoky *dashi* broth that is the base for many of Japan's classic dishes. *Katsuobushi* is often sprinkled over fresh *tōfu* or steamed greens like spinach.

Suita Shōten • 吹田商店
Tsukiji 4-11-1 • 中央区築地4-11-1
Tel. 03-3541-6931
SHOP • MAP PAGE 161, #12

Suita Shōten originated in Osaka in 1892 and sells more than one hundred types of kelp (*kombu*). The fourth-generation shop also sells other dried sea vegetables, like *hijiki* and *wakame*.

Maruryama Noriten Honten • 丸山海苔店本店
Tsukiji 4-8-8 • 中央区築地4-8-8
no phone
www.maruyamanori.com (Japanese)
SHOP • MAP PAGE 161, #7

In business for more than 150 years, Maruyama Noriten Honten

sells a variety of crisp, dark *nori* (laver) to more than 3,000 *sushi* shops. Much of the nori comes from the Ariake Sea, where the mineral-rich bay fed by rivers from the mountains provides ideal conditions for the cultivation of *nori*.

Yamamoto Shōten • 山本商店
Tsukiji 4-10-8 • 中央区築地4-10-8
Tel. 03-3541-2954
SHOP • MAP PAGE 161, #18

The boxes in front of Yamamoto Shōten are filled with colorful dried beans. Popular domestic beans include Tanba black beans and the highly regarded Hokkaido *azuki* beans. The store also sells sesame seeds, as well as other grains and millet.

Vegetable Ishibashi • ベジタブル石橋
Tsukiji 4-10-1 • 中央区築地4-10-1
Tel. 03-3545-1538
SHOP • MAP PAGE 161, #14

This corner shop has the best selection in the market of herbs, fresh *wasabi*, and seasonal vegetables. Heirloom vegetables of Kyoto (*Kyō yasai*) can also be found here.

Uogashi Meicha • 魚がし銘茶
Tsukiji 4-10-1 • 中央区築地4-10-1
Tel. 03-3541-3396
www.uogashi-meicha.co.jp/shop_03.html (Japanese)
SHOP • MAP PAGE 161, #15

Tea from this seventy-five-year-old shop finds its way to *sushi* shops and Japanese restaurants around the country. There are always several friendly guys behind the small counter pouring free samples of tea.

Karaimonya Takanashi • からいもん屋高梨
Tsukiji 5-2-1, Building #9 • 中央区築地5-2-1ビル9
Tel. 03-3541-0607 • www.karaimonya.com (Japanese)
SHOP • MAP PAGE 160, #30

Look for the large red chili pepper sign and follow your nose to this shop filled with a vast variety of spices and chilies. You'll also find hot sauces, curry powders, mustard, and the unusual salty citrusy paste (*yuzu koshō*), both green and red: 180 different spices in total. Pick up a small package of the shop's signature *maboroshi no shichimi*, the colorful seven-spice mixture used for topping hot *soba* noodles and *miso* soup.

Nakagawaya • 中川屋
Tsukiji 4-8-5 • 中央区築地4-8-5
Tel. 03-3541-6955
www5a.biglobe.ne.jp/~hirokazu/nakagawaya/profile.htm
(Japanese)

SHOP • MAP PAGE 161, #11

Perhaps the most colorful stand in the market is Nakagawaya, with its pickled fruits and vegetables. Some are pickled the day they are sold, like *asazuke*, or some are pickled for two to three years (Narazuke). Also, find the famous *betterazuke* of Tokyo, sweet *daikon* pickled in *kōji* yeast and sugar. Over the course of a year, almost four hundred different types of pickles rotate through the store by season.

Knife Shops
There are several knife shops in the market. Prices at all of the shops are comparable.

Tsukiji Masamoto • 築地正本
Tsukiji 4-9-9 • 中央区築地4-9-9
Tel. 03-3541-7155 • www.tukijimasamoto.co.jp/ (Japanese)

MAP PAGE 161, #10

Fifth-generation Tsukiji Masamoto has a friendly staff and, on some days, an English-speaking clerk.

Sugimoto Hamono • 杉本刃物
Tsukiji 4-10-2 • 中央区築地4-10-2
Tel. 03-3541-6980 • www.sugimoto-hamono.com/ (English)

MAP PAGE 161, #17

JAPANESE KNIVES

和包丁
WABOCHO

THERE IS NO BETTER PLACE TO INVEST IN A KNIFE than Japan. Although they are not inexpensive, if cared for properly, Japanese knives will last a lifetime. A good knife shop will also carry Western-style knives made in Japan that are sharpened on both sides.

Traditional Japanese knives are sharpened only on one side, and Westerners will find that cutting with them can take a bit of getting used to (be sure to let the shopkeeper know if you are right- or left-handed). Although most knives sold in the West do not rust, Japanese knives made from standard carbon steel rust easily. You may want to ask for a rust-resistant carbon steel that is easier to care for.

If this is your first time to purchase Japanese knives, you may want to start with three basic knives:

Deba bōchō 出刃包丁 Knife with a thick, wide surface, primarily used to prepare fish (to fillet, to gut, to cut through bones, and to remove the head)

Usuba bōchō 薄刃包丁 Knife with a broad, thin blade, used to peel and cut vegetables

Yanagiba bōchō 柳刃包丁 Long and slender knife with a pointed tip primarily used for cutting *sashimi*

Other kitchen tools you may find at knife shops:

Benrina-mandorin Japanese-made mandolin, less bulky than French ones

Honenuki Tweezers used for pulling bones out of fish fillets

Manaita Cutting board

Nukikata An implement in the shape of a seasonal motif, much like a cookie cutter, used to cut vegetables

Oroshigane A grater, ideal for grating ginger, *daikon*, and other vegetables (Note: graters for *wasabi*, made from sharkskin, are different from the ones for vegetables)

Otoshibuta Small, round, wooden lids that allow steam to escape while evenly distributing heat and gently cooking ingredients; they should be a bit smaller than the diameter of the pot

Tamagoyakiki Pan used to make Japanese-style omelet

Toishi Water stone used for sharpening knives

Uroko hiki Fish scaler

This reputable shop has been in business for more than two hundred years.

Aritsugu • 有次
Tsukiji 4-13-6 • 中央区築地4-13-6
Tel. 03-3541-6890 • www.aritsugu.jp/ (Japanese)
MAP PAGE 161, #23

If you plan on going to Kyoto, the Aritsugu shop in Nishiki Market has a larger selection of items than this one, and may be worth the wait.

Onoya Shōten • 大野屋商店
Tsukiji 4-9-1 • 中央区築地4-9-1
Tel. 03-3541-3051
MAP PAGE 161, #8

This shop boasts a variety of must-have supplies for professional and home kitchens alike, such as graters, bamboo strainers, steamers, cooking chopsticks, and bamboo baskets. The shop is a mishmash of goods, and it is best to go in with an idea of what you are looking for.

Hirayama Shōten • 平山商店
Tsukiji 5-2-1, Building #7 • 中央区築地5-2-1ビル7
Tel. 03-3541-6586
www.tsukijinet.com/tsukiji/kanren/hirayama/index.htm (Japanese)
MAP PAGE 160, #28

Hirayama is the one-stop shop for souvenirs: t-shirts with *kanji* symbols, plastic *sushi*, hats, bags, and much more. The store carries extra-large sizes, which are normally hard to find in Japan.

Urikiriya • うりきり屋
Tsukiji 4-7-2 • 中央区築地4-7-2
Tel. 03-3541-6644 • 8:00–17:30 Monday to Saturday;
11:00–17:30 Sunday and holidays
www.urikiriya.co.jp (Japanese)
MAP PAGE 161, #3

Just outside of the market is a great shop for housewares: gorgeous Japanese pottery, lacquerware, chopsticks, and more to decorate your table. There is a wide range of prices, and sale items are usually placed out on the sidewalk in front of the shop. If you walk to Ginza from Tsukiji along Harumi Dori, you will pass it on your left.

GINZA 銀座

METERS
0   100   200   300

FEET
0   300   600   900

Bic Camera **I**

YURAKUC STATIO

The Peninsula (hotel)

Kagoshima Yurakukan
かごしま遊楽館 6 **36**

YURAKUCHO I

YURAKUC

Imperial Hotel
(tea ceremony;
Kamon Restaurant)

Sony Building

UCHISAIWAICHO I

Tempura Kondō てんぷ

Pierre Marcolini ピエール マルニ

Confectionary West **20**   Kūya 空也

Ginza Natsuno 銀座夏野   **21 22**

Ginza Toyoda 銀座とよだ **23**

Ginza Bairin 銀座梅

24 Takumi たくみ

Toraya とらや **26**

Minamoto Kitchoan 源吉兆庵 **27**

Ginza Harutaka
銀座青空 **28**   Shiseido Parlou

29

Ginza Kyūbey 銀座久兵衛   Shiseido Parlou **30**

GINZA 8

SHINBASHI I

Gohiikini
ごひいきに
35

Shinbashi

32 Setouchi Shunsaikan せとうち旬彩館

SHINBASHI 2   Ogawaken 小川軒 **33**

SHINBASHI STATION   HIGASHI-SHINBASHI I

MUJI **2**

3 Okinawa Washita Antenna Shop
沖縄わしたショップ

Hokkaido Dosanko Plaza
北海道どさんこプラザ

4 **5** Mura Kara Machi
Kara Kan
むらからまちから館

Tokyo
otsu
aikan

Ginza-Itchome

6
New Castle ニューキャッスル

GINZA 1

7
Qu'il Fait Bon キルフェボン

SOTOBORI DORI

CHUO DORI

Ito-ya
8

GINZA 2

9 Birdland バードランド

10 Ginza Matsuzaki Sembei 松崎煎餅

Matsuya 松屋 **9**

GINZA 3

Kimuraya
木村家 Yamano (music store)
11

Cha Ginza
茶銀座

12 Ginza
Akebono
銀座あけぼの

Wako (department store)

14

15 KOBAN

16 Mitsukoshi 三越

GINZA 4

Fukumitsuya
福光屋

18 Kyūkyōdō 鳩居堂

19 Bunmeidō 文明堂

GINZA 5

HARUMI DORI

Higashi-Ginza

Kabukiza
(Kabuki Theater)

Chuo-ku

GINZA 6

GINZA 7

Ginza Ukai-tei 銀座うかい亭
31

TSUKIJI 4

Tokyo Expressway

Teuchi Soba Narutomi 手打ち蕎麦成富
34

TSUKIJI 5

GINZA

銀座

GINZA IS THE MAIN SHOPPING DISTRICT OF TOKYO. FROM MAJOR DEPARTMENT STORES AND FASHION labels to tiny boutiques, there is something for almost every whim or taste. You will find dozens of interesting shops in Ginza, too many to mention here. If something catches your attention, check it out, don't be afraid to poke your head in.

In this posh neighborhood, the crowd—and there is always a crowd—consists of young and old, locals and visitors. Centrally located, it is convenient to Tokyo Station. During the day, you'll see ladies who lunch; during the evening, Ginza turns into an entertainment district with many hostess clubs. Restaurants range from casual standing noodle bars to *kaiseki* restaurants that require a referral.

See *depachika* section for Ginza's two major department stores, **Mitsukoshi** and Matsuya.

Fukumitsuya • 福光屋
Chuo-ku, Ginza 5-5-8 • 中央区銀座5-5-8
Tel. 03-3569-2291 • 11:00—21:00 Monday to Saturday;
11:00—20:00 Sunday and holidays
www.fukumitsuya.co.jp/english/index.html (English)
SHOP • MAP PAGE 181, #14

Fukumitsuya is a *sake* shop representing a brewery from Kanazawa prefecture that opened in 1625. At the small tasting bar you can sip any *sake* you are interested in. Fukumitsuya has a wide selection including Kyoka, distinguished by the edible gold flakes which float in the *sake*; Hatsugokoro, an unusual aged *sake*; and *sake*-based sparkling cocktails in bottles or cans. The storefront is marked by a *sugidama* (cedar ball), which are traditionally hung outside *sake* breweries to announce the annual release.

Toraya • とらや
Chuo-ku, Ginza 7-8-6 • 中央区銀座7-8-6
Tel. 03-3571-3679 • 9:30—20:30 Monday to Saturday;
9:30—19:30 Sunday and holidays
www.toraya-group.co.jp/english/index.html (Japanese)
SHOP AND CAFÉ • MAP PAGE 180, #26

Toraya, one of the oldest confectioners in Japan, runs this gorgeous

shop with a café on the second floor. In the summertime you can cool down with a *kakigōri* (shaved ice sweet); on the menu you'll also find traditional Japanese pastries and sweets. See page 119 for more information on Toraya Akasaka Honten.

Teuchi Soba Narutomi • 手打ち蕎麦成富
Chuo-ku, Ginza 8-18-6, Futaba Building
中央区銀座8-18-6 二葉ビル
Tel. 03-5565-0055
11:30–15:00, 18:00–20:45 Monday to Friday;
11:30–15:00 Saturday;
closed Sunday, holidays, and third Saturday of the month
http://narutomi-soba.net/ (Japanese)
RESTAURANT • INEXPENSIVE • MAP PAGE 181, #34

Off the beaten path, and a favorite of Japanese food journalists, Narutomi Soba's white walls and dark wooden tables set the stage for handmade *soba* noodles. For an appetizer, start with the signature earthy *gobō tempura*, thin slices of burdock root fried to a crisp and sprinkled with salt. Follow with a serving of *soba* noodles, served with *tsuyu* dipping sauce that is on the sweet side, a nice match for the rustic noodles. The *sobagaki* is a dense buckwheat-flour cake eaten as a side dish. Another uncommon dish that is served here is *yakimiso* (grilled *miso* on a paddle), also often found only at restaurants like this that take the art of *soba* seriously. Narutomi's selection of gorgeous pottery on which the food is served is another reason for the restaurant's popularity.

Cha Ginza • 茶銀座
Chuo-ku, Ginza 5-5-6 • 中央区銀座5-5-6
Tel. 03-3571-1211 • 11:00–19:00;
closed most Mondays, check website
www.uogashi-meicha.co.jp/shop_01.html (Japanese)
SHOP AND CAFÉ • MAP PAGE 181, #12

This cool, sleek modern tea emporium is in the heart of Ginza and is a great place to recover from the rigors of shopping, with a healthy cup of green tea. Each floor of this three-story shop has a very different atmosphere. The first floor houses a mini-malist retail shop with a long wooden counter where you can sample and purchase tea, and be out the door. The second floor is a café filled with tables of chatting friends. The third floor is partially lit by a skylight, flooded with natural light, serene and quiet. The parent shop, **Uogashi Meicha**, has a stall in Tsukiji Market.

Bunmeidō • 文明堂
Chuo-ku, Ginza 5-7-10 • 中央区銀座5-7-10
Tel. 03-3574-0002 • Daily 11:00–21:00
www.bunmeido.com/ (Japanese)
SHOP AND CAFÉ • MAP PAGE 181, #19

The large coffee shop Bunmeidō is known for its *castella* cake—a sponge cake that is a specialty of Nagasaki—as well as Western-style sweets. A two-story, stained-glass window looms over the interior of this café, which also has a lunch menu with Western-style sandwiches and dishes, as well as some Japanese food with definite Western influences, such as *hayashi rice*, a dish of steamed rice and stewed beef. Other large windows overlooking the main street make this a great place to rest and do some people-watching.

Takumi • たくみ
Chuo-ku, Ginza 8-4-2 • 中央区銀座8-4-2
Tel. 03-3571-2017 • 11:00–19:00; closed Sunday and holidays
www.ginza-takumi.co.jp/ (Japanese)
SHOP • MAP PAGE 180, #24

Pottery and other crafts are showcased in this two-story shop on the outskirts of Ginza. There is a wide variety of regional pottery for daily use with reasonable prices, as well as teapots, baskets, and lacquerware. On the second floor, you'll find textiles and other artisan objects. The staff are friendly and knowledgeable about the selection.

Kūya • 空也
Chuo-ku, Ginza 6-7-19 • 中央区銀座6-7-19
Tel. 03-3571-3304 • 10:00–17:00; Saturday 10:00–16:00;
closed Sunday and holidays
www.wagashi.or.jp/tokyo/shop/0337.htm (Japanese)
SHOP • MAP PAGE 180, #21

This historic shop sells only one item, *monaka*, two delicate, crispy wafers sandwiching slightly sweet, crushed *azuki* beans. Kūya's *monaka* are so popular they must be ordered in advance; the store suggests calling a week ahead. When these delicacies are served to friends or given as gifts, they communicate to the recipient that much care and forethought has gone into the choice.

Okinawa Washita Antenna Shop • 沖縄わしたショップ
Chuo-ku, Ginza 1-3-9 • 中央区銀座1-3-9
Tel. 03-3535-6991 • Daily 10:00−19:00
www.washita.co.jp/info/shop/ginza/index.html (Japanese)
SHOP • MAP PAGE 181, #3

The cuisine of Okinawa, the southernmost islands of Japan, is very different from that of the rest of Japan. These tropical islands are rich with sea vegetables, pork, and the local *shōchū* called *awamori*, all products which are sold at this regional products shop. The basement is filled with *awamori*, a distilled beverage made from Thai rice. Other regional specialties include: fresh produce including a bitter squash (*gōya*), tropical fruits, a citrus juice *(shi-kuwa-sa-)* that is great for cocktails, as well as a very dense, rich *tōfu* (*shimadōfu*).

Ginza Kyūbey • 銀座久兵衛
Chuo-ku, Ginza 8-7-6 • 中央区銀座8-7-6
Tel. 03-3571-6523 • 11:30−13:30, 17:00−21:45;
closed Sunday and holidays
www.kyubey.jp/index_e.html (English)
RESTAURANT • LUNCH MODERATE, DINNER EXPENSIVE TO VERY EXPENSIVE • MAP PAGE 180, #29

Kyūbey Sushi is a famous top *sushi* restaurant. So popular—with Japanese as well as tourists—that it often turned away customers in the past. The restaurant now has opened an annex across the street to accommodate the overflow. The staff is accustomed to foreigners; English-speaking guests may be seated in front of an English-speaking chef. The *sushi* chefs here are so skilled that they can ever so slightly adjust the amount of rice or *wasabi* in each bite of *sushi* according to your preference. This is one of the few high-end *sushi* restaurants open at lunch, a meal that, here, is much more reasonably priced than the evening meal. It provides a nice option for a top-quality, classic Edo-style *nigirizushi*.

Minamoto Kitchoan • 源吉兆庵
Chuo-ku, Ginza 7-8-9 • 中央区銀座7-8-9
Tel. 03-3569-2360 • 10:00−21:00 Monday to Friday;
10:00−19:00 Saturday, Sunday, and holidays
www.kitchoan.co.jp (Japanese)
SHOP AND CAFÉ • MAP PAGE 180, #27

On the main street, Ginza Dori, sits Minamoto Kitchoan. The granite building has an impressive white banner with black calligraphy hanging from the second floor. A retail shop takes up the first two floors, a café on the third floor serves traditional sweets or a light meal, and a restaurant on floors four to six offers *kaiseki* meals. Kitchoan delights customers with seasonal sweets, many showcasing fresh fruit. One unique item offered in the summer is individual muscat grapes coated in sugar—jewel-like, bite-size sweets.

New Castle • ニューキャッスル
Chuo-ku, Ginza 2-3-1 • 中央区銀座2-3-1
Tel. 03-3561-2929
11:00–21:00; Saturday until 17:00; closed Sunday and holidays
RESTAURANT • INEXPENSIVE • MAP PAGE 181, #6

This old-style curry shop, in an old building in a very modern part of town, catches your eye. It looks as if little has changed since it opened in 1946. This mom-and-pop shop has long been famous for its curry rice, which can be topped with a sunny-side-up egg. The sole curry offered is a meat and vegetable version. The menu items are named after train stations on the Keihin-Tohoku train line, the difference being the portion size (small, medium, or large) and if it is topped with an egg or not.

Ginza Natsuno • 銀座夏野
Chuo-ku, Ginza 6-7-4 • 中央区銀座6-7-4
Tel. 03-3569-0952 • Monday to Saturday 10:00–20:00;
10:00–19:00 Sunday and holidays
www.e-ohashi.com (Japanese)
SHOP • MAP PAGE 180, #22

SHOPS FOR REGIONAL GOODS (ANTENNA SHOPS)

アンテナショップ

ANTENA SHOPPU

JAPAN IS A SMALL COUNTRY, ABOUT THE SIZE of California, yet each prefecture and region has its own distinctly local foods. There is no better expression of the diverse *terroir* of Japan than these local culinary commodities. The Japanese treasure these regional products.

Tokyo has numerous regional "antenna" shops from around the country that function as public relations offices offering tourist brochures. Antenna shops also offer items that are often hard to find outside of the region where they are produced. From local beverages like *nihonshu* and *shōchū*, to pickles, *miso*, and meats, these antenna shops offer great finds and are worth carefully perusing. If you are looking for pottery from a certain region (the pastel glazed Hagiyaki from Yamaguchi, for example), the regional antenna shop is a good place to start.

Some shops will have restaurants featuring local foods; these too are a great way to try food you normally would not have the chance to experience if you are not traveling outside of Tokyo during your visit to Japan.

Kagoshima Yurakukan • かごしま遊楽館
Chiyoda-ku, Yurakucho 1-6-4, Chiyoda Building
千代田区有楽町1-6-4千代田ビル
Tel. 03-3580-8821 • 10:00–20:00 Monday to Friday;
10:00–19:00 weekend and holidays
www3.pref.kagoshima.jp/foreign/english/profile/gaiyou/
yurakukan_main.html (English)

MAP PAGE 180, #36

Kagoshima, on the southern island of Kyushu, is known for its *shōchū*, in particular sweet potato *shōchū* (*imojōchū*); the shop has an unusually large selection. The restaurant on the second floor, Ichi Nii San, features a Berkshire pork (*kurobuta*)–based menu with a variety of dishes including breaded and fried pork cutlets (*tonkatsu*) or paper-thin sliced pork that is quickly heated in a hot broth (*shabu shabu*).

Hokkaido Dosanko Plaza • 北海道どさんこプラザ

Chiyoda-ku, Yurakucho 2-10-1, Tokyo Kotsu Kaikan
千代田区有楽町2-10-1東京交通会館
Tel. 03-5224-3800 • Daily 10:00—19:00
www.dosanko-plaza.jp/ (Japanese)

MAP PAGE 181, #4

The large northern island of Hokkaido is highly regarded for its agricultural products including kelp (*kombu*), potatoes, dairy products, and its rich variety of seafood, including salmon and crab. There are a few stands selling potato croquettes, soft ice cream cones, and trendy salted caramels, among other regional products.

Mura Kara Machi Kara Kan • むらからまちから館

Chiyoda-ku, Yurakucho 2-10-1, Tokyo Kotsu Kaikan
千代田区有楽町2-10-1東京交通会館
Tel. 03-5208-1521 • 10:00—19:30 Monday to Friday
10:00—19:00 weekends and holidays
http://murakara.shokokai.or.jp/ (Japanese)

MAP PAGE 181, #5

This antenna shop does not represent a single prefecture but carries a conglomeration of items from all over Japan. The shop is not very organized, so it helps to know what you are looking for. It is close to the Hokkaido shop. There are a wide variety of items including *miso*, fermented soybeans (*nattō*), *nihonshu*, Japanese confections (*wagashi*), pickles, and more.

Setouchi Shunsaikan • せとうち旬彩館

Minato-ku, Shinbashi 2-19-10 • 港区新橋2-19-10
Tel. 03-3574-7792 • Daily 10:00—20:00
www.setouchi-shunsaikan.com/ (Japanese)

MAP PAGE 181, #32

This shop is a collaboration of the Ehime and Kagawa prefectures on the island of Shikoku, set on the rich Setouchi inland sea. The shop offers a wide variety of seafood. Ehime is also famous for its *mikan*, a tangerine-like fruit that makes a refreshing juice. There is a restaurant on the second floor, Kaorihime, that specializes in *udon*.

There are many antenna shops sprinkled throughout the city—representing **Yamaguchi**, page 228, **Yamanashi**, page 228, **Shimane**, page 233, **Okinawa**, page 186, **Miyazaki**, page 268, **Hiroshima**, page 268, and **Niigata**, page 257.

This small shop is packed with a dizzying array of chopsticks, some handcrafted by artisans. A collection of seasonal chopstick rests (*hashioki*) changes throughout the year. The chopsticks are made from a variety of materials including lacquer and bamboo; some are tipped with gold or silver. Some of the designs are quite playful—there are chopsticks designed to look like colored pencils, others to look like trains. There are also different types of chopsticks designed specifically for certain foods, such as *sashimi*, *tōfu*, or *soba*. (The width, the texture, or the tip of the chopstick may be slightly different.) There are chopsticks for those who are still mastering their basic chopstick skills and short chopsticks for children. You'll find many other items for the table, as well. There are branches of Ginza Natsuno throughout the city.

Kimuraya · 木村家
Chuo-ku, Ginza 4-5-7 · 中央区銀座4-5-7
Tel. 03-3561-0091 · Daily 10:00–21:30
www.ginzakimuraya.jp (Japanese)
SHOP AND CAFÉ · MAP PAGE 181, #11

This busy shop in the heart of Ginza, across the street from the Mitsukoshi department store, is famous for its sweet buns. There's always a crowd lined up in front of the display case. The shop's signature bun (*anpan*) is filled with sweet *azuki* beans, but a wide assortment of other varieties is offered, including fruit jam, cream custard, cherry blossom (*sakura*), cream cheese, white bean paste (*shiroan*), green bean paste (*uguisu*), citrus (*yuzu*), chestnut (*kuri*), smooth *azuki* paste (*koshian*), and chunky *azuki* paste (*tsubuan*). Kimuraya also has an interesting selection of snack breads (*oyatsupan*), including deep-fried breads stuffed with curry (curry *pan*), breads filled with nuts and cheese—and even calzones. Kimuraya has branches in most *depachika*.

Pierre Marcolini · ピエール マルコリーニ
Chuo-ku, Ginza 5-5-8 · 中央区銀座5-5-8
Tel. 03-5537-0015 (chocolate shop)
Tel. 03-5537-2047 (ice cream shop)
11:00–20:00 Monday to Saturday;
11:00–19:00 Sunday and holidays
www.pierremarcolini.jp (Japanese)
SHOP · MAP PAGE 181, #17

In the heart of Ginza, Belgian Pierre Marcolini serves up chocolates and ice cream in two adjacent shops with cafés above each boutique.

Qu'il Fait Bon • キルフェボン

Chuo-ku, Ginza 2-4-5 • 中央区銀座2-4-5

Tel. 03-5159-0605 • Daily 11:00—21:00

www.quil-fait-bon.com/(Japanese)

SHOP AND CAFÉ • MAP PAGE 181, #7 & PAGE 255, #8

This picturesque *pâtisserie* with pots of flowers, plants, and trees by the front door looks like a doll house in the middle of a concrete jungle. It's a favorite with young Japanese women—the shop is often filled to overflowing with giggling girls. Best known for its beautiful seasonal fruit tarts, Qu'il Fait Bon also offers cakes available whole or by the slice. There are branches throughout the city, but this is the only one with a café (on the lower level).

Birdland • バードランド

Chuo-ku, Ginza 4-2-15, Tsukamoto Building B1

中央区銀座4-2-15 塚本素山ビル B1

Tel. 03-5250-1081

17:00—21:30; closed Sunday, Monday, and holidays

http://ginza-birdland.sakura.ne.jp/index.html (Japanese)

RESTAURANT • MODERATE • MAP PAGE 181, #9

This is considered by many to be the best *yakitori* restaurant in the city. Birdland is an anomaly among *yakitori* restaurants, which are usually smoky dives, often located near train stations, offering only the chicken skewers and cans of beer. Here, the art of grilling the chicken, and the quality of the chicken itself, is taken quite seriously. Wine is served in Riedel glasses; you may see kimono-clad women with men in designer business suits. Popular dishes include a rich chicken liver paté to start and an egg custard pudding for dessert, but it is the *yakitori* in between that brings the customers here. Birdland is located in the lower level of a building; the adjacent restaurant is the famous *sushi* shop, Sukiyabashi Jiro, where behind the counter you'll find the oldest chef in the world to hold three Michelin stars.

Ginza Matsuzaki Sembei • 松崎煎餅

Chuo-ku, Ginza 4-3-11 • 中央区銀座4-3-11

Tel. 03-3561-9811

10:00—20:00 Monday to Saturday;

11:00—19:00 Sunday and holidays

http://matsuzaki-senbei.com/ (Japanese)

SHOP AND CAFÉ • MAP 181, #10

Go to Matsuzaki (established in 1804) to purchase sweet, colorful crackers (*sembei*) made from flour, eggs, and sugar, artfully painted with seasonal designs such as flowers or fireworks. The selection of savory *sembei* include thin and delicate rice crackers in flavors like cheese, curry, or mayonnaise. The shop also prides itself on their *arare* and *okaki sembei* made from rice flour. Matsuzaki has a café on the second floor where you can enjoy teas and traditional sweets. In the summer, cool down with green tea syrup and *azuki* beans over shaved ice.

Ginza Akebono • 銀座あけぼの
Chuo-ku, Ginza 5-7-19 • 中央区銀座5-7-19
Tel. 03-3571-3640 • 9:00–21:00; Sunday until 20:00
www.ginza-akebono.co.jp/ (Japanese)
SHOP • MAP PAGE 181, #15

The very small Akebono sells an interesting assortment of modern, non-traditional *sembei* that include cheese, almond, fermented soybean (*nattō*), sea urchin (*uni*), and pine nut varieties. Some unusual versions such as *genkotsu sembei* are very tough and hard to chew and completely depart from the traditional crisp and delicate cracker. Akebono also has a wide assortment of Japanese confections (*wagashi*), including a sweet wafer sandwich cookie filled with chestnut paste (*kuri monaka*), two mini-pancakes with *azuki* paste (*dorayaki*), and buns stuffed with *azuki* paste (*manju*). In spring, don't miss the *ichigo daifuku*, a whole strawberry surrounded by *azuki* paste and wrapped in delicate sticky rice. Akebono has shops in most *depachika*.

Ginza Toyoda • 銀座とよだ

Chuo-ku, Ginza 7-5-4 La Viarre Ginza 2F
中央区銀座7-5-4ラヴィアーレ銀座ビル2F
Tel. 03-5568-5822
11:30—13:30, 17:30—20:30 Monday to Friday;
12:00—14:00, 17:30—20:30 Saturday; closed Sunday and holidays
www.tokyo-calendar.tv/dining/11428.html (Japanese)
RESTAURANT • LUNCH MODERATE, DINNER MODERATE TO
EXPENSIVE • MAP PAGE 180, #23

At this upscale *kappō ryōri*, Chef Okamoto dazzles customers with multiple courses of traditional Japanese cuisine. Ask to sit at the counter so you can watch him skillfully chopping ingredients and assembling gorgeous seasonal arrangements. Many *kappō ryōri* are only open for dinner, but Toyoda also serves lunch, providing a great opportunity to have this experience at a reasonable price. Ginza Toyoda is known for its extensive wine list, making this a favorite among Japanese, who appreciate the chance to dine on traditional cuisine paired with French wines.

Ginza Ukai-tei • 銀座うかい亭

Chuo-ku, Ginza 5-15-8 • 中央区銀座5-15-8
Tel. 03-3544-5252 • Daily 12:00—21:00; closed holidays
www.ukai.co.jp/ginza/en/index.htm (English)
RESTAURANT • MODERATE TO EXPENSIVE
MAP PAGE 181, #31

Opulent Ukai-tei provides glamorous private rooms in which a personal chef grills *wagyū* beef, seafood, and seasonal vegetables on a *teppan* (iron plate). This is a refined dining experience in a museum-like setting orchestrated by a skilled chef. At the close of the savory courses, diners are escorted to another beautiful room to select from a wide variety of sweets, displayed on several dessert carts.

Ginza Harutaka • 銀座青空

Chuo-ku, Ginza 8-5-8, Ginza Kawabata Building 3F
中央区銀座8-5-8かわばたビル3F
Tel. 03-3573-1144 • 17:00—24:00; Saturday until 22:30
closed Sunday and holidays
RESTAURANT • EXPENSIVE • MAP PAGE 180, #28

Chef Harutaka's *sushi* restaurant is popular with top chefs in the city. Harutaka honed his skills during twelve years at Michelin three-starred Sukiyabashi Jiro. A seat at the counter will afford a chance to watch the young, talented, soft-spoken chef at work. Part of the delight in dining here is the beautiful dishes you'll see throughout the evening.

Tempura Kondō • てんぷら近藤
Chuo-ku, Ginza 5-5-13, Sakaguchi Building 9F
中央区銀座 5-5-13坂口ビル9階
Tel. 03-5568-0923
12:00–13:30, 17:00–20:30 Monday to Saturday; closed Sunday
RESTAURANT • LUNCH MODERATE, DINNER EXPENSIVE
MAP PAGE 181, #13

This high-end *tempura* shop in the heart of Ginza is considered one of the best in the city. The signature items are deep-fried julienned carrots, sweet potatoes, and fava beans. Displayed behind the counter is a cornucopia of fresh seasonal vegetables waiting to be cut, battered, and deep-fried. The sound of the *tempura* sizzling in the hot oil is much appreciated by the Japanese. Watch the chefs: a *tempura* chef can hear when items are done by subtle changes in the sound of the sizzling; or, with chopsticks, feeling small changes in the vibration of the frying morsel.

Ginza Bairin • 銀座梅林
Chuo-ku, Ginza 7-8-1 • 中央区銀座7-8-1
Tel. 03-3571-0350 • Daily 11:30–20:45; closed holidays
www.ginzabairin.com/ (Japanese)
RESTAURANT • INEXPENSIVE • MAP PAGE 180, #25

This restaurant, opened in 1927, was the first *tonkatsu* restaurant to open in Ginza. At lunchtime, there may be a long line of customers waiting for the most popular item on the menu, the golden succulent deep-fried pork cutlets. At this casual, diner-like eatery, solo customers eat at the counter and groups of two or more at tables.

While in Ginza you may also want to visit:

Ito-ya
Chuo-ku, Ginza 2-7-15 • 中央区銀座2-7-15
Tel. 03-3561-8311 • 10:30–19:00 Sunday to Tuesday;
10:30–20:00 Wednesday to Saturday
www.ito-ya.co.jp/ (Japanese)
SHOP • MAP PAGE 181, #8

Ito-ya is a huge stationery shop spread out on several floors.

Kyūkyōdō • 鳩居堂
Chuo-ku, Ginza 5-7-4 • 中央区銀座5-7-4
Tel. 03-3571-4429 • 10:00–19:30 Monday to Saturday;
10:00–19:00 Sunday and holidays
www.kyukyodo.co.jp/ (Japanese)
SHOP • MAP PAGE 181, #18

This tiny shop near the main crossing has colorful *washi* (Japanese paper) and stationery.

MUJI
Chiyoda-ku, Yurakucho 3-8-3 • 千代田区有楽町3-8-3
Tel. 03-5208-8241 • Daily 10:00–21:00 • www.muji.net/ (Japanese)
SHOP • MAP PAGE 181, #2

This is a large branch of the popular design shop.

Bic Camera
Chiyoda-ku, Yurakucho 1-11-1 • 千代田区有楽町1-11-1
Tel. 03-5221-1111 • Daily 10:00–22:00
SHOP • MAP PAGE 180, #1

Bic Camera is an electronics megastore. Hidden on the second floor is a little-known but interesting *sake* department with bargains on whiskey, wine, champagne, and a respectable selection of *shōchū*.

ASAKUSA
浅草

MOST TOURISTS (BOTH JAPANESE AND NON-JAPANESE) WILL FIND THEIR WAY HERE TO HAVE THEIR PHOTO taken at the Kaminarimon large red lantern outside of the oldest Buddhist temple in Tokyo, Sensoji. The street leading up to the temple, Nakamise Dori, is home to many stalls selling traditional Japanese confections such as rice crackers, sweet potato cakes, and sticky rice dumplings. There are also many shops on the side streets that are worth seeking out. If you come during the cherry blossom season, then be sure to walk the few blocks to the Sumidagawa River. The river is lined with cherry trees and the sight of the blossoms is breathtaking.

All the addresses below are in Taito-ku 台東区.

Matsuki • 松喜
Kaminarimon 2-17-8 • 台東区雷門2-17-8
Tel. 03-3841-2983
SHOP • MAP PAGE 199, #19

This *wagyū* butcher shop is just across the street from the temple gate Kaminarimon. Take a peek at the marbled beef behind the refrigerated glass showcase. On the corner is a popular supermarket, Fresh Foods Ozeki. It is interesting to poke your head in to see what items are usually carried in a typical Japanese grocery store.

Mugitoro • むぎとろ
Kaminarimon 2-2-4 • 台東区雷門2-2-4
Tel. 03-3842-1066 • Daily 11:00–21:00
www.mugitoro.co.jp (Japanese)
RESTAURANT • MODERATE • MAP PAGE 199, #20

The entrance to this modern six-story building is marked by red paper umbrellas and benches. There is usually a line to get in. Mugitoro's signature dish is rice cooked with barley and topped with grated sticky potato (*yamaimo*). When the potato is grated, it creates a thick, creamy, slippery slurry. The meals here are based around *yamaimo*, which is served with a variety of small side dishes. In front of the shop is a menu board with photos of popular dishes you'll find offered here.

There is a small gift shop that carries an assortment of the restaurant's original confections. The *sandaime* cracker, also called *nuremochi*, is a rice cracker soaked in soy sauce—not crispy like

ASAKUSA/KAPPABASHI 浅草 / 合羽橋

SENZUKO 1

1 Otafuku 大多福

2 Oiwake 追分

Taitō-ku

33 Kappabashi Kissa 合羽橋喫茶

Okuda Lacquer
漆器のオクダ商店 **34**

Soi **35**

32 Nishiyama Shikki 西山漆器

NISHI-ASAKUSA 3

MATSUGAYA 3

Kondō Shōten
近藤商店 **36**

Fukuokaya Noren
福岡屋 **37**

31 Propack プロパック

30 Soba Salon Yabukita そばさろんやぶきた

MATSUGAYA 2

29 Komatsuya 小松屋

Asakusa Imahan 浅草今半

3

ASAKU
STATIC

Sankidō
三起堂 **38**

Kamata
かまた **39**

NISHI-ASAKUSA 2

28 Hashitō はし藤

Asakusa Sometarō 浅草染太郎

9

Maeda
まえ田 **40**

27 Arai Shōten 新井商店
26 Maizuru Honten まいづる本店
25 Fujita Shōji Pottery 藤田商事
◆Tokyo Honganji (temple)
24 Okuda Shōten Shiten オクダ商店支店
23 Takahashi Sōhonten 高橋総本店
41 Tanaka Shikkiten 田中漆器店

Iriyama Sembei 入山煎餅

NISHI-ASAKUSA 1

22 Tōan Yabukita 陶庵やぶきた

KOBAN **21**

Dengama 田窯

KAMINARIMON

Tawaramachi

KYOBASHI 1

ASAKUSA D

KAPPABASHI KITCHEN TOWN

METERS
0   100   200   300

FEET
0   300   600   900

ASAKUSA 3

26
25   27
23
24
16
28
29
5
30   31   32
7   33
34
Sensoji
(temple)

35
ASAKUSA 2   3   **4** Agemanjū Asakusa Kokonoe
5   **5** あげまんじゅう浅草九重
Kimuraya Ningyōyaki Honpo
木村家人形焼本舗

4
Yoshikami ヨシカミ   2   1
6 41
40   Daikokuya 大黒家
27   39   38   **7**
ASAKUSA 1   37   36   35
Umezono 梅園
11 Yagenbori やげん堀   31   **8**
28   29   32   34
22   **12**   30   33
Funawa Honten Kissashitsu 舟和本店喫茶室   TOBU-ASAKUSA
STATION
14   15   16   20   19
agurobito まぐろ人   17   Bairindō 梅林堂   2   Matsuya
7   6   5   **13**   **15**   (department
21   Aoi Marushin   18   Izumiya 和泉屋   store)
14 葵丸進.   4   **16**   **17**
3   2   Kamiya Bar 神谷バー
Tokiwadō Okoshi 常磐堂   □ *KOBAN*   **18**
Matsuki 松喜 **19**   *Kaminarimon*
(gate)
16   17   19   Azuma-bashi
18   *(bridge)*
15   20
14   13   12
8   9   10   1
KAMINARIMON 2   11
7   5   3
6   **20** Mugitoro むぎとろ

Sumidagawa (river)

most, but chewy and moist. The restaurant's signature cracker, *satochan*, is topped with black sesame seeds. If you like sweets, try the *tororintō*, coated with artisanal brown sugar.

Magurobito · まぐろ人
Asakusa 1-5-9 · 台東区浅草 1-5-9
Tel. 03-3844-8736 · 11:00–15:00, 17:00–22:00 Monday to Friday;
11:00–22:00 Saturday; 11:00–21:00 Sunday and holidays
www.maguro-bito.jp/ (Japanese)
RESTAURANT · INEXPENSIVE · MAP PAGE 199, #13

Magurobito is one of the better chains of *kaitenzushi* restaurants (plates holding *sushi* are placed on a revolving conveyor belt). It offers good value and a selection of seasonal fresh fish, so it's very popular. There is often a line, but it tends to move quickly. There

is a second shop in the area but it is a stand-and-eat (*tachigui*) and accommodates only a handful of customers.

Iriyama Sembei • 入山煎餅
Asakusa 1-13-4 • 台東区浅草1-13-4
Tel. 03-3844-1376 • 10:00—18:00; closed Thursday
www.prpub.jp/senbei/asakusa/iriyama.htm (Japanese)
SHOP • MAP PAGE 198, #10

The popular rice crackers (*sembei*) sold here are toasted until golden and then dipped into soy sauce. Each day 4,000 are grilled in this tiny shop by men in white t-shirts and thin, white cotton pants. Packages of the crackers are available, but are best eaten hot right off the grill. Iriyama have been toasting rice crackers since 1914.

Umezono ∙ 梅園
Asakusa 1-31-12 ∙ 台東区浅草1-31-12
Tel. 03-3841-7580
10:00—20:00; closed Wednesday and 2nd Tuesday of the month
www.asakusa-umezono.co.jp/ (Japanese)
SHOP AND CAFÉ ∙ MAP PAGE 199, #8

Just off the main shopping street, this corner café is easy to spot by the red paper umbrella and benches. Established in 1854, Umezono has a devoted following for Japanese confections, in particular the *oshiruko*, soup-like sweets including *azuki* paste, fruits, and sticky rice dumplings. Their signature dish, *awa zenzai*, one of the most popular Asakusa sweets, is a thick porridge served in a lacquer bowl and topped with some sweet *azuki* paste. The menu has a full selection of traditional sweets to enjoy inside the café; several of the sweets are packaged for takeaway.

Izumiya ∙ 和泉屋
Asakusa 1-1-4 ∙ 台東区浅草1-1-4
Tel. 03-3841-5501 ∙ 10:30—19:30; closed Thursday
www.asakusa.gr.jp/nakama/izumiya/ (Japanese)
SHOP ∙ MAP PAGE 199, #17

This quaint *sembei* shop packages its rice crackers in glass jars with tin lids. A wide variety of sweet and savory flavors include Japanese basil (*shiso*), rock sugar (*zarame*), and the very spicy *ookara*, covered with dried red pepper. You will also find the very delicate and thin *usuyaki*, *nori*-wrapped crackers, and an unusual type, the extra hard *genkotsu*.

Tokiwadō Okoshi ∙ 常磐堂
Kaminari Okoshi Kaminarimon Honpo
Asakusa 1-3-2 ∙ 台東区浅草1-3-2
Tel. 03-3841-5656
www.tokiwado.com (Japanese)
SHOP ∙ MAP PAGE 199, #16

This shop to the left of the main gate is a popular destination for tourists. Tokiwadō's lineup includes a variety of crackers and sweets, and a unique collection of *karintō* crackers in flavors such as sweet potato, *wasabi*, carrot, onion, and spicy burdock root; but *okoshi* are the shop's specialty. These colorful, pastel-colored, puffed rice crackers are made in flavors that include peanut, almond, sea vegetable, green tea, brown sugar, and black bean cocoa. You can watch the *okoshi* being made in a small kitchen behind a glass window.

Bairindō ⚬ 梅林堂

Asakusa 1-18-1 ⚬ 台東区浅草1-18-1

Tel. 03-3843-4311 ⚬ Daily 8:00–19:00

SHOP ⚬ MAP PAGE 199, #15

Bairindō has a collection of *okoshi* (see above), rice crackers, and cakes stuffed with *azuki* paste in shapes of famous Asakusa landmarks including the Kaminarimon gate and a five-tiered pagoda. The machine making the stuffed cakes always draws a crowd.

Aoi Marushin ⚬ 葵丸進

Asakusa 1-4-4 ⚬ 台東区浅草1-4-4

Tel. 03-3841-0110 ⚬ Daily 11:30–20:00

www.aoi-marushin.co.jp (Japanese)

RESTAURANT ⚬ INEXPENSIVE TO MODERATE

MAP PAGE 199, #14

This temple to *tempura* has seven floors and seats almost five hundred people. The front window has plastic samples of menu items. Shrimp is one of the most popular; other offerings include seafood and seasonal vegetables. Much *tempura* is light and crisp, but at this restaurant the crust is thick.

Asakusa Sometarō ⚬ 浅草染太郎

Nishi-Asakusa 2-2-2 ⚬ 台東区西浅草2-2-2

Tel. 03-3844-9502 ⚬ Daily 12:00–22:00

www.sometaro.com (Japanese)

RESTAURANT ⚬ INEXPENSIVE

MAP PAGE 198, #9

The Japanese have a sense of nostalgia when it comes to Sometarō, opened in 1946, and still housed in a traditional-style wooden cottage from that time, now surrounded by the modern city. Each table has its own iron griddle on which diners, sitting on *tatami*, cook their own food including savory pancakes (*okonomiyaki*), fried noodles and vegetables (*yakisoba*), and other grilled dishes.

Agemanjū Asakusa Kokonoe ⚬ あげまんじゅう浅草九重

Asakusa 2-3-1 ⚬ 台東区浅草2-3-1

Tel. 03-3841-9386 ⚬ Daily 9:30–19:00

www.agemanju.co.jp (Japanese)

SHOP ⚬ MAP PAGE 199, #4

There are five deep-fried *tempura*-style buns served here. Fillings include smooth *azuki* paste, sweet green tea paste, sweet potato with golden sesame seeds, squash, and chunky *azuki* with black sesame seeds.

Kimuraya Ningyoyaki Honpo • 木村家人形焼本舗
Asakusa 2-3-1 • 台東区浅草2-3-1
Tel. 03-3841-7055 • Daily 9:30–18:30
www.kimura-ya.co.jp (Japanese)
SHOP • MAP PAGE 199, #5

Opened in 1868, this shop on the Nakamise Dori continues to make cakes filled with *azuki* paste according to the original recipe. Watch the cooks working over the hot grill, pouring batter into the molds (in one of four shapes: pigeon, five-storied pagoda, lantern, and Zeus), then adding the *azuki* paste.

Funawa Honten Kissashitsu • 舟和本店喫茶室
Asakusa 1-22-10 • 台東区浅草1-22-10
Tel. 03-3842-2781 • Daily 9:30–20:00
www.asakusa-umai.ne.jp/umai/funawa.html (Japanese)
SHOP • MAP PAGE OO, #12

Funawa, opened in 1902, is known for its confections, eaten as a snack or dessert, made from sweet potatoes. You'll find small bite-sized balls in flavors such as strawberry, white bean paste, green tea, and creamy *azuki* paste.

Oiwake • 追分
Nishi-Asakusa 3-1-2 • 台東区西浅草 3-1-2
Tel. 03-3844-6283 • 18:00–24:00; closed Monday
www.oiwake.info/ (Japanese)
RESTAURANT • MODERATE • MAP PAGE 198; #2

For an entertaining and unique evening, attend this restaurant's live performances of *Tsugaru shamisen*, a type of music with an extremely fast and contagious beat played on a traditional instrument, the *shamisen*. Performers take turns singing on a narrow stage for an audience seated on *tatami* mats. On livelier evenings fellow customers will jump on stage and join in. There is a reasonable cover charge, but this is one of the few places in the city where you can see this traditional entertainment surrounded by Japanese. Very few tourists know about this authentic pub.

All the items on the menu—fried or grilled fish, pickles, rice balls, *edamame*, and vegetable *tempura*—go well with *sake*, which is the beverage of choice at this warm and friendly place. There are three performances each night (19:00, 21:00, and 22:30).

Kamiya Bar • 神谷バー
Asakusa 1-1-1 • 台東区浅草1-1-1
Tel. 03-3841-5400 • 11:30–21:30; closed Tuesday
www.kamiya-bar.com (Japanese)

BAR AND RESTAURANT • INEXPENSIVE TO MODERATE
MAP PAGE 199, #18

Kamiya is a classic neighborhood bar, opened in 1880. The pub menu has small bites like grilled chicken skewers, tuna *sashimi* in a vinegar and mustard sauce, and pickles. The bar's signature drink, Denki Bran, is a cocktail of brandy, gin, wine, curaçao, and herbs. Kamiya is an institution that draws an eclectic crowd of locals, tourists, the young and the old.

Asakusa Imahan • 浅草今半
Nishi-Asakusa 3-1-12 • 台東区西浅草3-1-12
Tel. 03-3841-1114 • Daily 11:30–20:30
www.asakusaimahan.co.jp/english/ (English)

RESTAURANT • INEXPENSIVE TO MODERATE
MAP PAGE 198, #3

Opened in 1895, Imahan is famous for its *sukiyaki* and *shabu-shabu* hot pots. Marbled Japanese beef (*wagyū*), cut into thin slices, is the main ingredient of the restaurant's signature dishes. On each table is a burner on which you cook your own hot pot. If you listen carefully, you will hear the sound of the pot bubbling *"gutsu gutsu."* Imahan has many shops in *depachika* throughout the city, including an eat-in counter at Takashimaya in Nihonbashi.

Otafuku • 大多福
Senzoku 1-6-2 • 台東区千束1-6-2
Tel. 03-3871-2521 • 17:00–23:00 Monday to Friday;
16:00–22:00 Saturday and holidays;
closed Sunday (sometimes other days, so best to call ahead
or check the online calendar)
www.otafuku.ne.jp (Japanese)

RESTAURANT • INEXPENSIVE TO MODERATE
MAP PAGE 198, #1

Otafuku serves fish cake stew (*oden*) in a style not often seen in Tokyo. The broth of the local style *oden* is usually made with soy sauce, dark and rich; Otafuku's version is pale and more delicately flavored. This popular restaurant, in the same family for five generations, is filled with dark wood and there is a long counter where you can see the chef standing over the large pot.

Yoshikami · ヨシカミ
Asakusa 1-41-4 · 台東区浅草1-41-4
Tel. 03-3841-1802 · 11:45−22:00; closed Thursday
www.yoshikami.co.jp/ (Japanese)
RESTAURANT−INEXPENSIVE TO MODERATE
MAP PAGE 199, #6

Yōshoku is Western-style food that has been adapted to the Japanese palate. The tagline for this *yōshoku* restaurant is *"umasugite mōshiwakenaisu"* (we apologize, our food is too delicious). The signature dish is a stew of tender beef in a rich demi-glace that melts in your mouth. The demi-glace sauce is also used on the hamburger served here. Other *yōshoku* dishes include croquettes, a tongue stew, and shrimp or crab gratin. Red-and-white-checked tablecloths line the tables of this dive, but it is the counter seats that are coveted. These are the front row seats from which you can watch the chefs prepare your meal. Westerners will be fascinated and baffled by the popularity of *omuraisu* (omelet over ketchup rice), a Japanese favorite.

Daikokuya · 大黒家
Asakusa 1-38-10 · 台東区浅草1-38-10
Tel. 03-3844-1111
11:10−20:30; Saturday and holidays until 21:00
www.tempura.co.jp/english/index.html (English)
RESTAURANT · INEXPENSIVE TO MODERATE
MAP PAGE 199, #7

You will see long lines outside of Daikokuya, famous for its shrimp *tempura*, served on a bed of rice with a sweet soy dipping sauce. The *tempura* is made to order; this isn't fast food, so order the local pickles, *daikon* slices pickled in *sake* lees (*betterazuke*) with a glass of beer while you wait. The first floor has tables and chairs and the second floor has *tatami* mat seating.

Yagenbori · やげん堀
Asakusa 1-28-3 · 台東区浅草1-28-3
Tel. 03-3626-7716 · Daily 10:00−19:00; closed holidays
www.rakuten.co.jp/edo-noren/828707/815847/ (Japanese)
www.norenkai.net/english/shop/yagenbori/index.html
SHOP · MAP PAGE 199, #11

Yagenbori, in business since 1625, is best known for the seven spice called *shichimi tōgarashi*. Based on dried chili pepper, Yagenbori's aromatic blend also includes: black sesame seeds, dried Satsuma orange peel, raw chili pepper, powdered Japanese prickly ash, white poppy seeds, and hemp seeds. This blend of spices is often

used to flavor *udon*, *miso* soup, *soba*, and can be sprinkled on top of pickles. Each of the ingredients of the *shichimi* are said to help the body in different ways (to relieve stress, for healthy skin, as an antioxidant, to aid digestion, and more).

What makes this store unique is that the spice can be blended to your specifications. There are three basic blends: *okara*, very spicy for those who prefer heat; *chūkara*, a medium blend and the most popular; and *kokara*, a milder mix with less chili pepper. Customers at Yagenbori can have these fine-tuned to their own taste buds. Yagenbori sells small wooden dispensers in the shape of a small bamboo or gourd which are traditionally used to store the spices.

While at Yagenbori, you may want to pick up some *kona sanshō* (powdered Japanese prickly ash), a seasoning often sprinkled on top of eel. It makes your tongue tingle and has an unforgettable smell.

Another notable shop in the area is Kurodaya (Asakusa 1-2-5), located to the right of the Kaminarimon gate, which sells gorgeous Japanese handmade paper, postcards, and other souvenirs that are light and easy to carry.

KAPPABASHI

合羽橋

A HUGE STATUE OF A CHEF TOWERING OVER THE MAIN INTERSECTION OF KAPPABASHI FROM ATOP A BUILDING, welcomes you to this wholesale district for kitchen equipment. Unlike the rest of Tokyo, this area is easy to navigate—it centers around a main thoroughfare less than a kilometer long that is lined with about 170 shops. Here you will find all the kitchen tools, vessels, and gadgets you need for your *batterie de cuisine*, from knives, pottery, and lacquerware to more esoteric items that are difficult to find outside of Japan such as *miso* strainers and *wasabi* graters.

Because these shops primarily serve the food industry, not much attention is paid to creating attractive displays. Recently a few shops have opened up that cater to the general public, and these are quite obvious because more care is taken to create appealing shop windows.

What distinguishes Kappabashi from restaurant supply districts in other large cities is the preponderance of the uniquely Japanese phenomenon of plastic food samples. Many restaurants display these plastic reproductions of the food items they serve, in order to lure customers by showing them exactly what they will be served. You will find realistic *nori*, *tempura*, *tonkatsu*, *sushi*, grilled fish, marbled beef, *ramen* noodles, ice cream sundaes, and much, much, much, much more. The plastic food key chains, magnets, and cell phone straps are fun, transportable souvenirs that "say" Tokyo.

Be aware that this neighborhood is, ironically, a black hole for restaurants. Conveniently, the Asakusa area is a short walk away; there are many good restaurants there (see page 197). Asakusa is also home to a historic temple, a beautiful site that should not be missed. Many of the shops in Kappabashi are closed on Sunday and holidays—but not all of them; on business days most of the shops open at 10:00 a.m. and close around 5:00 p.m. A few shops, and what they specialize in, are listed below. Some shops will deliver, so bring along the card of where you are staying. The service is usually next day, two days at most. Many shops sell the same items. If you are not in a rush, walk around a bit and compare prices, styles, etc.

Note that some of the shops share the same address and that all of these shops are in Taito-ku 台東区.

The following shops are listed in order going down one side of the street and returning on the other side.

Dengama • 田窯
Nishi-Asakusa 1-4-3 • 台東区西浅草1-4-3
Tel. 03-5828-9355 • Daily 10:00—19:00
www.kappabashi.or.jp/shops/101.html (Japanese)
SHOP • MAP PAGE 198, #21

Pottery overflows into the street from Dengama. The wide-open doors invite you in and showcase the cornucopia of designs, colors, and styles inside. Traditional pottery styles such as Arita, Mashiko, Shigaraki, Kutani, and Mino are all represented here. Dengama features pottery designed for daily use. Rice bowls, tea cups, serving dishes of different sizes, mortar and pestles, and *nabe* (hot pots) are affordable, sturdy, and durable. Don't miss the second floor with more upscale items. Sale items are often put in wooden boxes in front of the shop.

Tōan Yabukita • 陶庵やぶきた
Nishi-Asakusa 1-4-8 • 台東区西浅草1-4-8
Tel. 03-3842-2221
www.ybkt.co.jp/html/touan/touan.html (Japanese)
SHOP • MAP PAGE 198, #22

This is one of the prettier stores on the street, selling lacquer and glassware and specializing in Arita, Mino, and Shigaraki styles of pottery. Look for the beautiful large decorative platters and all shapes and sizes of plates and dishes.

Takahashi Sōhonten • 高橋総本店
Nishi-Asakusa 1-5-10 • 台東区西浅草1-5-10
Tel. 03-3845-1163
www.takaso.jp/contents/store/ceramic.html (Japanese)
SHOP • MAP PAGE 198, #23

Takahashi has a wide selection of pottery including ramen bowls, teapots, teacups, *nabe* rice cookers, and stoneware *shōchū* jars with spigots.

Okuda Shōten Shiten • オクダ商店支店
Nishi-Asakusa 1-5-10 • 台東区西浅草1-5-10
Tel. 03-3844-4511
www.kappabashi.or.jp/shops/32.html (Japanese)
SHOP • MAP PAGE 198, #24

This shop features bamboo products. Strainers, steamers, bamboo baskets for *soba*, tempura, or for large strainers, chopsticks, *handai* (large wooden bowls for making *sushi* rice), *bentō* boxes, and soup bowls are just a few of the hundreds of items.

Fujita Shōji Pottery • 藤田商事
Nishi-Asakusa 1-5-13 • 台東区西浅草1-5-13
Tel. 03-3841-0449
www.fujitashoji.com/mape.html (English)

SHOP • MAP PAGE 198, #25

Fujita Shōji has a wide variety of pottery, glass- and lacquerware, including a *soba* tray, dipping bowl, plate, and square pot for the cooking water; a covered tray for serving eel over rice; and covered orange lacquered bowls flecked with gold. Worldwide shipping is available and the English website is organized and easy to navigate.

Maizuru Honten • まいづる本店
Nishi-Asakusa 1-5-17 • 台東区西浅草1-5-17
Tel. 03-3843-1686
www.maiduru.co.jp/ (Japanese)

SHOP • MAP PAGE 198, #26

Plastic food samples including key chains, clocks, magnets, cell phone straps, and full-size samples.

Arai Shōten • 新井商店
Nishi-Asakusa 1-5-17 • 台東区西浅草1-5-17
Tel. 03-3841-2809
www.kappabashi.or.jp/shops/9.html (Japanese)

SHOP • MAP PAGE 198, #27

Specializing in equipment and implements for making sweets, both Japanese and Western, Arai Shōten will have anything you need for making confections at home. This friendly shop also carries kitchen gadgets for savory cooking.

Hashitō • はし藤
Nishi-Asakusa 2-6-2 • 台東区西浅草2-6-2
Tel. 03-3844-0723
www.hashitou.co.jp/ (Japanese)
SHOP • MAP PAGE 198, #28

Hashitō specializes in chopsticks and *hashioki* (chopstick rests).
The nice selection of decorative skewers, long picks, and toothpicks
will brighten up any appetizer plate.

Komatsuya • 小松屋
Nishi-Asakusa 2-21-6 • 台東区西浅草2-21-6
Tel. 03-3841-2368
www.tctv.ne.jp/members/moto/ (Japanese)

SHOP • MAP PAGE 198, #29

This massive store with a vast and attractive inventory offers a
wide selection of pottery, *ramen* bowls, teapots, serving dishes, hot
pots, and sake cups and pitchers.

Soba Salon Yabukita • そばさろんやぶきた
Nishi-Asakusa 3-7-3 • 台東区西浅草3-7-3
Tel. 03-5806-1717
www.yabukita.jp (Japanese)
SHOP • MAP PAGE 198, #30

While not many people are ambitious enough to make *soba* from scratch at home, this shop has all the essential tools you would need to do so. Large lacquer bowls for mixing the *sobako* (buckwheat flour) with water, wooden boards and rolling pins for rolling out the dough, and the uniquely shaped *soba* knives, comprise an inventory not seen outside of Japan. The knives alone are reason to visit the shop.

Propack • プロパック
Nishi-Asakusa 3-7-5 • 台東区西浅草3-7-5
Tel. 03-3843-2341
www.propack.jp/ (Japanese)
SHOP • MAP PAGE 198, #31

This shop with several floors is the largest on the street. It has a wide inventory of disposable *bentō* boxes (great for picnics), as well as kitchen gadgets, stationery, and gift wrap.

Nishiyama Shikki • 西山漆器
Nishi-Asakusa 3-24-3 • 台東区西浅草3-24-3
Tel. 03-3841-8831
www.shikki.jp/ (Japanese)
SHOP • MAP PAGE 198, #32

Nishiyama Shikki specializes in lacquerware including bowls, *bentō* boxes, and chopsticks. You'll find lacquered stacking boxes with gold designs, beautifully turned wooden trays, deep maroon lacquered teacup coasters, bright vermillion nesting bowls and hundreds of tempting objects for the home.

Kappabashi Kissa • 合羽橋喫茶
Nishi-Asakusa 3-25-11 • 台東区西浅草3-25-11
Tel. 03-5828-0308
RESTAURANT • INEXPENSIVE • MAP PAGE 198, #33

This stylish coffee shop at the far end of the street is the perfect place to rest your feet before retracing your steps back down the opposite side of the street. The simple menu offers sandwiches and desserts.

Return trip back on far side of the street:

Okuda Lacquer • 漆器のオクダ商店
Matsugaya 3-17-11 • 台東区松が谷3-17-11
Tel. 03-3844-1606
www.kappabashi.or.jp/shops/31.html (Japanese)
SHOP • MAP PAGE 198, #34

Lacquer shop including soup bowls, chopsticks, and more as well as a nice selection of wooden products including *manaita*, wooden cutting boards that are very gentle on knives, steamers, and *otoshibuta* (drop lids) that are essential in any Japanese kitchen.

Soi
Matsugaya 3-17-13 • 台東区松が谷3-17-13
Tel. 03-3843-9555
www.soi-s.jp/ (Japanese)
SHOP • MAP PAGE 198, #35

This interior design shop with its own wooden interior has a colorful selection of *tenugui* (hand towels), incredibly thin glassware, and artful pottery.

Kondō Shōten • 近藤商店
Matsugaya 3-1-13 • 台東区松が谷3-1-13
Tel. 03-3841-3372
www.kappabashi.or.jp/shops/56.html (Japanese)
SHOP • MAP PAGE 198, #36

This shop specializes in bamboo goods including strainers, chopsticks, baskets, toothpicks, and skewers.

Fukuokaya Noren • 福岡屋
Matsugaya 3-1-15 • 台東区松が谷3-1-15
Tel. 03-3844-4522
SHOP • MAP PAGE 198, #37

Noren are the decorative cloth banners hanging in front of stores and restaurants. They can also be used at home as room dividers in your home. Fukuokaya has a colorful array of *noren* in different sizes and colors as well as pillow covers.

Sankidō • 三起堂
Matsugaya 2-13-12 • 台東区松が谷2-13-12
Tel. 03-3841-2013 • no holiday • www.sankido.co.jp/ (Japanese)
SHOP • MAP PAGE 198, #38

This lacquer shop has chopstick rests, spoons, strainers, bowls, and more.

Kamata • かまた
Matsugaya 2-12-6 • 台東区松が谷2-12-6
Tel. 03-3841-4205 • www.kap-kam.com/(English)
SHOP • MAP PAGE 198, #39

Kamata has a large selection of Western and Japanese knives, Japanese whetstones for sharpening knives, and other kitchen gadgets.

Maeda • まえ田
Matsugaya 1-10-9 • 台東区松が谷1-10-9
Tel. 03-3845-2822
www.kappabashi.or.jp/shops/141.html (Japanese)
SHOP • MAP PAGE 198, #40

This pottery shop has *shōchū* cups, *donabe* pots for steaming rice, a special bowl and chopsticks for making *nattō* (fermented soybeans) extra sticky, mortar and pestle sets, and chopstick rests.

Tanaka Shikkiten • 田中漆器店
Matsugaya 1-9-12 • 台東区松が谷1-9-12
Tel. 03-3841-6755
www.kappabashi.or.jp/shops/97.html (Japanese)
SHOP • MAP PAGE 198, #41

It is hard to put down the shiny, silky lacquered bowls, chopsticks, ladles, trays, and chopstick rests at Tanaka. The staff can help you find a pair of chopsticks that will fit your hand size.

AMEYOKO
アメ横

YOU'LL FIND THIS BOISTEROUS OUTDOOR FOOD MARKET UNDER THE ELEVATED TRAIN TRACKS AT UENO station. It is not nearly as impressive as Tsukiji Market, but it is open seven days a week, and is a good alternative if Tsukiji is closed.

The fishmongers call out in husky voices offering discounts and bargains. "*Omake*" means "I'm offering a great discount;" you may also hear them shouting "*sen yen*" (1000 yen) and pointing to a tray loaded down with seafood. While bargaining is rarely done in Japan, it is acceptable here. You will find a bit of everything from seafood, fruits, and vegetables to dried foods.

At the end of the year, upwards of 400,000 people will squeeze into this narrow alley to pick up ingredients to make traditional New Year's dishes, including such as herring roe *(kazunoko)*, vinegared octopus *(sudako)*, and salmon. There are about four hundred shops squeezed in the many buildings along the 400-meter walkway. Ameyoko has always had the reputation for bargain shopping. http://www.ameyoko.net/e/ (English website)

This walk starts at Ueno station and goes south toward Okachimachi station. All of the addresses below are in Taito-ku 台東区.

Shimura Shōten • 志村商店
Ueno 6-11-3 • 台東区上野6-11-3
Tel. 03-3831-2454
Daily 9:00–19:00; closed holidays
http://homepage3.nifty.com/ameyoko/ (Japanese)
SHOP • MAP PAGE 218, #1

This candy shop, overflowing with chocolates and sweets, is much loved for its 1000-yen grab bags of miscellaneous candy. It's fun to watch the ebullient clerk and the excited customers banter back and forth ("More! More!") as he fills up a bag with candies, sweets, and snacks.

Fruits Shop Hyakkaen • 百果園
Ueno 6-10-12 • 台東区上野6-10-12
Tel. 03-3832-2625
Daily 10:00–20:00; no holidays
www.guidenet.jp/shop/083c/ (Japanese)
SHOP • MAP PAGE 218, #3

AMEYOKO アメ横

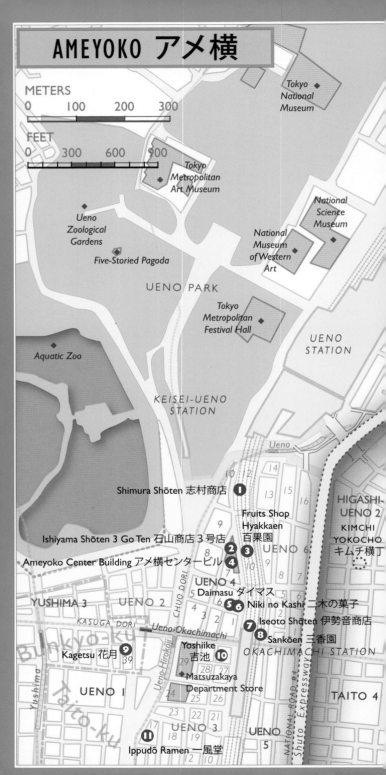

METERS
0   100   200   300

FEET
0   300   600   900

Tokyo National Museum

Tokyo Metropolitan Art Museum

Ueno Zoological Gardens

Five-Storied Pagoda

National Science Museum

National Museum of Western Art

UENO PARK

Tokyo Metropolitan Festival Hall

UENO STATION

Aquatic Zoo

KEISEI-UENO STATION

Ueno

Shimura Shōten 志村商店 **❶**

Fruits Shop Hyakkaen 百果園

HIGASHI-UENO 2

KIMCHI YOKOCHO キムチ横丁

Ishiyama Shōten 3 Go Ten 石山商店 3 号店 **❷** **❸**

UENO 6

Ameyoko Center Building アメ横センタービル **❹**

UENO 4

Daimasu ダイマス **❺**

YUSHIMA 3

UENO 2

Niki no Kashi 二木の菓子 **❻**

CHUO DORI

KASUGA DORI

Ueno-Okachimachi

Iseoto Shōten 伊勢音商店 **❼**

Sankōen 三香園 **❽**

OKACHIMACHI STATION

Kagetsu 花月 **❾**

Yoshiike 吉池 **❿**

Matsuzakaya Department Store

BUNKYO-KU

Ueno-Hirokoji

UENO 1

UENO 3

UENO 5

TAITO 4

Taito-ku

Ippudō Ramen 一風堂 **⓫**

NATIONAL ROAD #4
Shuto Expressway

This shop sells seasonal fresh fruit skewered on disposable chopsticks. Depending on the time of year, you may find a kebab of strawberries, a chunk of pineapple, or a slice of melon, a refreshing, portable snack.

Ishiyama Shōten 3 Go Ten • 石山商店3号店
Ueno 4-7-8 • 台東区上野4-7-8
Tel. 03-3833-6668
9:00–19:00; closed the 3rd Wednesday of the month except for
December, when the shop is open daily
SHOP • MAP PAGE 218, #2

Ishiyama specializes in *sashimi*-quality tuna. You'll see large red glistening blocks of meat as well as *saku* cuts (to make *sushi* or *sashimi* at home). This fishmonger also sells other seafood products including crab, salmon, and other seasonal fish.

Ameyoko Center Building • アメ横センタービル
Ueno 4-7-8, Ameyoko Center Building
台東区上野4-7-8アメ横センタービル
no phone (this is a building)
10:00–20:00; closed the 3rd Wednesday of the month except for
December, when the shop is open daily
www.ameyoko-center-bldg.com/ (Japanese)
SHOP • MAP PAGE 218, #4

A handful of shops in the basement of the Ameyoko Center Building also sell fresh seafood, meat, and dry goods, and is worth visiting for the inventory of spices, fresh herbs, and produce for Southeast Asian cooking. Here you will find many ingredients for cooking Thai, Vietnamese, Chinese, and Malaysian food—rice paper, curries, noodles, fish sauce, and other ingredients that are often not sold at local supermarkets are available here.

Iseoto Shōten • 伊勢音商店
Ueno 6-4-10 • 台東区上野6-4-10
Tel. 03-3831-4411 • Daily 9:00–19:00
www.iseoto.com/ (Japanese)
SHOP • MAP PAGE 218, #7

This shop, dating from 1876, specializes in bonito flakes (*katsuobushi*), kelp (*kombu*), *shiitake*, dried anchovies, and other products for making *dashi*. The shop is redolent with the aroma of the smoked and dried bonito. The products are sold from wooden barrels that spill out into the street. This top-quality *katsuobushi*

is aged longer than most. The shop also sells dried squid and dried
scallop ligaments, which are delicious snacks.

Daimasu · ダイマス
Ueno 4-6-13 · 台東区上野4-6-13
Tel. 03-3831-5023
9:00–18:30;
closed the 2nd, 4th, and 5th Thursday of each month
www.daimasu.net/ (Japanese)
SHOP · MAP PAGE 218, #5

This tiny shop has a colorful display of dried beans, grains, rice,
sesame seeds, millet, and more.

Sankōen · 三香園
Ueno 6-10-3 · 台東区上野6-10-3
Tel. 03-3831-1579
10:00–19:00; closed Sunday
SHOP · MAP PAGE 218, #8

This large shop specializes in dried laver (*nori*) and tea. There are
many types of *nori* including Korean-style, flavored with sesame
oil and salt, and Japanese-style, both seasoned with a sweet *mirin*
or unseasoned, for making *sushi* at home.

Niki no Kashi · 二木の菓子
Ueno 4-6-1 · 台東区上野4-6-1
Tel. 03-3833-405
Daily 9:30–19:30
www.nikinokashi.co.jp (Japanese)
SHOP · MAP PAGE 218, #6

Niki no Kashi may be one of Ameyoko's most famous vendors.
In business since 1947, this large discount shop for sweets and
candies has an unusually wide selection of *dagashi*. *Dagashi*
are inexpensive snacks and sweets, popularized in the 1940s
and 1950s. There are a few shops around the city that still
sell *dagashi*; often each piece sells for about ten yen. You hear
shoppers there saying "*natuskashii*," meaning that this reminds
them of the old days.

The selection also includes European chocolates, rice crackers,
and Japanese confections. You may want to try the bean sweets
(*mamegashi*), different beans that have been cooked in a simple
syrup, then rolled in sugar crystals, or the deep-fried crackers
with a sweet coating (*karintō*). There are savory chips and snacks,

both Japanese and imported, as well as packaged foods including pickles, curries, and spices.

Yoshiike • 吉池
Ueno 3-27-12 • 台東区上野3-27-12
Tel. 03-3831-0141 • Daily 9:30–24:00
www.yoshiike-group.co.jp/ (Japanese)
SHOP • MAP PAGE 218, #10

Since 1920, Yoshiike has been a prominent shop in this area of Ueno. This large store has a supermarket in the basement and a large seafood department on the first floor. The second floor is a liquor shop, with wine, *sake*, *shōchū*, and spirits as well as *sake* cups and decanters.

It is the seafood department that makes this shop worth visiting. The fresh seafood area is impressive with a colorful array of fish, crabs, shellfish and other seafood. But that is just a tiny part of this expansive floor. There is marinated fish, dried fish, smoked salmon, spicy cod roe (*mentaiko*), deep-fried or steamed fish cakes, canned seafood, and much more.

In the middle of the floor, there is a refrigerated case with reasonably priced *sashimi* platters and *sushi* to go, if you want to have an impromptu picnic in nearby Ueno Park. You can pick up some chilled *sake* from the second floor.

Ippudō Ramen • 一風堂
Ueno 3-17-5 • 台東区上野3-17-5
Tel. 03-5807-2772 • Daily 11:00 (a.m.)–03:00 (a.m.)
www.ippudo.com/ (Japanese)
RESTAURANT • INEXPENSIVE • MAP PAGE 218, #11

This well-known *ramen* shop started in 1985, with fifteen counter seats. It now has dozens of locations throughout Japan and even a branch in New York City. The specialty is pork bone (*tonkotsu*) *ramen* made with very thin noodles. Other popular dishes on the menu include dumplings, fried rice, and rice topped with spicy cod roe.

Near Ameyoko

If you are interested in Korean food, walk to the other side of the tracks to an area called Kimchi Yokocho. Within a few blocks there, you'll find a handful of shops and restaurants specializing in Korean food. Kimchi Yokocho (ムチ横丁) http://panda .starfleet.ac/~kaeru/kimuti/kimuti.html

NIHONBASHI 日本橋

Mandarin Oriental (hote

Bank of Japan ◆

Ogura Oden おぐ羅お

OTEMACHI 1

NIHONBASHI-
HONGOKUCHO 2

NIHONBASHI
HONGOKUCHO

METERS

| 0 | 100 | 200 | 300 |

FEET

| 0 | 300 | 600 | 900 |

Otemachi

OTEMACHI 2

Shuto Expressway

Nihonb

Sh

Konaya 古奈屋

14

6

MARUNOUCHI 1

7

Chiyoda-ku

10

EITAI DORI

YAESU 1

8

Otakō お多幸 **19**

2

TOKYO
STATION

Shōchū Authority 焼酎オーソリティ

21

Fuji no Kuni Yamanashi Kan Antenna Sh
富士の国山梨館 **22**

3

Hasegawa Saketen
はせがわ酒店 ●

Oidemase Yamaguchi Kan Antenna Shop
おいでませ山口館 **23**

26

Daimaru 大丸

1 **27**

Nihonbashi Naga
日本橋長門

9

30

Nihonbashi Yukari 日本橋ゆかり **29**

2

Tōkyō Ramen Street

Sapporoya 札幌や **31**

3

YAESU DORI

4

CHUO DORI

YAESU 2

YAESU 2

1

KYOBASHI 1

2

*Bridgeston
Museum
of Art*

4

3

Iseihiro Kyobashi Honten 伊勢廣京橋本店 **32**

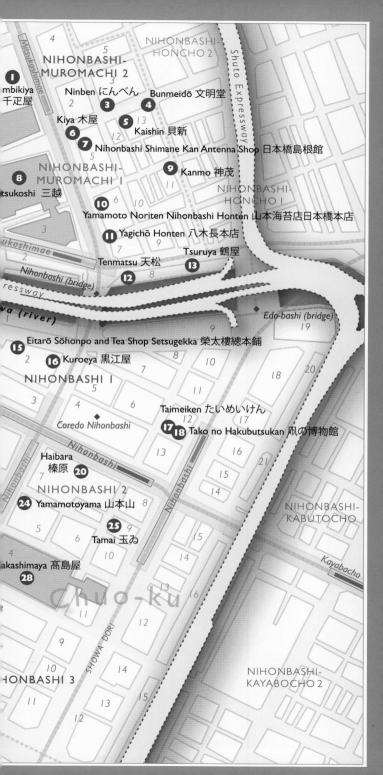

1 mbikiya 千疋屋

NIHONBASHI-MUROMACHI 2

4

5

3

3 Ninben にんべん

4 Bunmeidō 文明堂

6 Kiya 木屋

2

13

5

7 Kaishin 貝新

12

7 Nihonbashi Shimane Kan Antenna Shop 日本橋島根館

NIHONBASHI-MUROMACHI 1

8 tsukoshi 三越

9 Kanmo 神茂

NIHONBASHI HONCHO 2

Shuto Expressway

NIHONBASHI-HONCHO 1

11

10 6 10

Yamamoto Noriten Nihonbashi Honten 山本海苔店日本橋本店

ukoshimae

3

11 Yagichō Honten 八木長本店

2

7 9

Nihonbashi (bridge)

12 Tenmatsu 天松

8

13 Tsuruya 鶴屋

ressway

wa (river)

9

Edo-bashi (bridge)

19

15 Eitarō Sōhonpo and Tea Shop Setsugekka 榮太樓總本鋪

16 Kuroeya 黒江屋

2

8 10

18

20

NIHONBASHI 1

7

11

5

3 4 6

Coredo Nihonbashi

Taimeiken たいめいけん

12 17

17 **18** Tako no Hakubutsukan 凧の博物館

13

16

21

Haibara 榛原 **20**

Nihonbashi

15

14

NIHONBASHI 2

24 Yamamotoyama 山本山

8

NIHONBASHI-KABUTOCHO

5

25 9

6 Tamai 玉ゐ

10

15

14

Kayabacho

4

akashimaya 髙島屋

28

13

16

Chuo-ku

11

12

9

SHOWA DORI

14

HONBASHI 3

10

13

15

11

12

NIHONBASHI-KAYABOCHO 2

NIHONBASHI
日本橋

THE NIHONBASHI DISTRICT IS HOME TO SOME OF THE OLDEST SHOPS IN THE CITY AS WELL AS TWO OF THE BEST *depachika*, Takashimaya and Mitsukoshi. Centrally located, it is a short walk from Tokyo station. This is a traditional neighborhood that adheres to the old practices, so many shops are closed on Sundays and national holidays.

Nihonbashi is the name of the first wooden bridge to be built across the Nihonbashi River, in 1603 by the Shogun Tokugawa Ieyasu. All points in Japan are measured from a marker in the middle of the bridge that designates the starting point for the famous "Five Routes," the most famous being the Tokaido connecting Edo (former name for Tokyo) to Kyoto. The bridge and the area around it became the central point for commerce and culture in the seventeenth century.

Tokyo's main seafood market was originally here on the banks of the Nihonbashi River. It was moved to its current location after the great Kanto Earthquake of 1923.

Japan's first department store, Mitsukoshi, opened here in 1904, and Takashimaya followed in 1916 on the opposite side of the river. To this day, both department stores attract customers from around the country.

Addresses listed below are all in Chuo-ku 中央区. "Nihonbashi Muromachi" are on the Mitsukoshi side of the river while "Nihonbashi" are on the Takashimaya side.

See the *depachika* section for information on **Takashimaya** and **Mitsukoshi**.

Nihonbashi Yukari ● 日本橋ゆかり
Nihonbashi 3-2-14 ● 中央区日本橋3-2-14
Tel. 03-3271-3436
11:30–14:00, 17:00–22:00; closed Sunday and holidays
www.nihonbashi-yukari.com (Japanese–some English)
RESTAURANT ● LUNCH INEXPENSIVE TO MODERATE, DINNER
MODERATE TO EXPENSIVE ● MAP PAGE 222, #29

For exquisite *kaiseki* and *kappō ryōri*, dine at Nihonbashi Yukari, home of third-generation Chef Kimio Nonaga, the 2002 Iron Chef winner. Go at lunch if you are on a budget, but a dinner here will be one you will not forget. For lunch, you can reserve a special *bentō* ahead of time or order one of the daily specials. There are

private *tatami* rooms in the basement, but the coveted seats are at the counter where you can watch Chef Nonaga's artistry from a front row seat. Beverages include a nice selection of Japanese wine and an original beer that chef Nonaga created to specifically complement Japanese food.

Chef Nonaga takes prides in preparing food by traditional techniques. And, unlike many chefs who are on the shy side, chef Nonaga is happy to talk about his food and how it is prepared. He is a strong proponent of using local ingredients, both vegetables and seafood.

Yamamotoyama • 山本山
Nihonbashi 2-5-2 • 中央区日本橋2-5-2
Tel. 03-3281-0010 • Daily 10:00–18:00
www.yamamotoyama.co.jp/(Japanese)
www.yamamotoyama-usa.com/ (English for USA site)
SHOP • MAP PAGE 223, #24

The historic tea and *nori* shop, Yamamotoyama, established in 1690, stands next door to an Illy Espressamente coffee shop, an

interesting contrast of old and new. The teas are exquisite and there is a wide range to select from. *Kukicha*, in particular, is an unusual tea that is not often found outside of Japan, made from the stems and leaves of the tea plant. Yamamotoyama has two small seating areas in which to enjoy tea and traditional sweets.

Kuroeya • 黒江屋
Nihonbashi 1-2-6 • 中央区日本橋1-2-6
Tel. 03-3272-0948
9:00–17:00; closed weekends and holidays
www.norenkai.net/english/shop/kuroeya/index.html (English)
SHOP • MAP PAGE 223, #16

Kuroeya's dizzying selection of about 1,500 types of lacquer vessels are squeezed into this second-floor shop. The wide variety includes chopsticks, bowls, cups for tea and *sake*, spoons, forks, vases, and much more. This historic shop dates back to 1689. The entrance isn't obvious; you'll pass a security guard in what looks like an office building, before climbing a flight of stairs in the rear of the lobby. If there are sale items, they are placed up front near the register. These tend to be very good bargains, so it is worth poking your head into the shop if you are in the neighborhood.

Fuji no Kuni Yamanashi Kan Antenna Shop
富士の国山梨館
Nihonbashi 2-3-4, Nihonbashi Plaza Building
中央区日本橋2-3-4日本橋プラザビル
Tel. 03-3241-3776 • Daily 10:00—19:00
www.yamanashi-kankou.jp/tokyo/tokyo001.html (Japanese)
SHOP • MAP PAGE 222, #22

Yamanashi prefecture, west of Tokyo, is home to Mount Fuji, Japan's most treasured symbol. It's an area famous for fruit such as strawberries, cherries, peaches, and grapes, some of which find their way into the regional wine. If you are curious about Japanese wine, then you will not want to miss this shop, which has an unusually large selection from this area.

Oidemase Yamaguchi Kan Antenna Shop
おいでませ山口館
Nihonbashi 2-3-4, Nihonbashi Plaza Building
中央区日本橋2-3-4日本橋プラザビル
Tel. 03-3231-1863 • Daily 10:30—19:00
www.oidemase-t.jp/ (Japanese)
SHOP • MAP PAGE 222, #23

The show windows display a tempting selection of pastel-colored Hagiyaki pottery, characteristic of Yamaguchi prefecture. The teacups and teapots in particular are nice; they show their age as the tiny cracks in the glaze darken over time with use. Yamaguchi is famous for seafood, *sake* (Dassai is a popular brand), and fruit. The shop sells a refreshing 100% *mikan* (tangerine) juice.

Nihonbashi Nagato • 日本橋長門
Nihonbashi 3-1-3 • 中央区日本橋3-1-3
Tel. 03-3271-8966
10:00—18:00; closed Sunday and holidays
www.wagashi.or.jp/tokyo/shop/0318.htm (Japanese)
SHOP • MAP PAGE 222, #27

This tiny sweets shop has space for only three customers at a time. In front of the store is a red banner with white calligraphy and a dark wooden sign above the door, also with white calligraphy. A small window showcases seasonal Japanese confections (*wagashi*). Nagato is famous for its soft and jelly-like *warabi mochi* sprinkled with toasted soybean powder (*kinako*), *azuki* paste cakes (*yōkan*), and beautiful, seasonal *wagashi*.

Sapporoya · 札幌や
Nihonbashi 3-3-5, B1 · 中央区日本橋3-3-5, B1
Tel. 03-3275-0024
11:00–21:30 Monday to Friday; Saturday until 16:00;
closed Sunday and holidays

RESTAURANT · INEXPENSIVE · MAP PAGE 222, #31

At lunchtime, this simple, basement shop often has a line of salarymen out the door. Avoid the peak lunch crowd if you can—go in the late afternoon or early evening. While the shop has hot bowls of *ramen*, it is the cold *ramen* noodles (*hiyashi chūka goma dare*) that the shop is known for: a large, shallow bowl of chilled noodles topped with julienned cucumbers, ham, tomatoes, a hard-boiled egg, bamboo shoots, pickled ginger, and shredded *nori*. What brings the dish together is the savory and slightly sweet sesame dressing. There is nothing better on a hot, steamy summer day. Don't be afraid to pick up the wide bowl to slurp the broth.

Tamai • 玉ゐ
Nihonbashi 2-9-9 • 中央区日本橋2-9-9
Tel. 03-3272-3227
11:00—14:00, 17:00—21:00 Monday to Friday;
11:30—15:00, 16:30—20:00 weekends and holidays
http://anago-tamai.com/ (Japanese)
RESTAURANT • INEXPENSIVE • MAP PAGE 223, #25

Tamai, a small shop in the backstreets behind Takashimaya, marked with a large blue and white kite-like banner, specializes in saltwater eels (*anago*). The historic building itself has a simple interior. Fans of *unagi*, the freshwater eel, may also enjoy *anago*, which is tender and a bit more delicate and fatty. Like *unagi*, it is served either simmered or grilled in a lacquer box over hot rice. You can add an order of *hone chazuke*, a small bowl of rice topped with the fried bones of the *anago* that is topped with hot tea. (Yes, the bowl of rice is topped with hot tea so you are eating a soupy bowl of hot tea, rice, and the fried *anago* bones.)

Otakō • お多幸
Nihonbashi 2-2-3 • 中央区日本橋2-2-3
Tel. 03-3243-8282
11:30—13:30, 17:00—22:30 Monday to Friday;
16:00—22:00 Saturday and holidays; closed Sunday
www.tokyo-gourmet.net/restaurants/otako/index.html (Japanese)
RESTAURANT • INEXPENSIVE TO MODERATE
MAP PAGE 222, #19

The *oden* at Otakō is Kanto-style, served in a dark, intense, richly flavored sweet and hot broth (*amakara ni*). The signature dish, *tōmeishi*, is a large block of *tōfu* over hot rice that is topped with the rich broth.

Taimeiken · たいめいけん
Nihonbashi 1-12-10 · 中央区日本橋1-12-10
Tel. 03-3271-2465 · 11:00–20:30 Monday to Saturday;
11:00–20:00 Sunday and holidays
www.taimeiken.co.jp/ (Japanese)
RESTAURANT · MODERATE · MAP PAGE 223, #17

Yōshoku is the term for Western foods that have been adapted to the Japanese palate; popular examples include beef stew, pasta, hamburgers, and croquettes. Taimeiken's *yōshoku* menu has been attracting customers since 1931. You can expect long lines at lunch. The restaurant's signature dish, *omuraisu*, is a three-egg omelet folded around ketchup-flavored rice and chopped ham. If you love watching chefs in action, a standing *ramen* bar on the right side of the restaurant overlooks the kitchen. It can only hold a few people at a time, but is one of the best places in the city to observe the frenetic activity.

Kiya · 木屋
Nihonbashi Muromachi 1-5-6 · 中央区日本橋室町1-5-6
Tel. 03-3241-0110
10:00–18:00; Sunday and holidays 11:15–17:45
www.kiya-hamono.co.jp/english/index.html (English)
SHOP · MAP PAGE 223, #6

The compact corner shop, opened in 1792, displays a shining collection of knives, pots, pans, and many kitchen implements, including graters, pepper grinders, and tweezers for pulling bones out of fish, as well as scissors and gardening tools. The friendly staff is patient and helpful.

Nihonbashi Shimane Kan Antenna Shop • 日本橋島根館

Nihonbashi Muromachi 1-5-3, Fukushima Building

中央区日本橋室町1-5-3福島ビル

Tel. 03-5201-3310

Daily 10:00–19:00; closed holidays

www.shimanekan.jp/ (Japanese)

SHOP • MAP PAGE 223, #7

Shimane prefecture on the Sea of Japan is rich with seafood. Popular items in this shop include the *himono*, fish that is butterflied, salted, and dried. There are often tastings of the local *sake* (*jizake*) in the front of the store. There are more than eight hundred different food items to select from.

Kanmo • 神茂

Nihonbashi Muromachi 1-11-8 • 中央区日本橋室町1-11-8
Tel. 03-3241-3988 • 10:00–18:00 Monday to Friday;
10:00–17:00 Saturday; closed Sunday and holidays
www.hanpen.co.jp/ (Japanese)

SHOP • MAP PAGE 223, #9

Kanmo, established in 1688, specializes in *hanpen*, a savory, fluffy cake made from egg whites and fish meat. *Hanpen* can be served with *wasabi* and soy sauce or in a clear broth soup, but it is most commonly found in *oden* along with other types of fish cakes.

The refrigerated cases at Kanmo showcase many ingredients for *oden* including deep-fried fish cakes mixed with burdock root, squid, sardines, or wood ear mushrooms. A seasonal selection of fish cakes includes laver, bamboo shoots, shrimp, and ginger. Do not miss Kanmo's fish cakes with vegetables (*yasai-age*) such as *edamame*, corn, Japanese basil, and broccoli.

Yamamoto Noriten Nihonbashi Honten
山本海苔店日本橋本店

Nihonbashi Muromachi 1-6-3 • 中央区日本橋室町1-6-3
Tel. 03-3241-0290 • Daily 9:00–18:30
www.yamamoto-noriten.co.jp/english/ (English)

SHOP • MAP PAGE 223, #10

This large shop on the main street, Chuo Dori, offers many types of laver (*nori*). Classic offerings include grilled *nori*, used to wrap *sushi*, and seasoned *nori* (*ajitsukenori*), which is slightly sweet and sticky, and often a part of traditional Japanese breakfasts. *Nori chazuke* is a dry mix of *nori* and toasted rice crackers that is served over rice and then topped with a hot green tea. *Nori Tsukudani* is a sweet *nori* paste that is often used to top rice. Some modern *nori* offerings include snack *nori*, much like potato chips, in flavors like plum, sea urchin, spicy cod roe, leeks and *miso*, salmon, and sesame.

Tenmatsu • 天松

Nihonbashi Muromachi 1-8-2 • 中央区中央区日本橋室町1-8-2
Tel. 03-3241-5840
11:00–14:00, 17:00–21:00 Monday to Friday;
11:00–14:30, 17:00–21:00 weekends and holidays
www.tenmatsu.com/english/index.htm (English)

RESTAURANT • LUNCH INEXPENSIVE, DINNER MODERATE
MAP PAGE 223, #12

The aroma of sesame oil is hard to miss when you get close to this *tempura* restaurant. Ask to be seated at the first or second floor

counter where you can watch the *tempura* chefs cut vegetables and seafood, dip the pieces into a thin batter, and gingerly place them into hot oil. The lacy pieces are presented to you one by one as they come out of the pot. Use the sweet soy dipping sauce with grated radish or simply sprinkle with salt. The meal finishes with a steaming bowl of white rice, pickles, and a bowl of red *miso* soup.

Yagichō Honten • 八木長本店
Nihonbashi Muromachi 1-7-2 • 中央区日本橋室町1-7-2
Tel. 03-3241-1211 • Daily 10:00–18:00
www.yagicho-honten.jp/profile.html (Japanese)
SHOP • MAP PAGE 223, #11

This eighth-generation dried goods store (*kanbutsuya*) dates back to 1737. All of the items here are lightweight and have a long shelf life, making perfect items to take home in your suitcase. You'll find dried kelp (*kombu*) and bonito flakes (*katsuobushi*) for making stock, or if you prefer, convenient *dashi* packs—similar to teabags but filled with kelp and bonito flakes—that are superior to instant *dashi* that may have additives. Other dried items in the shop include sea vegetables, shiitake mushrooms, beans, sesame seeds, and dried chili peppers, as well as noodles such as *sōmen*, *soba*, and *udon*.

Eitarō Sōhonpo and Tea Shop Setsugekka • 榮太樓總本鋪
Nihonbashi 1-2-5 • 中央区日本橋室町1-2-5
Tel. 03-3271-7785 • 9:00–18:00; closed Sunday and holidays
www.eitaro.com/ (Japanese)
www.norenkai.net/english/shop/eitaro/index.html (English)
SHOP AND CAFÉ • MAP PAGE 223, #15

This Japanese confection shop dating from 1857 is also a café/restaurant with a lunch menu that includes noodles, rice, and a hearty soup filled with vegetables (*kenchinjiru*). The signature hard candies in flavors like *mattcha* and brown sugar are some of the shop's most popular items as are the sweet beans called *amanattō*. In recent years the venerable shop had trouble attracting a younger generation with disposable income and responded by creating a line of modern confections including trendy lollipops, candy-flavored lipgloss, and other hip products that aren't available at the historic flagship store, but can be found at **Isetan** *depachika* in Shinjuku at Ameya Eitarō.

Tsuruya • 鶴屋
Nihonbashi Muromachi 1-8-8 • 中央区日本橋室町1-8-8
Tel. 03-3243-0551 • 9:00–18:00; closed Sunday
www.tsuruya.co.jp (Japanese)
SHOP • MAP PAGE 223, #13

Tsuruya's history can be traced back to 1803. Here you will find a selection of both traditional and modern Japanese confections in the Kyoto tradition, including interesting jellies in flavors such as strawberry, grape, and melon. The exquisite, thin, sweet rice crackers (*hanasembei*) have seasonal flower petals baked into them.

Bunmeidō • 文明堂
Nihonbashi Muromachi 1-13-7 • 中央区日本橋室町1-13-7
Tel. 03-3241-0002 • 8:30–18:00; closed Sunday and holidays
www.bunmeido.co.jp/ (Japanese)
SHOP • MAP 223, #4

Bunmeidō is the place to try *castella* sponge cake. Vanilla and cheese versions are always available, and there are flavors such as salt or almond caramel that change with the seasons. You may also want to sample the delectable stuffed pancakes (*dorayaki*) in flavors like *mattcha*, black sesame, and chestnut with chunky *azuki* paste.

Ninben • にんべん
Nihonbashi Muromachi 2-3-1 • 中央区日本橋室町2-3-1
Tel. 03-3241-0241 • 10:00–18:00; weekends until 17:00;
closed some Sundays, check website
www.ninben.co.jp/ (Japanese)
SHOP • MAP PAGE 223, #3

Ninben is synonymous with bonito flakes (*katsuobushi*); this shop's history dates back to 1699. The smell of freshly shaven *katsuobushi* permeates the street. There is a huge variety of dried flavorings and condiments based on *katsuobushi* that can be added to rice, soups, and noodles.

Kaishin • 貝新
Nihonbashi Muromachi 1-13-5 • 中央区日本橋室町1-13-5
Tel. 03-3241-2734 • 10:00—18:00 Monday to Friday;
10:00—16:00 Saturday; closed Sunday and holidays

SHOP • MAP PAGE 223, #5

This shop specializes in seafood and sea vegetables that have been marinated in a sweet soy sauce (*Tsukudani*). The original shop in Mie prefecture dates back to 1597. When you enter the shop, the aroma of sweet soy is overwhelming. Behind the glass counter are red lacquer trays filled with the marinated items that are perfect for spooning over a hot bowl of rice.

Sembikiya • 千疋屋
Nihonbashi Muromachi 2-1-2 • 中央区日本橋室町2-1-2
Tel. 03-3241-0877 • Daily 9:00—19:00; closed holidays
www.sembikiya.co.jp/ (Japanese)

SHOP AND RESTAURANT • LUNCH INEXPENSIVE TO
MODERATE, DINNER MODERATE • MAP PAGE 223, #1

Shop here for flawless fruit for gift-giving, including melons and mangoes presented in wooden boxes with price tags in the hundreds of dollars. This boutique is a pristine and beautifully designed backdrop for fresh fruit, preserves, and exquisite fruit pastries. On the second floor is a restaurant serving fruit-based dishes including the signature mango curry rice, pineapple beef stew, and parfaits. On the first floor next to the fruit shop is a casual café for freshly squeezed fruit juices, mango curry rice, and soft ice cream: Café di FESTA.

Ogura Oden • おぐ羅おでん
Nihonbashi Muromachi 2-1-2, Nihonbashi Mitsui Tower B1
中央区日本橋室町2-1-2日本橋三井タワー B1
Tel. 03-3516-1775
11:30—14:30, 17:00—22:30 Monday to Friday;
11:30—14:30, 17:00—22:00 Saturday, Sunday, and holidays
www.mitsuitower.jp/shop/ogura/index.html (Japanese)
RESTAURANT • LUNCH INEXPENSIVE TO MODERATE,
DINNER MODERATE • MAP PAGE 222, #2

This *oden* restaurant is hidden in the basement of the Mitsui Tower. Ogura's main restaurant in Ginza is perpetually crowded and open only for dinner, but this location is open for lunch as well as dinner, and on weekends and holidays. The delicate broth made here, praised by connoisseurs, is made from kelp, bonito flakes, and salt, and because no soy sauce is used, the color is light and clear. The most popular items are rolled cabbage, *daikon*, and *tōfu*. A chilled *sake* is the preferred drink to accompany *oden*.

While in Nihonbashi there are a few interesting shops worth visiting.

Haibara • 榛原
Nihonbashi 2-7-6 • 中央区日本橋2-7-6
Tel. 03-3272-3801 • 10:00—18:30; Saturday until 17:00;
closed Sunday and holidays • www.haibara.co.jp/ (Japanese)
SHOP • MAP PAGE 223, #20

Haibara, a paper shop dating back to 1806, sells dainty and delicate Japanese paper, stationery, postcards, and small gifts.

Tako no Hakubutsukan • 凧の博物館
Nihonbashi 1-12-10, 5th Floor • 中央区日本橋1-12-10, 5F
Tel. 03-3275-2704 • 11:00—17:00; closed Sunday and holidays
MUSEUM • MAP PAGE 223, #18

On the fifth floor of the building that houses the restaurant **Taimeiken** is a kite museum with over three thousand colorful Japanese kites.; only 200 yen to enter

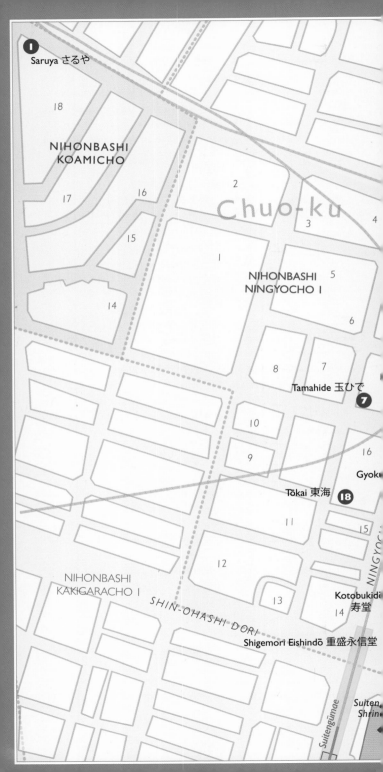

① Saruya さるや

18

NIHONBASHI KOAMICHO

17   16

15

14

Chuo-ku

2

3

4

1

NIHONBASHI NINGYOCHO 1

5

6

8   7

Tamahide 玉ひで **⑦**

10

9

16

Gyok

Tōkai 東海 **⑱**

15

11

12

NIHONBASHI KAKIGARACHO 1

SHIN-OHASHI DORI

13

14

Kotobukid
寿堂

Shigemori Eishindō 重盛永信堂

NINGYO

Suitengūmae

Suiten
Shrin

NINGYOCHO 人形町

Ningyocho

NIHONBASHI
NINGYOCHO 3

19

6

7

Kintame 近為

2

5

3 Kizushi 㐂寿司

4 Nihonbashi Hiyama 日本橋日山

8

Uokyū 魚久

5

24

6 Hamanoin 浜乃院

8

4

9 Ningyocho Imahan 人形町今半

kuraya
蔵屋

Morinoen 森乃園

9

22

23

10 11 Futaba Tōfu 双葉

10

Toritada 鳥忠

12

13

Ningyocho Shinoda Zushi Sōhonten
人形町 志乃多 寿司 総本店

14

堂で

3

15

AMAZAKE YOKOCHE

21

Yanagiya 柳屋

11

Kameidō 亀井堂

16

17 Sōkaya 草加屋

2

20

12

13

19

16

17

14

NIHONBASHI
NINGYOCHO 2

sukushi つくし

15

NIHONBASHI
KAKIGARACHO 2

NINGYOCHO

人形町

THIS HISTORIC NEIGHBORHOOD, NINGYOCHO, IS SOMETIMES ALSO REFERRED TO AS NIHONBASHI Ningyocho. If you are Japanese, this is a much loved area, but visitors seem to be unaware that the small shops have a rich history. Part of the old downtown (*shitamachi*) area, one street in particular, Amazake Yokocho, has several food shops worth visiting. There used to be many shops selling *amazake* on this street, a low- or non-alcoholic drink made from rice *kōji*, and while most of them have long disappeared, you can still try it at **Futaba Tōfu**. This traditional drink is often seen at shrines in Kyoto or at Shinto shrines throughout the country during the New Year holidays. *Amazake* is sweet, thick with soft grains of rice, and is flavored with a hint of ginger. In the summer it is served chilled and in the winter it is served warm. In addition to the food shops, you will see shops selling artisanal goods like lacquer boxes, colorful cloths (*tenugui*), and the traditional stringed instrument, the *shamisen*. A major attraction in the area is the Suitengu shrine.

Note that many shops are closed on Sunday and national holidays.

Addresses listed below are all in Chuo-ku 中央区.

Toritada • 鳥忠
Nihonbashi Ningyocho 2-10-12
中央区日本橋人形町2-10-12
Tel. 03-3666-0025
9:00−19:00; closed Sunday and holidays
www9.ocn.ne.jp/~toritada/index2.html (Japanese)
SHOP • MAP PAGE 241, #12

This smart shop specializes in top-quality chicken. You will also find a nice selection of *yakitori* and grilled chicken. Toritada is famous for their omelets (*tamagoyaki*), one kind in particular, the mother and child (*oyakoyaki*). Only thirty are made each day. *Oyakoyaki* are juicy, rich with flavor, and filled with chicken and the herb *mitsuba*, which is rolled in at the last minute, creating a nice contrast between the green leaves and the yellow eggs. You can see the omelets being made early in the day through a window that overlooks the kitchen.

Gyokueidō • 玉英堂
Nihonbashi Ningyocho 2-3-2 • 中央区日本橋人形町2-3-2
Tel. 03-3666-2625
9:30–21:00 Monday to Saturday; Sunday and holidays
until 17:00; closed the last Sunday of each month
www.ningyocho.or.jp/shop/a28.html (Japanese)
SHOP • MAP PAGE 241, #14

Gyokueidou is a four-hundred-year-old shop from Kyoto known
for two sweets, the *dorayaki*, pancakes stuffed with *azuki* paste,
and the *gyokuman*, a large sweet stuffed bun that is filled with a
chestnut, *azuki* paste, and pink and white bean paste.

Ningyocho Shinoda Zushi Sōhonten
人形町志乃多寿司総本店
Nihonbashi Ningyocho 2-10-10 • 中央区日本橋人形町2-10-10
Tel. 03-5614-9300 • Daily 9:00–19:00; closed holidays
www.norenkai.net/english/shop/shinodazushi/index.html
(English)
SHOP • MAP PAGE 241, #13

Shinoda specializes in *inarizushi*, deep-fried *tōfu* that is simmered
in a brown sugar broth and made into a parcel that is filled with
vinegared rice. The *sushi* shop also has rolled *sushi* surrounded
with *nori* (*norimaki*), pressed *sushi* (*oshizushi*), and *sushi* wrapped
with a thin omelet (*chakinzushi*).

Kameidō • 亀井堂
Nihonbashi Ningyocho 2-20-4 • 中央区日本橋人形町2-20-4
Tel. 03-3666-6654 • 9:00–18:30 Monday to Saturday;
10:00–17:30 Sunday and holidays
www.kameido.ne.jp (Japanese)
SHOP • MAP PAGE 241, #16

This modern shop is known for sweet, crunchy, flour-and-egg
cookies, *kawara sembei*, in decorative shapes, that are eaten plain
or iced with a thin layer of *mattcha* frosting. Kameido also sells
ningyōyaki, the signature sweet of the area, a pancake batter
surrounding *azuki* paste, baked in figurative molds.

Futaba Tōfu • 双葉
Nihonbashi Ningyocho 2-4-9 • 中央区日本橋人形町2-4-9
Tel. 03-3666-1028 • Daily 7:00–19:30
www.futaba-tofu.jp/menu/menu02.html (Japanese)
SHOP • MAP PAGE 241, #11

Among the impressive selection of soy products at Futaba Tōfu, you'll find the shop's signature jumbo deep-fried *tōfu* ball (*ganmo*). Stuffed with gingko nuts, chestnuts, and vegetables, it's ten times larger than the version you'll find elsewhere. For sweets, look for doughnuts, pudding, and soft ice cream, all made from soy milk. Don't miss the signature traditional drink *amazake*.

Tamahide · 玉ひで

Nihonbashi Ningyocho 1-17-10 · 中央区日本橋人形町1-17-10
Tel. 03-3668-7651 · 11:30—13:00, 17:00—22:00;
16:00—21:00 Saturday; closed Sunday and holidays
www.tamahide.co.jp/ (Japanese)
RESTAURANT · LUNCH INEXPENSIVE,
DINNER MODERATE TO EXPENSIVE · MAP PAGE 240, #7

It's easy to find Tamahide—look for the long line out the front door. Opened in 1760, this fifth-generation shop is synonymous with a dish called *oyakodon*, literally, "mother and child." The dish is made from chicken cooked in a sweet soy broth to which eggs are added and cooked for just a moment, then poured over a bowl of rice. Alternatives to the chicken are duck or ground chicken. Seating is communal at low tables, with a trough under the table in which to put your feet. In the evening a multi-course chicken *sukiyaki* meal is served.

Kintame · 近為

Nihonbashi Ningyocho 2-5-2 · 中央区日本橋人形町2-5-2
Tel. 03-3639-9439 · 9:30—18:30; closed Sunday
www.kintame.co.jp (Japanese)
SHOP · MAP PAGE 241, #2

Next door to Hiyama is Kintame, a branch of the famous Kyoto shop. See page 68 for more information.

Ningyocho Imahan · 人形町今半

Nihonbashi Ningyocho 2-9-12 · 中央区日本橋人形町2-9-12
Tel. 03-3666-7006 · Daily 11:00—22:00; closed holidays
www.imahan.com/e-guide/ningyocho_shop.html (English)
RESTAURANT · LUNCH MODERATE, DINNER MODERATE TO
EXPENSIVE · MAP PAGE 241, #9

Pop into this restaurant for *sukiyaki*, *shabu shabu*, and grilled *wagyū* steak. The large two-story red building with a black-tile roof sits on the corner. The entrance is to the right behind the blue banner. Sit grillside at the *teppanyaki* counter or if you plan to order one of the hot pots, *sukiyaki,* or *shabu shabu,* ask for a table in the dining room.

Hamanoin • 浜乃院

Nihonbashi Ningyocho 2-9-3 • 中央区日本橋人形町2-9-3
Tel. 03-3639-0231 • 10:00—19:00 Monday to Friday;
10:00—18:00 Saturday, Sunday, and holidays
www.hamanoin.co.jp (Japanese)
SHOP • MAP PAGE 241, #6

Although this shop specializes in *miso*-marinated seafood, such as salmon, cod, mackerel, and *fugu* to be grilled at home, you'll also find seafood snacks to munch on, including bite-size bits of processed smoked sea urchin, fish crackers, and dried scallops.

Nihonbashi Hiyama • 日本橋日山

Nihonbashi Ningyocho 2-5-1 • 中央区日本橋人形町2-5-1
Tel. 03-3666-5257
11:30—14:00, 17:00—21:00; closed Sunday and holidays
www.hiyama-nihonbashi.co.jp (Japanese)
RESTAURANT • LUNCH MODERATE, DINNER EXPENSIVE
MAP PAGE 241, #4

Behind the unremarkable façade is a retail shop and, on the second floor, a handsome, high-end restaurant specializing in Japanese beef (*wagyū*). At the restaurant indulge in *sukiyaki, shabu shabu,* or steak, always accompanied by the traditional seasonal pickles, *miso* soup, and rice.

Kizushi • 㐂寿司

Nihonbashi Ningyocho 2-7-13 • 中央区日本橋人形町2-7-13
Tel. 03-3666-1682 • 11:45—14:30, 17:00—21:30 Monday to Friday;
11:45—21:00 Saturday; closed Sunday and holidays
RESTAURANT • LUNCH MODERATE, DINNER MODERATE TO
EXPENSIVE • MAP PAGE 241, #3

The third-generation owner works with his sons behind the counter at this traditional *sushi* restaurant. The *sushi* that is served in a classic manner—not onto a plate, but placed onto the narrow counter in between the chef and diner. Eat the *sushi* with your fingers, and wipe them with the small wet napkin that is presented in a small basket. The seafood, some of which still may be alive and moving, is displayed in small refrigerated cases on straw trays. Dinner may be pricey; lunch is more affordable. Note: some of these old-style *sushi* shops have the reputation for being unfriendly, but here you will be warmly greeted and well looked after.

Uokyū · 魚久

Nihonbashi Ningyocho 1-1-20 · 中央区日本橋人形町1-1-20
Tel. 03-5695-4121 · 9:00–19:00 Monday to Friday
9:00–18:00 Saturday; closed Sunday and holidays
www.uokyu.co.jp/ (Japanese)

SHOP AND RESTAURANT · LUNCH INEXPENSIVE, DINNER
MODERATE · MAP PAGE 241, #5

Uokyū is a take-out shop and restaurant known for its seafood marinated in *sake* lees, a method not often used outside of Japan. Unlike popular *miso*, with its inherent sweetness, *sake* lees impart an aromatic and intense flavor.

Yanagiya · 柳屋

Nihonbashi Ningyocho 2-11-3 · 中央区日本橋人形町2-11-3
Tel. 03-3666-9901 · 12:30–18:00; closed Sunday

SHOP · MAP PAGE 241, #15

There is often a line here, but you won't be bored because you can watch the staff making the fish-shaped hotcakes stuffed with *azuki* beans, the iconic and only item made here. There are hundreds of shops making *taiyaki*, but this is one of the "big three" in Tokyo; the other two are **Naniwaya** and Wakaba in Yotsuya.

Tōkai · 東海

Nihonbashi Ningyocho 1-16-12 · 中央区日本橋人形町1-16-12
Tel. 03-3666-7063 · 9:00–19:00; closed Sunday and holidays

SHOP · MAP PAGE 240, #18

Japanese-style waffles folded over apricot jam are the specialty at this popular Japanese confectionary shop. The rarely found *kimishigure*, bite-size pink sweets that literally melt in your mouth, are also made here along with a small selection of other *wagashi*. Across the street is a well-stocked *nihonshu* shop.

Morinoen · 森乃園

Nihonbashi Ningyocho 2-4-9 · 中央区日本橋人形町2-4-9
Tel. 03-3667-2666
9:00–21:00 Monday to Friday;
11:00–18:00 Saturday, Sunday, and holidays
www.morinoen.co.jp/ (Japanese)

SHOP AND CAFÉ · MAP PAGE 241, #16

You can smell the *hōjicha* tea leaves roasting at Morinoen as soon as you exit the nearby train station. Brown in color, this green tea is unusual in that it is roasted. It can be served hot or cold, steeped with milk and sugar. The café on the second floor serves traditional Japanese sweets and tea.

Sōkaya • 草加屋

Nihonbashi Ningyocho 2-20-5 • 中央区日本橋人形町2-20-5

Tel. 03-3666-7378

8:00—20:00; closed Sunday

SHOP • MAP PAGE 241, #17

Sōkaya's *sembei* are sold from bamboo baskets in front of the shop. The front of the shop overlooks the workspace where you can watch the rice crackers being grilled over charcoal. The wide variety of crackers ranges from sweet to savory.

Kotobukidō • 寿堂

Nihonbashi Ningyocho 2-1-4 • 中央区日本橋人形町2-1-4

Tel. 0120-48-0400 (toll-free number in Japan)

9:00—21:00; closed Sunday

SHOP • MAP PAGE 240, #19

Only a handful of people can fit in this confection shop from which the unmistakable aroma of cinnamon wafts into the street. The signature sweet, *koganei imo*, is a small cake made from white bean paste, egg yolk, and sugar, which is then dusted with cinnamon and baked. This is primarily a take-out shop, but if you order just one of the *koganei imo*, the staff will serve it to you with a cup of tea and invite you to sit for a moment.

Itakuraya • 板蔵屋

Nihonbashi Ningyocho 2-4-2 • 中央区日本橋人形町2-4-2

Tel. 03-3667-4818

9:00—18:00; closed Sunday and holidays

www.itakuraya.com/global/ (English)

SHOP • MAP PAGE 241, #8

Look for red lanterns with black writing in front of this shop famous for its small grilled *azuki*-stuffed cakes (*ningyōyaki*). You'll find the cakes in the shape of the seven gods of fortune, fish, or pretty decorative patterns. The shop offers a large selection of sweet crackers in flavors such as black sesame, ginger, peanut, *miso*, and Japanese basil—be sure not to miss the winter specialty, gorgeous *sembei* garnished with colorful, edible flower petals (*hanaichirin*).

Shigemori Eishindō · 重盛永信堂
Nihonbashi Ningyocho 2-1-1 · 中央区日本橋人形町2-1-1
Tel. 03-3666-5885
9:00—20:00; Saturday and holidays until 17:30
closed Sunday
SHOP · MAP PAGE 240, #20

Near the Suitengu shrine, and commanding the corner with its large display of stuffed cakes and sweet crackers, is Shigemori Eishindō. Try the sweet, chewy *ningyōyaki* cakes, filled with *azuki* paste which you can see being made at the rear of the shop.

Tsukushi · つくし
Nihonbashi Ningyocho 2-1-12 · 中央区日本橋人形町2-1-12
Tel. 03-3664-7357
Daily 8:00—20:00
www.ntv.co.jp/burari/030329/info02.html (Japanese)
CAFÉ · MAP PAGE 241, #21

Although Tsukushi is a sweets café that offers a multitude of classic *azuki* confections, most Japanese go there for one of the few desserts made without *azuki* beans, the signature *purin*, a dense, rich egg custard with an intense caramel sauce, much like *crème caramel*, which is served alone or with *azuki* beans and canned fruit.

Just in front of the Suitengu shrine, look for two small candy shops. These small vintage emporiums are regarded with great nostalgia by the older generation because they sell *dagashi*, sweets and crackers that were popular in the early twentieth century.

Saruya · さるや
Nihonbashi Koamicho 18-10 · 中央区日本橋小網町18-10
Tel. 03-3666-3906
9:00—17:00; closed Sunday, holidays,
and 3rd Saturday of the month
http://www.norenkai.net/english/shop/saruya/index.html
(English)
SHOP · MAP PAGE 240, #1

A bit of a walk, but worth the effort is the only shop in Japan specializing in traditional, handcrafted toothpicks. Yes, toothpicks. And for three hundred years. The toothpicks are packaged in wooden boxes and decorative papers.

TSUKISHIMA 月島
and TSUKUDA 佃

METERS

0   100   200   300

FEET

0   300   600   900

Chuo-ku

TSUKUDA 1

2   1

① Tenyasu Honten 天安本店
② Tanakaya 田中屋

3
4

TSUKUDA OHASHI

TSUKUDA 2

TSUKISHIMA 1

MONJAYAKI STREET

1

3   4

Okame Hyottoko Ten
おかめひょっとこ店

6   5   **③**   9

18   TSUKISHIMA 3

17   Hazama はざま   10

④   11

⑤   12

Monja Kondō Honten
もんじゃ近どう本店

5   16   13

14

TSUKISHIMA 4

Tsukishima

sukishima

KIYOSUME DORI

TSUKISHIMA 2

TSUKISHIMA AND TSUKUDA

月島   佃

TSUKISHIMA AND TSUKUDA ARE ON AN ISLAND IN THE SUMIDAGAWA RIVER WHERE IT FLOWS INTO TOKYO BAY. This neighborhood is a short walk from Tsukiji Market.

The Monjayaki Association has a stand near the exit of the subway station where you can pick up a map of the area. If you know where you want to go, the people manning the stand can direct you there but don't rely on them for recommendations.

Tsukishima near Tsukiji is one of the few places where you can find the local Tokyo dish *monjayaki* that is similar to the more famous *okonomiyaki* of Osaka, but is based on a thinner batter. Diners cook their own *monjayaki* and eat the thin, crisp, savory pancake right off of the iron grill (*teppan*) with a small, metal spatula. The setting lends itself to drinking beer or other chilled drinks to keep cool as you cook the sizzling entrée. You probably won't find this local specialty outside of this neighborhood.

Have the wait staff make the first *monjayaki* for you to demonstrate how it is done. There are many variations. A popular combination is spicy cod roe (*mentaiko*), sticky rice taffy (*mochi*), and cheese. An Italian version would be tomatoes, cheese, and pesto; a Korean version may include *kimchi* and thin sliced pork. Inquire if the restaurant has any original recipes—that's bound to be the best.

The best time to come is in the evening as the main street, Nishi Naka Dori Shōtengai, is closed off to cars making it easy to carefully peruse the shops before deciding on one. Most of the restaurants have low tables with *tatami* mats but if you don't want to sit on the floor, there are restaurants with tables and chairs. Not all of the places are comfortable with non-Japanese speakers, so in selecting a shop, choose one that extends a warm welcome.

All these addresses are in Chuo-ku 中央区.

Monja Kondō Honten • もんじゃ近どう本店
Tsukishima 3-12-10 • 中央区月島3-12-10
Tel. 03-3533-4555 • Daily 17:00—22:00
RESTAURANT • INEXPENSIVE • MAP PAGE 249, #5

Kondō is one of the original *monjayaki* shops. Recommended is the *mochi*, cheese, and *mentaiko monjayaki*.

Okame Hyottoko Ten ∙ おかめひょっとこ店
Tsukishima 3-8-10 ∙ 中央区月島3-8-10
Tel. 03-5548-1508 ∙ Daily 11:00—22:00; closed holidays
RESTAURANT ∙ INEXPENSIVE ∙ MAP PAGE 249, #3

Okame Hyottoko is open for lunch if you come during the day.
The friendly staff can help you navigate more than one hundred
options. Okame has two other shops in the area; if this one is full,
ask them to direct you to the other ones.

Hazama ∙ はざま
Tsukishima 3-17-18 ∙ 中央区月島3-17-18
Tel. 03-3534-1279 ∙ Daily 12:00—22:00; closed holidays
RESTAURANT ∙ INEXPENSIVE ∙ MAP PAGE 249, #4

Hazama, located on one of the side streets is tiny and very popular. The seafood comes from Tsukiji, minutes away, and so is very fresh. The signature dish, *Hazamamonja*, is filled with seafood like scallops, shrimp, squid, and octopus. There are other items on the menu in addition to *monjayaki* including grilled tuna steaks (*maguro sute-ki*).

This neighborhood is known for another Tokyo speciality that is eaten throughout Japan but originated here. Down the street, in the area known as Tsukuda, you will find purveyors of the intensely flavored sweet, soy-simmered seafood or sea vegetables called *Tsukudani*. Popular *Tsukudani* include clams (*asari*), tiny anchovies (*shirasu*), tiny shrimp (*ami*), kelp (*kombu*), and shrimp (*ebi*), best enjoyed with a hot bowl of rice.

Tenyasu Honten ・ 天安本店
Tsukuda 1-3-14 ・ 中央区佃1-3-14
Tel. 03-3531-3457 ・ Daily 9:00–18:00; closed holidays
www.tenyasu.jp/ (Japanese)
SHOP ・ MAP PAGE 249, #1

This specialty food shop, housed in an old two-story building, on the banks of the Sumidagawa River, was founded in 1837.

Tanakaya ・ 田中屋
Tsukuda 1-3-13 ・ 中央区佃1-3-13
Tel. 03-3531-2649 ・ 9:30–17:30 Monday to Saturday;
10:00–17:00 Sunday and holidays
SHOP ・ MAP PAGE 249, #2

Next door to Tenyasu is Tanakaya, another purveyor of *Tsukudani*.

There are many types of *Tsukudani* (佃煮); these are some of the more common ones:

Ami Tiny opossum shrimp
Anago Conger eel
Asari Littleneck clams
Ebi Shrimp
Funa Prussian carp
Hamaguri Orient clam
Hoshi shiitake Dried *shiitake*
Hotate Scallops
Ikanago Sand lance
Inago Locust
Kaki Oysters
Koayu Baby sweetfish
Koi Carp
Kombu Kelp
Konago Sand eel
Kurumi konago Walnuts and sand eel
Nori Laver
Shijimi Corbicula clam
Shirauo Japanese icefish
Unagi Freshwater eel
Wakasagi Japanese smelt

14

← HARAJUKU STATION (50m.)

❶
13 12 *10* *8*
Kyūshū Jangara Ramen 九州じゃんがららーめん

32
27

JINGUMAE 1
9
11 *28* *24*
31 *26* *25* *21*

JINGUMAE 6
30 *20*
29 *OMOTESANDO*

4
3
5 *2*
10 *6* *7* *1* **Omotesando Ukai-tei**
9 **❸ 表参道うかい亭**
Harajuku Mizuho 原宿瑞穂 ❷ *10* **❹**
11 *8* **Omotesando Hills**
表参道ヒルズ

12 *13* *11* *8*
14 *12* *9*
17 *15* *17* *16* *13* **JINGUMAE 5**
16 *6*

18 *15* *Tenrism*
Shrine
25 *21* *14* *5*
27 *24* *19* *39*
26 *20* *41* *4*
28 *22* *40* *3*
31 *23* *42* *45*
33 *36* *44* *46*
37 *43* *47* *48*
35 *38*

34

Shibuya-ku

5

53 **Kyō Hayashiya 京はやしや ⑬**
52

SHIBUYA 1

AOYAMA DORI

OMOTESANDO 表参道

METERS

0 .... 100 .... 200 300

FEET

0 .... 300 .... 600 900

JINGUMAE 3

23

17

16

15

7

JINGUMAE 4

14

8

6

5

Maisen まい泉

5

13

9

1

10

4

11

6 Niigata Kan Nesupasu 新潟館ネスパス

3

7 Ginza Natsuno Aoyama Ten 銀座夏野青山店

2

Zenkoji (temple)

Omote-Sando

KITA-AOYAMA 3

11

12

KOBAN

13

MINAMI-AOYAMA 3

1

Omote-Sando/Omote-Sando

18

8

14

Qu'il Fait Bon

HIGASHIYA man

9

17

1

Prada (shop) •

MINAMI-AOYAMA 5

2

10 Yanmo やんも

3

11

50

5

Yoku Moku

NATIONAL ROAD #246

9

Pierre Hermé ピエール・エルメ

7

4

10

8

KOTTO DORI

Minato-ku

HIBUYA 4

11

OMOTESANDO
表参道

OMOTESANDO IS THE HIGH-END SHOPPING DISTRICT WHERE YOU WILL NOT ONLY FIND LADIES WHO LUNCH after shopping in international luxury boutiques, but also young girls who dress in frilly, lacy Lolita-crossed-with-Goth-Little-Bo-Peep style carefully perusing the shops on the famous Takeshita Dōri side street in the adjacent neighborhood Harajuku. Many Japanese fashion designers are present, too, including Issey Miyake and Rei Kawakubo of Comme des Garçons. While you're in the neighborhood, you may want to visit Meiji Jingu Shrine. Architects come to check out Herzog & de Mueron's Prada building and Tadao Ando's Omotesando Hills complex. Kiddyland is a popular shop for the latest gadgets, toys, electronics, and Hello Kitty trinkets.

Niigata Kan Nesupasu • 新潟館ネスパス
Shibuya-ku, Jingumae 4-11-7 • 渋谷区神宮前4-11-7
Tel. 03-5771-7711 • Daily 10:30–19:30
www.nico.or.jp/nespace/index.html (Japanese)
SHOP • MAP PAGE 255, #6

Just behind the impressive Omotesando Hills is the antenna shop of Niigata prefecture. The shop has an impressive selection of local *sake* and *sake*-friendly snacks, many made from seafood, and the rice, *soba*, and seafood that the region is known for. There is a restaurant in the basement if you want to try some of the local *sake* and food.

Kyō Hayashiya • 京はやしや
Shibuya-ku, Jingumae 5-52-2, O-baru Building B1
渋谷区神宮前5-52-2オーバルビルB1
Tel. 03-3498-8700 • Daily 11:30–22:00
CAFÉ • MAP PAGE 254, #13

This ultra-modern and sleek café with a luminous white, minimalist interior serves traditional Japanese desserts based on *mattcha*, soy bean powder and black sugar syrup. You'll also find stylish fusion sweets such as *mattcha* financiers, *mattcha* crème caramel, and a marron glacés *mattcha* parfait.

Yanmo • やんも

Minato-ku, Minami Aoyama 5-5-25, T Place Building B1

港区南青山5-5-25, B1

Tel. 03-5466-0636 • 11:30—13:30 Monday to Friday;

12:00—14:00 Saturday and holidays; 18:00—21:30 Monday to

Saturday and holidays; closed Sunday

www.yanmo.co.jp (Japanese)

RESTAURANT • LUNCH INEXPENSIVE, DINNER MODERATE •

MAP PAGE 255, #10

Located on a backstreet behind Comme des Garçons, this shop attracts smartly dressed staff from the fashion boutiques as well as area salarymen. The waters off the Izu peninsula provide fresh fish that is featured daily on the simple menu. You'll find the day's catch prepared a variety of ways including *sashimi*, *miso*-marinated, or grilled, served with soup, rice, and side dishes. Although it is in the basement, a part of the restaurant overlooks a small garden. There is a counter where you can watch the chefs as they prepare the fish.

Maisen • まい泉

Shibuya-ku, Jingumae 4-85 • 渋谷区神宮前4-85

Tel. 03-3470-0071 • Daily 11:00—10:30

http://mai-sen.com/ (Japanese)

RESTAURANT • INEXPENSIVE • MAP PAGE 255, #5

Tokyoites love Maisen's panko-crusted and deep-fried pork cutlets (*tonkatsu*). The menu includes different pork cuts, shrimp, and croquettes. If you are not in the mood for something fried, try the ginger-flavored stir-fry pork (*shōgayaki*). The long line at this large restaurant usually moves quickly. There is a take-away stand in front of the shop.

HIGASHIYA man

Minato-ku, Minami Aoyama 3-17-14 • 港区南青山3-17-14
Tel. 03-5414-3881 • Daily 10:00—20:00
www.higashiya.com/e/man/index.html (English)

SHOP • MAP PAGE 255, #9

This tiny and stylish steamed-buns (*manju*) shop is a branch
of the popular Higashiya confectionary shop that specializes in
updated *wagashi* including interesting items like roasted tea
crème caramel and green tea *blanc manger*. The shop offers a
tempting selection of seasonal sweets, pictured and described in
a month-by-month calendar on the website.

Kyushu Jangara Ramen • 九州じゃんがららーめん

Shibuya-ku, Jingumae 1-13-21 • 渋谷区神宮前1-13-21
Tel. 03-3404-5405 • Daily 10:45 a.m.–2:00 a.m.
www.kyusyujangara.co.jp/ (Japanese)

RESTAURANT • INEXPENSIVE • MAP PAGE 254, #1

Order a bowl of *tonkotsu*, a thick, dense pork-bone broth with thin
noodles topped with a hard-boiled egg, tender pork, and bamboo

shoots—you'll find the shop filled with young kids from the neighborhood slurping up this quick, inexpensive, and satisfying ramen. The addition of spicy cod roe (*mentaiko*) to the hearty bowl will add another rich layer of flavor.

Yoku Moku
Minato-ku, Minami-Aoyama 5-3-3 • 港区南青山5-3-3
Tel. 03-5485-3330 • Daily 10:00–18:30
www.yokumoku.co.jp/store/aoyama-honten.html (Japanese)
SHOP AND CAFÉ • MAP PAGE 255, #11

If you missed the Yoku Moku boutique at *depachika*, it's not too late to pick up an assortment of sweets, much loved by the Japanese as hostess gifts, packaged in a tin or wrapper printed with seasonal motifs such as autumn leaves or cherry blossoms. At the newly renovated café, the Blue Brick Lounge, you can also have coffee or tea with a slice of cake or pick up a bite-size pastry to go.

Harajuku Mizuho • 原宿瑞穂
Shibuya-ku, Jingumae 6-8-7 • 渋谷区神宮前6-8-7
Tel. 03-3400-5483
8:30–18:00 (or until quantities last); closed Sunday
SHOP • MAP PAGE 254, #2

Mame daifuku is the signature item here, and it is considered to be among the best in the city. *Mame daifuku* is a delicate layer of sticky rice studded with beans surrounding smooth and not-too-sweet *azuki* paste. The shop closes when everything is sold out—go early.

Omotesando Ukai-tei • 表参道うかい亭

Shibuya-ku, Jingumae 5-10-1, Omotesando Gyre 5F

渋谷区神宮前5-10-1表参道ジャイル5F

Tel. 03-5467-5252 • 12:00–14:30, 17:30–21:00 Monday to Friday;
12:00–21:00 weekends and holidays

www.omotesando-ukaitei.jp (English)

RESTAURANT • LUNCH EXPENSIVE, DINNER EXPENSIVE TO
VERY EXPENSIVE • MAP PAGE 254, #3

Plan on two hours for lunch or dinner at this luxurious *teppanyaki* restaurant with opulent Western décor—no expense spared, no detail overlooked, no accoutrement too elaborate. There is a cocktail terrace overlooking the city, private rooms with a personal chef, and a menu that includes top-quality Japanese beef (*wagyū*), seasonal seafood, and a separate dessert lounge.

Omotesando Hills • 表参道ヒルズ

Shibuya-ku, Jingumae 4-12-10, Omotesando Hills

渋谷区神宮前4-12-10表参道ヒルズ

www.omotesandohills.com/english/ (English)

RESTAURANTS, SHOPS, CAFÉS • INEXPENSIVE TO MODERATE
MAP PAGE 254, #4

There are several interesting shops in this shopping complex designed by Tadao Ando, including the restaurant Yasaiya Mei, where vegetables take center stage. Toraya Café is a sleek eatery serving modern *wagashi* including a cake made from *azuki* beans and cocoa, a soymilk and *mattcha* pudding, and other sweets that marry East and West. R style by Ryoguchiya Korekiyo is another creative confectionary café where you'll find, among other delicacies, a blossoming "flower" of cream cheese and *azuki*; or, cook a skewer of rice taffy balls (*amiyaki dango*) on a small tabletop grill. The parent company, Ryoguchiya Korekiyo, has been producing *wagashi* since 1634. Last but not least, don't miss Hasegawa Saketen, a small *sake* shop with a standing bar serving small *sake*-friendly bites.

Ginza Natsuno Aoyama Ten • 銀座夏野青山店

Shibuya-ku, Jingumae 4-2-17 • 渋谷区神宮前4-2-17

Tel. 03-3403-6033 • 10:00–20:00 Monday to Saturday;
10:00–19:00 Sunday and holidays

www.e-ohashi.com/natsuno/index.html (Japanese)

SHOP • MAP PAGE 255, #7

A branch of the chopsticks shop in Ginza (see page 187).

Shinjuku Hormone 新宿ホルモン11 **①**

SHINJUKU 2

SHINJUKU DORI

Saiseisakaba 再生酒場 **②**

Shinjuku Gyoen National Garden

Isetan 伊勢丹 **③**

Tempura Tsunahachi 天ぷらつな八 **④**
Tonkatsu Santa とんかつ 三太 **⑤**

SHINJUKU 3 **⑥**

Takano 高野

SHINJUKU 4

SENDAGAYA 5

Takashimaya 髙島屋 **⑦**
Tōkyū Hands 東急ハンズ **⑧**

SHINJUKU STATION

Kinokuniya 紀伊國屋書店 (bookstore)

KOSHU-KAIDO

Odakyū **⑨**

Keio **⑩**

Hiroshima Yume Terasu
広島ゆめてらす
Shinjuku Sazan Terrace
⑪ ⑫
Shinjuku Miyazaki Kan KONNE
新宿みやざき館KONNE

Shinjuku

Shibuya-ku

YOYOGI 2

SHINJUKU 新宿

METERS
0 · 100 · 200 · 300

FEET
0 · 300 · 600 · 900

NISHI-SHINJUKU 1

Shinjuku-ku

FUREAI DORI

Tokyo Metropolitan Government Office

YOYOGI 3

NISHI-SHINJUKU 3

⑬ Park Hyatt Tokyo
パークハイアット東京

SHINJUKU

新宿

SHINJUKU IS KNOWN FOR ITS SKYSCRAPERS THAT ARE HOME TO MANY HOTELS SUCH AS THE PARK Hyatt Tokyo, Keio Plaza, Hyatt Regency, and Hilton Tokyo. It is also the home to Tocho, Tokyo's Metropolitan Government Towers—and to the Kabukicho red-light district. The area has a very modern feeling, and though it lacks the charm of historic Asakusa and other older parts of the city, Shinjuku should not be missed, if only to visit the food hall (*depachika*) at Isetan department store.

Shinjuku has a starring role in Sofia Coppola's film *Lost in Translation*, which was filmed in the area. But what really shines in the movie is the Park Hyatt Tokyo, where many of the scenes take place. The hotel has several good restaurants and offers unparalleled views of the city. If the weather is good, go during the day and have lunch on Chef Kenichiro Oe's classical Japanese cuisine at Kozue. If you are on a budget, have a drink at the Peak Bar and Lounge from which you have the same breathtaking vista. Both of these restaurants have a bird's-eye view of Mount Fuji when the weather is clear. Alternatively, go in the evening and have dinner or drinks at the New York Bar and Grill, where the city sparkles below you and you can indulge in a simply-grilled *wagyū* steak.

Shinjuku is also a large commuting hub, with subway and rail lines extending out towards the western suburbs. Shinjuku station is the busiest in the world: more than 3.5 million commuters pass through its thirteen lines daily. Trying to navigate the crowds during rush hour can be intimidating, and leaving the station by the wrong exit can also be a source of frustration. Avoid both by familiarizing yourself with the exit closest to your destination, and by traveling during non-peak times, if possible.

See the chapter on *depachika* for **Isetan** and **Takashimaya**.

Park Hyatt Tokyo • パークハイアット東京
Shinjuku-ku, Nishi-Shinjuku 3-7-1-2 • 新宿区西新宿3-7-1-2
Tel. 03-5322-1234 • See hours of operation on website for each restaurant (hours differ).
http://tokyo.park.hyatt.com/ (English)
BAR AND RESTAURANT • MODERATE TO EXPENSIVE (SEE ABOVE)
MAP PAGE 263, #13

Tonkatsu Santa • とんかつ 三太
Shinjuku-ku, Shinjuku 3-33-10 • 新宿区新宿3-33-10
Tel. 03-3351-5861
11:30–14:00, 17:00–21:30 Tuesday to Friday;
11:30–21:30 Saturday, Sunday, and holidays;
if Monday is a holiday, the store will be open,
and closed on Tuesday.
www.shinjuku.or.jp/kirin/washoku/santa/ (Japanese)
RESTAURANT • INEXPENSIVE • MAP PAGE 263, #5

Tonkatsu Santa has a following for its deep-fried pork *tonkatsu*, breaded with an unusual *panko* (Japanese bread crumbs): rather than flakes, the bread is julienned. The counter seating on the first floor is great for watching the staff expertly slice cabbage for salad and cook the crisp golden pork morsels.

Tempura Tsunahachi • 天ぷらつな八
Shinjuku-ku, Shinjuku 3-31-8 • 新宿区新宿3-31-8
Tel. 03-3352-1012
Daily 11:30–22:30
www.tunahachi.co.jp/ (Japanese)
RESTAURANT • LUNCH INEXPENSIVE, DINNER INEXPENSIVE
TO MODERATE • MAP PAGE 263, #4

Tempura Tsunahachi has been the favored local *tempura* spot in Shinjuku since 1924. The old building it is housed in, feels a bit out of place in this modern part of the city. The best seats are at the counter, where you can watch the seasonal ingredients dipped into batter and deep-fried. Tsunahachi has seven other branches in the Shinjuku area, but this, the original store, has the most character.

Takano • 高野
Shinjuku-ku, Shinjuku 3-26-11 • 新宿区新宿3-26-11
Tel. 03-5368-5147
Daily 10:00–20:00 (fruit shop);
Daily 11:00–20:30 (fruit restaurant)
http://takano.jp/ (Japanese)
RESTAURANT • INEXPENSIVE • MAP PAGE 263, #6

Takano Fruits is spread over several floors. One floor is dedicated to fruit baskets and whole fruits intended to be given as gifts, including a tiny room dedicated to melons, some of which cost hundreds of dollars. The staff will graciously explain the method used to cultivate the flawless orbs. Another floor displays fruit parfaits, cakes, and individual desserts, and includes

a counter where you may enjoy a glass of freshly squeezed juice, or a fruit platter. The other floors house a restaurant where full-course meals based on seasonal fruit are served. These unique meals, comprised of sweet and savory courses, are a must for fruit lovers.

Shinjuku Miyazaki Kan KONNE
新宿みやざき館KONNE

Shibuya-ku, Yoyogi 2-2-1, Shinjuku Sazan Terrace
渋谷区代々木2-2-1新宿サザンテラス内
Tel. 03-5333-7764 • Daily 11:00—21:00
Station: Shinjuku JR Station's Minami Guchi (South Exit)
www.konne.jp/ (Japanese)
SHOP • MAP PAGE 263, #12

This shop sells food specialties from Miyazaki, on the southern island of Kyushu, a region known for its pork, chicken, and *shōchū*. The casual café features charcoal-grilled chicken, a chilled *miso* soup, and tender, braised Berkshire pork. There is a wide variety of *shōchū*, including limited-releases that are available for sale on the first day of each month. Pickles, sweets, fruit, tea, and barley *miso* are also some of what you will find here.

Hiroshima Yume Terasu • 広島ゆめてらす

Shibuya-ku, Yoyogi 2-2-1, Shinjuku Sazan Terrace
渋谷区代々木2-2-1新宿サザンテラス内
Tel. 03-5354-3206 • 11:00—21:00 Monday to Saturday;
Sunday and holidays until 20:30
www.pref.hiroshima.lg.jp/tokyo/ (Japanese)
SHOP • MAP PAGE 263, #11

This is the regional products shop of Hiroshima prefecture. Select among local *sake*, fish products, and *miso*. The restaurant's offerings include popular dishes like *Hiroshimayaki* (two thin savory pancakes surrounding stir fried noodles).

Saiseisakaba • 再生酒場

Shinjuku-ku, Shinjuku 3-7-3, Marunaka Building 1st floor
新宿区新宿3-7-3丸中ビル
Tel. 03-3354-4829 • Daily 17:00—24:00
www.ishii-world.jp/brand/motsu/nihonsaisei/shinjuku3/
(Japanese)
BAR AND RESTAURANT • INEXPENSIVE TO MODERATE
MAP PAGE 263, #2

You'll find this friendly standing bar (*tachinomi*) on the back streets of Shinjuku Sanchome—and since it's designed with items from the fifties, entering the bar feels like stepping back in time. The shop specializes in grilled innards, and, because they're so fresh, some are available *sashimi*-style (raw brains are creamy, and the boiled tongue is tender). If you can, grab a spot at the counter and notice how vigilant the staff is at keeping cutting boards spotless. You can also watch everything being grilled as well as see what's coming out of the kitchen (including the young, handsome men on staff).

Shinjuku Hormone • 新宿ホルモン
Shinjuku-ku, Shinjuku 3-12-3 • 新宿区新宿3-12-3
Tel. 03-3353-4129
Daily 17:00—24:00
www.ishii-world.jp/brand/motsu/shinjuku-horumon/
shinjukuhoru/ (Japanese)
BAR AND RESTAURANT • INEXPENSIVE TO MODERATE
MAP PAGE 263, #1

Shinjuku Hormone and Saiseisakaba are both part of a chain of restaurants managed by Ishii Group. They are *the* specialists in offal (*naizō*), evident by the top-quality products served, the knowledgeable staff, and the wide variety of items on the menus.

If you like to cook, you'll love the experience here. Each party has its own charcoal stove to grill the offal. If you are adventurous, here you can try *pai* (teat) or *sao* (tip of the penis).

Tōkyū Hands • 東急ハンズ
Shibuya-ku, Sendagaya 5-24-2, Times Square Building
渋谷区千駄ヶ谷5-24-2タイムズスクエアビル
Tel. 03-5361-3111
Daily 10:00—20:30 (no regular holiday, but may close
once a month, call ahead)
http://shinjuku.tokyu-hands.co.jp/ (Japanese)
SHOP • MAP PAGE 263, #8

Tōkyū Hands offers a wide variety of items for the home. There is a vast selection of modestly priced kitchenware and housewares, including *bentō* boxes in every shape, size, and color; chopsticks in fabric sleeves; and myriad pots, pans, and gadgets. Tōkyū Hands is located in the same building as Takashimaya department store.

KAGURAZAKA

神楽坂

ONE OF THE MOST CHARMING PARTS OF THE CITY IS KAGURAZAKA. THE NARROW STREETS WITH COBBLED stones are reminiscent of some parts of Kyoto. There is a chance that you will see a geisha on one of the side streets—this is still an entertainment district. The neighborhood is sometimes referred to as Petit Paris with *crêperies*, *fromageries*, bistros, and wine bars dotting the streets. You'll also find several high-end *kaiseki* restaurants such as Ishikawa and Toyoda, as well as Tenko, a top-class, famous *tempura* establishment. The main street leads up to Bishamonten temple on the left, marked by the red gate and a row of white lanterns.

All the addresses listed here are in Shinjuku-ku 新宿区.

Fujiya ⬩ 不二家
Kagurazaka 1-12 ⬩ 新宿区神楽坂1-12
Tel. 03-3269-1526 ⬩ 10:00—22:00 Monday to Friday;
11:30—19:00 weekends and holidays
www.fujiya-peko.co.jp (Japanese)
SHOP AND CAFÉ ⬩ MAP PAGE 273, #1

This branch is the only shop in Japan where you can purchase a small, soft, cookie in the shape of Pekochan, the darling mascot of the Fujiya sweets chain. Customers are usually grannies or mothers with children lined up outside the shop, waiting to buy this tidbit filled with *azuki*, chocolate, or seasonal flavors like mango or *mattcha*. The windows allow you to watch the cakes being made as you wait. Not a gastronomic mecca, to say the least, this café serves a simple menu including Japanese-style hamburgers, pasta, and desserts, and provides an amusing glimpse of Japanese culture.

Kinozen ⬩ 紀の善
Kagurazaka 1-12 ⬩ 新宿区神楽坂1-12
Tel. 03-3269-2920
11:00—21:00 Monday to Saturday; 12:00—18:00 Sunday and holidays; closed 3rd Sunday of the month
SHOP AND CAFÉ ⬩ MAP PAGE 273, #2

Located next door to Fujiya, Kinozen too often has a line out the door, patiently waiting to be seated and order from the menu of traditional Japanese sweets. The one foray into modernism is the *mattcha babaloa*, similar to *panna cotta*, made from *mattcha*, topped with chunky *azuki* and whipped cream—a nice ensemble of flavors and textures. In summer, the shaved ice colored with flavored syrups (*kakigōri*) offers a respite from the heat and humidity.

Kintokiya ▪ きんときや
Kagurazaka 2-10 ▪ 新宿区神楽坂2-10
Tel. 03-3260-4151
10:00–20:00; Sunday and holidays until 19:00
www.kintokiya.com (Japanese)
SHOP ▪ MAP PAGE 273, #3

This tiny Japanese sweets shop has items made with sweet potatoes and with chestnuts. In summer, try the purple sweet potato ice cream. There are also some classic sweets on the menu, including *azuki* bean cakes and skewers of sticky rice balls with drizzled toppings.

KAGURAZAKA 神楽坂

Ushigome-Koagurazaka

Kagurazaka

IWATOCHO

Shinjuku-ku

Baikatei 梅花亭 ⑩
KAGURAZAKA 6

OKUBO DORI

FUKUROMACHI

Isuzu 五十鈴 ⑨
Genpin Fugu 玄品ふぐ料理 ⑧ KAGURAZAKA 5

⑦ Fukuya 福屋

Bishamonten temple
(Zenkokuji)

⑥ Rakuzan 楽山
KAGURAZAKA 4
⑤
Kagurazaka 50ban 神楽坂五十番

WAKAMIYACHO

④ Futaba 二葉

WASEDA (KAGURAZAKA) DORI

KAGURAZAKA
3

KAGURAZAKA 2

TSUKUDOCHO

SOTOBORI DORI

③ Kintokiya きんときや
② Kinozen 紀の善
① Fujiya 不二家

AGEBACHO

KAGURAZAKA I

Chiyoda-ku

KAGURAGASHI

Iidabashi

Iidabashi

IIDABASHI
STATION

METERS
0   100   200   300

FEET
0   300   600   900

Futaba • 二葉
Kagurazaka 3-2, K Building • 新宿区神楽坂3-2Kビル
Tel. 03-3260-0853
11:30–13:30, 17:30–21:30; closed Sunday and holidays
RESTAURANT • LUNCH INEXPENSIVE, DINNER MODERATE TO
EXPENSIVE • MAP PAGE 273, #4

On the side street is Futaba, famous for its "scattered" *sushi* (*bara chirashi-zushi*), in which *sushi* ingredients are cut into small pieces and served over rice in a bowl. Sixteen ingredients, which change seasonally, are presented in one bowl and may include abalone, shrimp, tuna, salmon roe, eel, squid, egg, Japanese basil, pickles, and ginger among them.

Kagurazaka 50ban • 神楽坂五十番
Kagurazaka 3-2 • 新宿区神楽坂3-2
Tel. 03-3260-0066
9:00–23:00; Sunday and holidays until 22:00
www.50ban.com (Japanese)
SHOP AND RESTAURANT • INEXPENSIVE
MAP PAGE 273, #5

The lines at the top of the hill prove the popularity of the savory and sweet steamed buns (*chūkaman*) that are a specialty of 50ban. Choose among two dozen types that include shrimp, pork, scallops, cheese, and curry, as well as sweet varieties such as custard or coconut.

Rakuzan • 楽山
Kagurazaka 4-3 • 新宿区神楽坂4-3
Tel. 03-3260-340 • 19:00–20:00; closed Sunday
www.rakuzan.co.jp (Japanese)
SHOP • MAP PAGE 273, #6

This gorgeous tea shop is lined with shelves packed with tea, cups, pots, and storage tins. Traditional music plays in the background. There is a small area to relax while you sample a cup of green tea. The colorful window display celebrates the changing seasons.

Fukuya • 福屋
Kagurazaka 4-2 • 新宿区神楽坂4-2
Tel. 03-3269-3388
10:00–20:00, Saturday until 18:00; closed Sunday and holidays
www.kagurazaka.net/shiga/fukuyatennai.mov
SHOP • MAP PAGE 273, #7

This small cracker shop across the street from the Bishamonten temple offers *sembei*, hand-roasted and dipped in soy sauce. The modern shop has a restrained and somber look. There are small packs of bite-size crackers, sweet, deep-fried crackers, and thin *ususembei*.

Isuzu • 五十鈴
Kagurazaka 5-34 • 新宿区神楽坂5-34
Tel. 03-3269-0081
9:00—20:00; closed Sunday and holidays
http://shinjukuku-kushouren.net/itten/isuzu/ (Japanese)
SHOP • MAP PAGE 273, #9

There is a confection here to satisfy every sweet tooth: sweet beans (*amanattō*), chestnuts, and soft pastry shells filled with raisins and *azuki* or walnuts and white bean paste, as well as a changing menu of seasonal sweets.

Baikatei • 梅花亭
Kagurazaka 6-15 • 新宿区神楽坂6-15
Tel. 03-5228-0727
Daily 10:00—19:30
www.baikatei.co.jp (Japanese)
SHOP • MAP PAGE 273, #10

This small shop displays its skillfully handcrafted sweets—flower motifs in vibrant pastels—on antique dressers. Look for *ume monaka*, delicate crispy wafers in the shape of plum blossoms. Also featured is *dorayaki*, an unusual waffle-style pastry filled with *azuki* paste.

Genpin Fugu • 玄品ふぐ料理
Kagurazaka 5-35 • 新宿区神楽坂5-35
Tel. 03-5225-3029
12:00—14:00, 16:30—22:00 Monday to Friday;
12:00—22:00 weekends and holidays
www.tettiri.com/(Japanese)
RESTAURANT • LUNCH INEXPENSIVE, DINNER MODERATE
MAP PAGE 273, #8

Genpin Fugu is a restaurant chain that specializes in *fugu* cuisine (see page 96). The décor is basic, the main event here is the poisonous puffer fish, which is prepared in a variety of ways: sashimi, grilled, deep-fried, and hot pot–style. The chain has many branches throughout the city, all reliable.

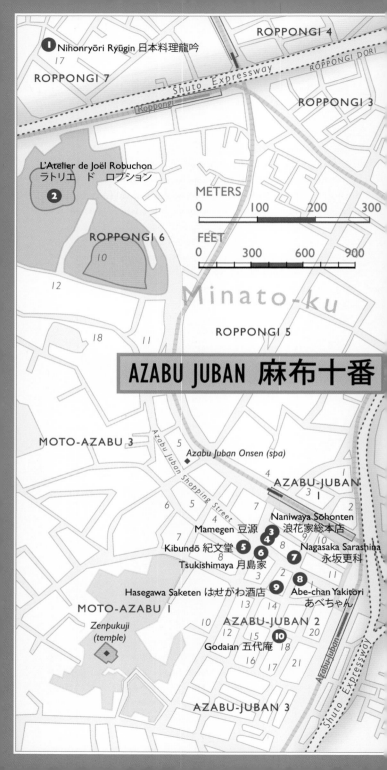

❶ Nihonryōri Ryūgin 日本料理龍吟
17

ROPPONGI 7

ROPPONGI 4

Shuto Expressway

ROPPONGI DORI

Roppongi

ROPPONGI 3

L'Atelier de Joël Robuchon
ラトリエ ド ロブション
❷

METERS
0   100   200   300

ROPPONGI 6

10

FEET
0   300   600   900

12

Minato-ku

18   *11*

ROPPONGI 5

AZABU JUBAN 麻布十番

MOTO-AZABU 3

Azabu Juban Shopping Street

5   Azabu Juban Onsen (spa)

4   AZABU-JUBAN

6   *5*   *7*   *3*   *1*

1   *2*

Naniwaya Sōhonten
浪花家総本店

4   Mamegen 豆源 **❸**
❹   *8*   Nagasaka Sarashina
永坂更科

Kibundō 紀文堂 **❺**
8   **❻**   *3*   *9*   *10*

Tsukishimaya 月島家   *2*   *11*

Hasegawa Saketen はせがわ酒店   **❾**   **❽**
13   *14*   Abe-chan Yakitori
あべちゃん

MOTO-AZABU 1

Zenpukuji
(temple)

10   AZABU-JUBAN 2   *20*

12   *15*   *18*
Godaian 五代庵   **❿**

16   *17*   *21*

AZABU-JUBAN 3

Shuto Expressway

Azabu-Juban

AZABU JUBAN
麻布十番

AZABU JUBAN IS A MODERN NEIGHBORHOOD IN THE HEART OF THE CITY WITH A FEW POCKETS OF FOOD shops that make for a fun afternoon of grazing. It is also home to the city's famed Azabu Juban *onsen*, so if you need to soak in the hot springs, this is the place to do so (Minato-ku, Azabu-Juban 1-5-22). Azabu Juban hosts a popular festival (Azabu Juban *matsuri*), usually held in late August, filled with international food booths. Azabu Juban is an easy neighborhood to navigate. All the addresses here are in Minato-ku 港区.

Godaian · 五代庵
Azabu-Juban 2-18-11, Park Azabu Juban Building
港区麻布十番2-18-11
Tel. 03-6436-9119 · 10:00—19:00; closed Wednesday
www.godaiume.co.jp/ (Japanese)
SHOP · MAP PAGE 276, #10

This temple to *umeboshi* is dedicated to the bite-size pickled apricots, often referred to mistakenly as pickled plums. *Umeboshi* often garnish a bowl of hot rice, or are added to a rice ball. (*Umeboshi* is sometimes placed on rice in a *bentō* box, the small red circular pickle on a rectangular field of white symbolizing the Japanese flag.) Originally established in Wakayama prefecture, this tenth-generation shop has several boutiques around the city; this is one of the most beautiful. What makes Godaian's unique is that they are pickled twice, a process that results in a tender, soft, and not too tart or salty *umeboshi*.

Abe-chan • あべちゃん
Azabu-Juban 2-1-1 • 港区麻布十番2-1-1
Tel. 03-3451-5825
11:30–13:00, 15:00–21:30; closed Sunday
www.ehills.co.jp/rp/dfw/EHILLS/townguide/
lunch/116abechan.php (Japanese)
RESTAURANT • INEXPENSIVE • MAP PAGE 276, #8

This second generation shop opened in 1934. The shop is famous for its tender, stewed offal (*nikomi*) as well as grilled chicken skewers (*yakitori*). The dipping sauce for the *yakitori* is a "descendant" of the original sauce; that is, each day, the sauce is replenished with the ingredients for the original recipe. The pot has never been emptied, only added to. At the front of the shop, you can see the large pot, a source of great pride for the owner, Abe-chan.

Lunch is a bargain for *yakitori don* (*yakitori* on a bowl of hot rice) or *nikomi teishoku* (the set lunch menu with the signature *nikomi*). Dinner fills up quickly with salarymen and locals. The grill, set up at the front window wafting charcoal smoke into the street, lures customers in. If the restaurant is full, you will be directed to a sister shop just around the corner.

Nagasaka Sarashina • 永坂更科
Azabu-Juban 1-8-7 • 港区麻布十番1-8-7
Tel. 03-3585-1676
11:30–20:00; Sunday and holidays until 19:00
www.nagasakasarasina.co.jp (Japanese)
RESTAURANT • INEXPENSIVE • MAP PAGE 276, #7

The bamboo-slatted doors and the red *noren* (banner) with white lettering mark the entrance to Nagasaka Sarashina. This nineteenth-century *soba* shop is famous for pure, white *sarashina* noodles. Unlike most *soba* noodles that are brown and earthy, *sarashina* are made from buckwheat that is polished to the core, resulting in silky noodles. The basic cold noodles (*mori soba*) are served with two dipping sauces, sweet (*amakuchi*) and spicy (*karakuchi*) and garnished with *wasabi* and julienned green onions.

Tsukishimaya • 月島家
Azabu Juban 2-3-1 • 港区麻布十番2-3-1
Tel. 03-3452-0991 • 10:00—20:00; closed Tuesday
SHOP • MAP PAGE 276, #6

It would be easy to walk by this small window selling *imagawayaki*, the round, grilled sweet snack cakes filled with *azuki* paste, custard, or cheese; keep an eye out for the red, white, and blue *noren* in front. Tsukishimaya also offers *inarizushi*, sweet, deep-fried *tōfu* parcels filled with rice, *shiitake*, and crunchy pickled lotus root (*renkon*). You can't fail to be impressed by the tiny space in which the elderly couple works.

Mamegen • 豆源
Azabu Juban 1-8-12 • 港区麻布十番1-8-12
Tel. 03-3585-0962
10:00—20:00; Tuesday until 19:00;
Friday and Saturday until 20:30
www.mamegen.com (Japanese)
SHOP • MAP PAGE 276, #4

A brick building on the corner with a brown banner over the door, Mamegen opened in 1865 and has been in the same family for six generations. Peer into the window to watch the addictive salted rice crackers (*shio okaki*) frying in sesame oil. The nutty aroma wafts into the street. On display are more than ninety varieties of sweet and savory ball-shaped snacks filled with beans, nuts, or peas. Choose from flavors such as green apple, sea urchin, wasabi, coffee, squid ink, crab, or curry. Mamegen has shops in most *depachika*.

Naniwaya Sōhonten • 浪花家総本店
Azabu Juban 1-8-14 • 港区麻布十番1-8-14
Tel. 03-3583-4975
11:00—19:00; closed Tuesday and 3rd Wednesday of the month
www.wagashi.or.jp/tokyo/shop/0510.htm (Japanese)

SHOP AND CAFÉ • MAP PAGE 276, #3

This was the first shop in Japan to sell *taiyaki (tai* is sea bream, a fish used in celebratory events and *yaki* means to grill), fish-

shaped cakes stuffed with sweet *azuki* paste. Opened in 1909, it has become an institution; *taiyaki* fans from around the country make pilgrimages here. Three cooks are squeezed into the narrow space, pouring batter into hot fish-shaped molds, and then adding a dollop of *azuki* paste. The cakes are grilled until crisp. There is a small café in back that also serves stir-fried noodles and shaved ice with sweet syrups.

Kibundō • 紀文堂
Azabu Juban 2-4-9 • 港区麻布十番2-4-9
Tel. 03-3451-8918 • 9:30—19:00; closed Tuesday
http://jin3.jp/kameiten2/kibundo.htm (Japanese)

SHOP • MAP PAGE 276, #5

Kibundō is a third-generation shop. The signature item is *Shichifukujin ningyoyaki*, small sweet grilled cakes stuffed with *azuki* in the shape of the seven gods of fortune. They also make small waffles stuffed with custard and apricot (*anzu*) jam and nine different types of rice crackers that are all hand-grilled. You can see the delicacies being made at the back of the narrow shop behind a glass window.

Hasegawa Saketen ● はせがわ酒店
Azabu Juban 2-2-7 ● 港区麻布十番2-2-7
Tel. 03-5439-9498
12:00—20:00; closed Sunday and holidays
www.hasegawasaketen.com/english/index.html (English)
www.hasegawasaketen.com/tenpo_azabu.html (Japanese)
SHOP ● MAP PAGE 276, #9

The entrance to the shop is marked by a hanging cedar ball, which sake brewers traditionally set out in front of their breweries each year when the *sake* is ready. The staff at this friendly, well-stocked shop can help you select from among the wine, *sake*, *shōchū*, and *umeshu* offered. Hasegawa Saketen has many branches throughout Tokyo, including a shop in the basement of Tokyo Station, a convenient location for those boarding the bullet train.

CHAPTER 5

....

CULINARY ITINERARIES

IN TOKYO

....

THE QUESTION I AM MOST FREQUENTLY ASKED BY VISITORS TO TOKYO—VISITORS INTERESTED IN THE food scene—is, "I only have one or two days here—where should I go?" The city is huge and hard to navigate, the choices are overwhelming.

The following itineraries are intended for the visitor who only has a limited time in the city. See the specific chapters for detailed information.

ONE-DAY TOUR

- **Tsukiji Market** (page 159)—the world's largest seafood market is in the heart of the city. If Tsukiji is closed, go to the market in **Ameyoko** near Ueno Station (page 217).

- *Depachika*—the vast, varied, and impressive food halls of major department stores. From Tsukiji Market, walk down Harumi Dori to Ginza. During this short (15-minute) walk, you will pass the Kabukiza (Kabuki Theater) on your right. In Ginza, you have a choice of department stores with *depachika*—if you can only visit one, it should be **Mitsukoshi** (page 47). There are two floors dedicated to food; be sure to visit both. If you can time your visit for the store's opening at precisely 10 a.m., you'll receive an impressive welcome, with bowing staff at the main entrance (corner of Harumi Dori and Chuo Dori). While you are in Ginza, you may want to make a quick detour to **Ito-ya**, an incredible (nine-floors!) stationery shop (page 195).

- Lunch in **Ginza** (see restaurant recommendations, page 182), or head up to **Asakusa** via subway or taxi and have lunch there (see restaurant recommendations, page 197).

- Visit the **Asakusa** area near the Sensoji temple (page 197) to walk along the Nakamise Dori street, which is filled with many specialty food shops. Nibble your way down the narrow and boisterous street, filled with food stalls on either side. You'll be tempted by rice crackers, pastries, sweet-bean-paste-filled cakes, sticky rice balls, and more.

- From Asakusa, it is a short walk to the **Kappabashi** neighborhood (page 209), the kitchen supply district famous for its plastic food samples. (There are not many restaurants in this area, so have lunch before you come here.)

If you are enamored of *depachika* and still have the energy, finish your day at the food floor at **Isetan** in **Shinjuku** (page 46). This is the best *depachika* in the country.

TWO-DAY TOUR

THIS TOUR DIVIDES TOKYO DOWN THE MIDDLE. THE first day is focused on the east side, and day two will take you through the west side.

Day One
- **Tsukiji Market** (page 159), the world's largest seafood market. Alternatively, if Tsukiji is closed, the market at **Ameyoko** (page TK).

- **Kappabashi** (page 209). Most stores open at 10 a.m., so don't arrive before then.

- **Asakusa**—for lunch and the Nakamise Dori street (see above).

- Spend the afternoon in the old downtown areas of **Ningyocho** (page 242) and **Nihonbashi**, the historic areas of Tokyo (page 225). The area is filled with some of the oldest food shops in Tokyo. Tokyo's original fish market was located in Nihonbashi.

- End your day in **Ginza** at the **Mitsukoshi** *depachika* (page 47) or Matsuya (map page 181 #9).

- If you want to visit a large supermarket, and get a panoramic view of the culinary culture of Japan, **Itō Yōkadō** (see page 286) in Kiba is just three stops on the Tozai line from Nihonbashi, and is one of the largest markets close to the city center. You'll note the contrasts between the size of the seafood department and the meat department, the attention paid to presentation even in this chain superstore, the variety of soy products, and the array of Japanese-made kitchen equipment and gadgets, and much much more.

Day Two

- **Isetan**—begin your day at the city's top *depachika* in **Shinjuku** (page 46) or Odakyū (map page 263 #9) or Keio (map page 263 #10).

- **Times Square**, the south side of Shinjuku station is home to **Takashimaya**, with another grand *depachika* (page 47), **Tōkyū Hands** for kitchen gadgets and tableware (page 269), and **Kinokuniya** bookstore for cookbooks in English.

- Spend the afternoon in **Omotesando** (page 257), the elegant and fashionable shopping area, to see the high-end chocolate, pastry, and *wagashi* shops.

- If time permits, **Kagurazaka** (page 271), the historic entertainment district, is a nice area to walk around and sample simple street food like steamed buns.

CULINARY SOUVENIRS

WHAT FOODIE DOES NOT LOVE SHOPPING FOR ITEMS TO COOK WITH? HERE ARE SOME SPICES, INGREDIENTS, and kitchen gadgets to buy in Tokyo—many not available elsewhere, or available, but not as well made—that will help you to enjoy Japan in your home kitchen.

For one-stop shopping, consider going to **Itō Yōkadō** in the

Kiba neighborhood, four stops on the Tozai subway line from the Otemachi Station (which is connected to Tokyo Station by an underground passage). This is a superstore including a supermarket as well as a housewares department.

Itō Yōkadō • イトーヨーカドー
Koto-ku, Kiba 1-5-30 • 江東区木場1-5-30
Tel. 03-5606-5234 • Daily 10:00—23:00; closed holidays
www.itoyokado.co.jp/ (Japanese)
SHOP

Other places to explore are the shopping arcades (*shōtengai*) scattered throughout the city. Kichijoji Station on the Chuo line has a large *shōtengai* just north of the station. *Shōtengai* are fun places because many are still full of family-owned ma-and-pa shops specializing in certain foods such as *tōfu*, meat, seafood, and produce.

Items to pick up at shops:

Cha Different varieties of tea including *sencha*, *genmaicha*, and *hōjicha*

Katakuriko A thickening agent

Katsuobushi Dried, smoked flakes of bonito, an essential for making dashi

Kokuto Brown sugar from Okinawa and nearby islands

Kombu The base for making any *dashi*

Kuzu A trendy ingredient used as a thickening agent; popular with top chefs throughout the world

Mattcha powder Traditional *mattcha* is expensive and can be hard to work with in the kitchen, you can find instant versions to make *mattcha* lattes at home or to mix into vanilla ice cream.

Miso koshi Strainer for incorporating *miso* into soup stock

Strainers Fine-meshed strainers excellent for straining soup stocks; there is also a special strainer used for getting *tōfu* out of hot broths

Umeboshi Salty, tart pickled apricots

Wasabi: Tubes of *wasabi*; ask for *hon wasabi* or *nama wasabi* for 100% *wasabi* (Much of what is served outside of Japan is actually horseradish paste mixed with food coloring.)

Yuzu Look for dried *yuzu* citrus peels if you like to make homemade pickles.

Yuzu koshō A salty and citrusy condiment (good quality *yuzu koshō* is very different from the kind at 100 yen shops); there are two types, green and red

There are dollar shops scattered throughout the city filled with great kitchen gadgets and items with which to stock your home pantry. Look for 100 yen shops (also called 99 yen shops), where everything costs 100 (or 99) yen. Daisō is a 100 yen shop near Harajuku Station.

Daisō • ダイソー

Shibuya-ku, Jingumae 1-19-24 • 渋谷区神宮前1-19-24

Tel. 03-5775-9641 • Daily 10:00−21:00; closed holidays

www.daiso-sangyo.co.jp/english/ (English)

SHOP • MAP PAGE 156, #12

At 100 yen shops you will most likely find:

Goma Toasted black (*kuro*) or white (*shiro*) sesame seeds. Crush the seeds
and add sugar and soy sauce for a dressing for cooked vegetables. Try
crushed black sesame seeds with sugar over ice cream.

Hashi Long chopsticks (for cooking) and regular chopsticks (for eating)

Hashioki Chopstick rests available in seasonal designs

Ichimi Crushed, dried red chili pepper

Kinako Flour made from roasted soybeans, a great topping for ice cream
or to mix into a cold glass of milk

Kushi Long bamboo skewers used for grilling

Makisu Rolling mat for making *sushi* rolls at home

Misoshiru gu Packs of dried ingredients that, when making *miso* soup,
simply need to be tossed into the soup

Neriume Tube of *umeboshi* (salted apricot) paste; some *umeboshi* is mixed
with *shiso* leaves (*shiso iri*); use to mix into salad dressings or for rolled *sushi*

Ochoko and tokkuri *Tokkuri* are small carafes for *sake*, and *ochoko* are
small cups. If you are a casual drinker of *sake*, these cups are perfect as
they are sturdy and can be thrown into the dishwasher. .

Shamoji Rice paddles; the Japanese versions are plastic, studded, and easy
to use because rice does not stick to them

Shichimi Seven-spice mix to top *miso* soups or noodle bowls

Yukari Packets of dried purple *shiso* leaves; used for making rice balls

Yuzu koshō *Yuzu* and salt in a paste; try mixing it with mayonnaise to
spice up sandwiches or as a dip for crudités

DAY TRIPS FROM TOKYO

There are many options for day trips from Tokyo; in addition to the
vineyard excursions on pages 148−149, consider the following:

Yanesen 屋根千

Yanesen is the area comprised of Yanaka, Nezu, and Sendagi in
the northern part of Tokyo. Filled with many small shops and
shopping arcades (*shōtengai*), Yanesen is a popular destination for
Tokyo foodies. Food and wine writer Junko Nakahama offers walking tours in English. http://omiyage.yanesen.org/ (English)

Utsunomiya 宇都宮

Utsunomiya, a city in Tochigi prefecture about an hour from Tokyo,
is famous for pot stickers (*gyōza*) and has more than thirty shops
selling the dumplings. The city sponsors a *gyōza* festival each fall.

Kawagoe 川越

Kawagoe, a city in Saitama prefecture, also about an hour outside of Tokyo, is nicknamed "Little Edo," as it was a center of commerce during the Edo period. Do not miss the knife shop Machi-kan; the confectioners street, Kashiya Yokocho; or the nostalgic main street in the downtown area, Kurazukuri Street, which is lined with historic buildings dating back to the Edo period. Here you will be tempted with pickles, rice crackers, candies, and traditional *wagashi* confections.

KYOTO'S NISHIKI MARKET

京都錦市場

KYOTO'S NISHIKI ICHIBA

THIS SECTION IS A BRIEF LIST OF SOME OF THE SHOPS IN NISHIKI ICHIBA, A SHORT BUT REMARKABLE market street in the heart of Kyoto. It is a destination for both the professional chef and the general public and should not be missed. The market is easy to navigate (it is a short narrow street) and dates back four centuries.

Here you will find a taste of almost all that Kyoto is famous for. There are pickles sold from wooden barrels, whose tart, vinegary aroma penetrates the air. You'll find soy in many forms from *tōfu* and *yuba*, to soy doughnuts and soymilk ice cream. The colorful Kyoto heirloom vegetables appear throughout the market. Knives and kitchen tools are showcased at a gorgeous stall.

Nishiki is also called "Kyoto's kitchen." It opens at 10 a.m. when you may see some chefs carefully perusing the market. Later in the day, housewives come to do their shopping. Both chefs and home cooks depend on Nishiki to provide the ingredients for *obanzai*, the traditional home cooking developed over centuries by natives of Kyoto.

All of the shops below offer food to go which you can nibble on as you stroll down the street, a bit of a breach of Japanese etiquette, but not considered as offensive here in the market district, as it is elsewhere in the city. They are listed in the order in which you will see them walking east (*higashi*) to west (*nishi*).

Takakuraya Pickles ● 高倉屋
Tel. 075-231-0081 ● Daily 10:00—18:00
www.takakuraya.jp/ (Japanese)

SHOP

Pickles, pickles, and more pickles. The entry to the shop is topped
with rows of white paper lanterns. Above, large wooden barrels
are filled with . . . pickles. Eggplant, cucumbers, radishes, cabbage,
daikon, ginger, squash, turnips, and dozens of Japanese vegetables
are cured with a variety of pickling agents. The selection changes
seasonally and is available to sample.

Aritsugu ● 有次
Tel. 075-221-1091 ● Daily 9:00—17:30
www.aritsugu.jp (Japanese)

SHOP

In addition to the beautifully organized and displayed knives in
this famous shop, in business since 1560, you will also find an
enticing selection of other essential tools for the kitchen including
handcrafted pots, graters, and peelers. Aritsugu also has a shop in
Tsukiji Market in Tokyo, which caters to fishmongers; this shop
has a wider selection and is more welcoming to tourists.

Yubakichi ● 湯波吉
Tel. 075-221-1372 ● 10:00—18:00; closed Sunday and
the 4th Wednesday of the month

SHOP

Yubakichi dates back to 1790. The delicate soymilk skin (*yuba*)
made here is available both dried and fresh. The fresh *yuba* is
creamy and has a light sweetness to it and can be served simply
with *wasabi* and soy sauce.

Yamadashiya ● やまだしや
Tel. 075-223-5272 ● 10:00—18:00; closed Wednesday

SHOP

The aroma of roasted *hōjicha* tea wafts into the street in front
of Yamadashiya. This stall sells more than a dozen types of tea,
displayed in large wooden crates.

Tsunoki ● 津之喜
Tel. 075-221-2441 ● 10:00—18:00; closed Monday and
2nd Wednesday of the month ● www.tsunoki.co.jp/ (Japanese)

SHOP

The nearby Fushimi neighborhood is Japan's second largest

sake brewing area with about three-dozen breweries. If you can't make the short twenty-minute trip to Fushimi to visit the breweries, you can find a good variety of local *sake* at this shop. Tsuki no Katsura is a reliable producer and makes an unusual sparkling cloudy *sake* (*nigorizake*). Tsunoki has been the *sake* shop in the market for more than two hundred years.

Kuromame Cha An Kitao • 黒豆茶庵北尾
Tel. 075-221-5003 • Daily 9:30–18:00
www.kitaoshoji.co.jp/ (Japanese)
SHOP AND CAFÉ

Kitao specializes in beans, including black beans, soybeans, and *azuki*. There is a small café in the back serving bean-based sweet dishes. Place your order; it will be brought to you with a small bowl of dried black beans that you then grind into a powder in a large stone mortar that sits on your table, and then sprinkle over your dessert.

Miki Keiran • 三木鶏卵
Tel. 075-221-1585 • Daily 8:00–18:30
SHOP

Miki Keiran's savory omelets are rich in flavor yet delicate and light, the result of a unique method in which the uncooked eggs are poured into rectangular pans and cooked layer by layer over the fire as the chefs turn the omelets with long chopsticks.

Mochitsukiya • もちつき屋 つき屋
Tel. 075-223-1717 • 11:00–17:30 Monday to Friday;
11:00–18:00 Saturday, Sunday, and holidays
www.nishiki-mochitsukiya.com/ (Japanese)
SHOP AND CAFÉ

If you pass this shop at the right time, you will see sticky rice taffy (*mochi*) being made in a huge stone mortar, a two-person operation with one person pounding and the other turning the dough. It's rather unusual to see a *mochi* shop at all—this is a food usually eaten at home—and even more unusual to see it topped with peanut butter, spicy cod roe, pickled apricots with bonito flakes, or cheese, which are offered here. *Mochi* is also served here in classic sweet style, with *azuki* beans.

Notoyo Nishiten • のとよ西店
Tel. 075-231-0815 • 8:00–18:00; closed Monday
SHOP

Notoyo Nishiten Restaurant (on the 2nd floor)
Tel. 075-231-0813 • 11:00–15:00; closed Monday
RESTAURANT • INEXPENSIVE

Notoyo specializes in river fish, in particular, eel (*unagi*), which is available charcoal-grilled in an aromatic ginger soy sauce. Another delicacy is eel liver (*unaginokimo*) threaded on bamboo skewers, grilled, and dipped in sauce. The shop also sells *unagi* bones that have been deep-fried, a great snack to accompany beer. The restaurant on the second floor serves the same specialties.

Marukame • 丸亀
Tel. 075-221-2434 • Daily 8:00–17:30
SHOP

The irresistible deep-fried fish cakes come in a variety of types, including cheese, shrimp, and octopus with Japanese basil (*takoshiso*). Elsewhere fish cakes are called *Satsuma-age*, but here in the market the locals call them *tempura*.

Chūō Beikoku • 中央米穀
Tel. 075-221-2026 • Daily 9:00–18:00
www.okomenochuoo.jp/index.html (Japanese)
SHOP

Rice balls (*omusubi*) that are showcased in this tiny stall include flavors like prickly ash berries with kelp (*sanshō kombu*), dried anchovies with prickly ash berries (*chirimen sanshō*), and ground chicken and *miso* (*torisoboro miso*).

Kyō Yasai Kanematsu • 京野菜かね松
Tel. 075-221-0088 • Daily 10:00–18:00
SHOP

Kanematsu has an impressive display of the heirloom vegetables of Kyoto, *Kyō yasai*, (see page 67). This famous shop has the widest variety in the market; do not miss it.

Yaoya no Nikai • かね松やお屋の二かい
Tel. 075-221-0089 • 11:00–until lunch is sold out;
closing day is not fixed so call ahead
RESTAURANT • INEXPENSIVE

On the second floor of Kanematsu is a restaurant serving dishes that showcase *Kyō yasai*. Each day the restaurant offers a set menu that may include *tempura*, vegetables dressed with sesame dressing, pickles, *yuzu*-infused rice, and *miso* soup. Call ahead to make a reservation at this very popular shop.

Chinami • 千波

Tel. 075-241-3935 • Daily 9:00—18:30

www.kyoto-wel.com/shop/S81182/index.html (Japanese)

SHOP

Chinami specializes in *Tsukudani*, seafood and sea vegetables simmered in sweet soy. You can also pick up two local condiments that are most commonly sprinkled over a hot bowl of rice—fresh Japanese prickly ash berries (*sanshō*) and tiny dried anchovies with *sanshō* (*chirimensanshō*).

Hirano • 平野

Tel. 075-221-6318 • Daily 9:30—18:30; closed holidays

www.e385.net/hirano/ (Japanese)

SHOP

Over seventy varieties of colorful side dishes (*obanzai*) tempt customers at this handsome shop. The dishes include seafood and meats, but are rich with vegetables and soy products.

Fuka • 麩嘉

Tel. 075-231-1584 • 9:30—17:30; closed Monday and last Sunday of the month from February to August

SHOP

This corner shop has different flavors of fresh wheat gluten (*nama fu*), including unusual ones such as bacon, basil, or cheese as well as more traditional flavors like pumpkin and sesame. Logs of *fu* are displayed in a small refrigerated case much like cheese would be in the United States.

Konna Monja • こんなもんじゃ

Tel. 075-255-3231 • Daily 10:00—18:00

www.kyotofu.co.jp/shop/monja/ (Japanese)

SHOP

Soymilk doughnuts and ice cream are the most popular items at this *tōfu* shop. There is a small eat-in space.

Dintora Spice Shop • ぢんとら

Tel. 075-221-0038 • 9:00—18:00; closed Tuesday (if Tuesday is a holiday, it will be open, and closed Wednesday)

http://homepage2.nifty.com/dintora/ (Japanese)

SHOP

Add a taste of Japan to your pantry with spices from this tiny specialty shop including dried citrus peel (*yuzu* or *chinpi*), dried chili powder (*ichimi*), seven-spice powder (*shichimi*), and

Japanese mustard (*karashi*). The *chinpi* (dried citrus peel) can be mixed with honey and hot water for a cold remedy, or added to the bath.

Daiyasu • 大安
Tel. 075-221-0246
8:30—18:00; closed Sunday and holidays
BAR • INEXPENSIVE

Behind the blue banner with white calligraphy is a popular bar for grilled seafood and small dishes served with *sake*, wine, or beer.

RESOURCES

....

www.metropolis.co.jp Website of the weekly magazine

www.tasteofculture.com Cookbook author Elizabeth Andoh's site; Andoh offers classes and market tours

www.sake-world.com *Sake* authority John Gauntner's site; Gauntner offers *sake* classes

omiyage.yanesen.org Food writer Junko Nakahama offers tours of Yanesen

Cool Tools: Cooking Utensils from the Japanese Kitchen by Kate Klippensteen, Kodansha International

Dashi and Umami: The Heart of Japanese Cuisine by Cross Media

The Decorative Art of Japanese Food Carving by Hiroshi Nagashima, Kodansha International

A Dictionary of Japanese Food: Ingredients and Culture by Richard Hosking, Tuttle Publishing

The Insider's Guide to Sake by Philip Harper, Kodansha International

Japanese Cooking: A Simple Art by Shizuo Tsuji, Kodansha International

Japanese Kitchen Knives: Essential Techniques and Recipes by Hiromitsu Nozaki, Kodansha International

Kaiseki: The Exquisite Cuisine by Kyoto's Kikunoi Restaurant by Yoshihiro Murata, Kodansha International

Nihonshu ga Umai Otona no Izakaya/Tokyo Sake Pub Guide (bilingual) by John Gauntner, Ebisu Kosyo Publication

Tsukiji: The Fish Market at the Center of the World by Theodore Bestor, University of California Press

Washoku: Recipes from the Japanese Home Kitchen by Elizabeth Andoh, Ten Speed Press

INDEX

ABOUT THE AUTHOR

....

Trained as a chef and baker at the French Culinary Institute and as a sommelier at the American Sommelier Association, Yukari Sakamoto (坂本ゆかり) has worked as a sommelier at the prestigious New York Bar and Grill in the Park Hyatt Tokyo and at Takashimaya department store. She teaches classes on food, wine, and *shōchū*, the popular Japanese distilled spirit, and she was the first non-Japanese to pass the rigorous exam to become a "*shōchū* advisor," essentially a *shōchū* sommelier. She conducts culinary tours of Tokyo's shops and markets, as well as hands-on cooking classes.

Her writing has been featured in such publications as *Food & Wine*, *Travel & Leisure*, *Time*, *Saveur*, and *The Japan Times*, and she writes a column in *Metropolis* magazine to help foreigners in Tokyo access the food culture of Japan. She and her husband, Shinji, a Japanese fishmonger, divide their time between Tokyo and New York City.

ABOUT THE PHOTOGRAPHER

....

Takuya Suzuki, (鈴木拓也) a Tokyo native, specializes in food and travel photography. His work can be seen in many Japanese magazines.

A NOTE ON DESIGN MOTIFS The pattern on the book's end-papers is a traditional Japanese design motif depicting fish scales; the small round symbol flanking each page number and in several other locations in the book is a traditional plum blossom motif.